Gestalt Graphology

Gestalt Graphology

Exploring the Mystery and Complexity of Human Nature Through Handwriting Analysis

Felix Klein

iUniverse, Inc.
New York Bloomington

Gestalt Graphology
Exploring the Mystery and Complexity of Human Nature Through Handwriting Analysis

iUniverse books may be ordered through booksellers or by contacting:

iUniverse
1663 Liberty Drive, Suite 200
Bloomington, IN 47403
www.iuniverse.com
1-800-Authors (1-800-288-4677)

ISBN: 978-0-595-44307-9 (pbk)
ISBN: 978-0-595-88636-4 (ebk)

Printed in the United States of America

Contents

Contents

Acknowledgments

By Janice H. Klein

Dedicated to my daughter, Valerie Bottenus, daughter also of the late Ralph P. Bottenus and stepdaughter of Felix Klein, without whose perseverance, intelligence, and technical assistance this book might never have seen the light of day (and Valerie wants to add a thank-you to her friend Jerry Diaz, whose computer expertise was invaluable).

Peter P. Papay, who studied Felix's courses with me but never had an opportunity to know the man whose work he has done so much to keep alive, is an individual of great generosity and persistence, and I will never be able to thank him enough for his dedication to the task of preserving Felix's legacy. Peter began by scanning the three correspondence courses, sharpening the illustrations, and providing me with computer discs of all three. Next he undertook the scanning and formatting of the Felix Klein Dachau Concentration Camp Memoir, which is now in the archives of the Yad Vashem Holocaust Memorial Museum in Jerusalem.

Now Peter has completed the most important project of all, making Felix's monographs available in this volume for present and future generations to enjoy.

Peter is not only a Professional member of the National Society for Graphology, but in 2004 NSG's Board awarded him the rarely bestowed title of Honorary member. (As if all that weren't enough, Peter—who lives in Louisiana—is also NSG's Southeast Regional Advisor!)

His wonderful wife, Maj. Bonnie M. McEwan, USAF (Ret.), deserves a special thank you from me, as she has cheerfully and competently proof-read countless pages of copy for this book and other material.

My gratitude to you both, Peter and Bonnie!

Acknowledgments

[illegible]

Preface

By Peter P. Papay

Some graphologists write books to help others learn this art-science, while others just want to see their names in print. Since Felix Klein never wrote a book he could easily slip into oblivion as a result, whereas lesser graphologists might prevail simply because they had published books. Felix did, however, write numerous monographs which can and should be preserved. Because the papers were written over a period of many years, there was some variety in their formats and a few needed a little care.

So, I went about consolidating the ones Janice Klein felt were his best, and in addition I put them on a computer disk (CD-ROM), with the result that Felix's work can be preserved for future generations of graphologists.

I am one of the many people who have studied Felix's correspondence courses with Janice Klein, having taken all three courses and been Professionally certified by the National Society for Graphology. There's a saying that when a need arises someone will appear to provide the solution, and apparently I was that person. Although in general I'm not a "do-gooder," in this case an inner voice was telling me to take on this project, and with my wife's support and help was able to finish it.

Now I feel honored to have been instrumental in helping to preserve Felix's legacy, and am gratified to know that my contribution will make these monographs accessible to others for years to come.

List of Publications

Rhythm, Groundrhythm and Beyond

Human Character Types (Erich Fromm)

Male and Female in Handwriting

Combining Indicators

Character Structure of Neuroses (Revd. Wittlich Method)

Extremes in Handwriting Analysis

Comparison Between Thematic Apperception Test (TAT) and Graphology, conducted by Hunter College, N. Y., complete with reprint from the magazine "Perceptual and Motor Skills," 1973, and 10 handwriting analyses by Felix Klein

Priorities (A New Typology, Based on Alfred Adler)

Emotional Release in Handwriting

The Ductus: The Quality of the Stroke

Rhythm, All Roads Lead To

The Power of Form (Revised and expanded edition)

The Unconscious in Handwriting

The Addictive Personality as Seen in Handwriting

The Psychology of the Handwriting of the Child

Foreword

The author of these monographs, Felix Klein, was born on January 17th, 1911, in Vienna, Austria. He was to become a teacher extraordinaire and an inspiration to thousands over a period of more than fifty years, all of this while pursuing innovative research in graphology, instructing, lecturing, and in 1972 founding the National Society for Graphology, headquartered in New York City.

Before the war, when his cousin, Robert Goldsand (later to become a renowned concert pianist), had his handwriting analyzed while he and Felix (both 13) were at a hotel in the Tyrolian Alps with their parents, Felix was so astounded at the accuracy of the analysis that he asked how he could learn this art. The analyst gave him the title of a certain book and Felix began saving his allowance until he could buy it.

As a young boy in Vienna, Felix had hopes of becoming a physician, but being the only son of a department store owner, he was sent to a business school to prepare him to follow in his father's footsteps. In May of 1938, the young Felix, already married and working in the family store, was arrested by the Nazi invaders and shipped first to Dachau for six months and then to Buchenwald for six months more. While in those camps he formulated his theory of *Directional Pressure* as a result of studying changes in the handwriting of his fellow inmates.

Fortunately, in May of 1939, through an English friend of his wife, Marie Lisa, (who had been able to go ahead to the United States), Felix received the requisite sponsorship in London and was released from Buchenwald. His goal of rejoining "Lisl" in New York City was achieved in 1940 through the sponsorship of George Seibel, Director of the Carnegie Free Library of Pittsburgh and an active member of the National Coordinating Committee for Refugees.

Although when Felix arrived in the United States in 1940 (still a Depression-era year) he was unable to earn more than a tiny income from teaching and doing handwriting analyses in his spare time, he did hold fast to his dream of one day being able to devote full time to graphology. In the meantime, in order to support his growing family (sons born in 1943, 1945, and 1948) he studied watchmaking and eventually bought a small jewelry store.

It wasn't until 1969 that he made the daring decision to open an office on West 57th Street, a prime New York City business area, and to begin his full-time career as Manhattan Handwriting Consultant, doing extensive work in personnel selection and vocational guidance.

Over the years he would become a consultant to the United Nations, to AT&T, and to the State of New York. He was a top-ranked document examiner and had testified in over 150 court cases in New York, New Jersey, Connecticut, New Mexico and Nevada, as well as in Geneva, Switzerland, and the island of St. Vincent's. In 1979 he was called to Ghana, Africa, to testify in a case involving a major political figure. In 1987 he presented two lectures at Oxford University before the 1st British Symposium on Graphological Research. In 1985 he spoke before the First Israeli Conference on Scientific Graphology, in Jerusalem. In 1989 and 1991 he lectured at Cambridge University before the 2nd and 3rd British Symposiums.

Felix Klein was also the founder and a past president of the National Bureau of Document Examiners, and was a past president of the American Association of Handwriting Analysts. He appeared on many television and radio shows and was the subject of numerous magazine articles. A prominent clinical psychologist once wrote to Felix, "… with your knowledge of graphology and psychology, you're the only one I know who speaks and understands both 'languages.'"

It is probably as a teacher that Felix Klein was best known and loved. He offered classes four nights a week at his office in all levels of graphology: Elementary, Intermediate, Advanced, Master Research, and Psychology for Graphologists. He also offered private lessons, as well as correspondence courses at all levels and had students from all over the U.S., Canada, Europe, and Israel.

Out of his many monographs, the best are presented here. His contribution to the scientific validity of graphology is described in the paper 'Comparison Between Thematic Apperception Test (TAT) and Graphology', a research project conducted at Hunter College, New York, in 1973. Later, in conjunction with Roger Rubin, he did the graphological research for George Langer, Ph.D. (Adelphi University) for his doctoral dissertation entitled *Graphology in Personality Assessment.*

After the death of his first wife, Felix married Janice Bottenus, a former student who became his secretary, and who herself was widowed. She carries on his teaching and other work today. What has always impressed her most, as it did everyone who knew Felix, was that he hadn't become bitter or cynical as a result of his concentration camp suffering, but always believed, like Anne Frank, that most people were good at heart. In a letter to one of his students he explained that he learned his deep love for humanity from his mother, because she always felt that love for others was the key to happiness.

Felix Klein, described by one of his students as "a man with a golden heart," died on July 26, 1994, following a series of strokes, but he lives on in the hearts of all who knew him.

Of course, no write-up about him would be complete without mentioning the famous *Cheese Sandwich Incident.* In case the reader is not familiar with the story, it demonstrates his 'golden heart' well. In the concentration camps he used his graphology skills to survive. One freezing November day in 1938, at Buchenwald, a German SS officer, who had heard he analyzed handwriting, demanded an analysis for himself. Felix was escorted into the cozy warmth of the officer's quarters where he managed to stretch the analysis into an all day event. When Felix was finished, the officer was so delighted with the results that he wanted to reward him. At first he offered some cigarettes. Since Felix didn't smoke, he promised to give him some food instead. When the prisoners were lined up to be marched back to the barracks that evening, a foot soldier came with a paper bag and asked for "the man who does the handwriting." The rule required that prisoners and guards never be any closer to one another than the length of a bayonet at the end of the gun. With this in mind, the guard put the bag on the end of his bayonet and handed it to Felix. When they got back to the barracks, seventeen men came and asked what was in the paper bag. He opened it, and it contained a cheese sandwich. He hadn't tasted cheese in six months, so it was extremely valuable to him. Felix invited the seventeen men to a party to be on the next day, Sunday, a non-working day. That sandwich was cut into seventeen pieces and relished by his fellow inmates. That is *agape* (unselfish) love!

Rhythm, Groundrhythm and Beyond

Felix Klein

Rhythm, Groundrhythm and Beyond

A Lecture Delivered at the Fifth Annual Convention of the American Association of Handwriting Analysts

What is Rhythm

Defining rhythm becomes easier when we understand what is meant by regularity in handwriting. Once regularity has been defined, we will point out the difference between regularity and rhythm.

For judging regularity we do not insist on the exact repetition of the forms or letters—we are simply concerned with four criteria of the downstrokes of the handwriting. These are:

1. Height of the middle zone downstrokes.
2. Distance between the middle zone downstrokes.
3. Direction (angle with the base line) of middle zone downstrokes.
4. Direction of the downstrokes of the long letters.

Now you can see that in regularity we expect a "monotonizing" of the handwriting. Regularity has a tendency to reduce originality of forms. Good regularity and legibility are not always companions. Regularity can be compared to the German word "takt" or in the English translation "beat" which comes from the Latin. The word rhythm comes from the Greek and it means to flow.

Klages, the well-known German graphologist makes a very clear distinction between beat and rhythm. Beat is the recurrence of the same criteria in the same interval. Rhythm is the recurrence of similar criteria in similar intervals.

Here is an interesting example. It is well known how easy it is to learn the exercises necessary to be able to swim. Every beginner finds out pretty soon that to do the motions does not necessarily mean that one can swim. Why should that be? Possibly because the change from a regular motion to a rhythmic one must occur. If this is correct, the observation is important that after the rhythmic motion has succeeded, a conscious control of the motion is unwanted. In fact, the thinking process is disturbing to the rhythm. And this is not only true for swimming. Going down a flight of steps quickly can be done best by not willfully thinking about it, but permitting the legs to do the work without the conscious mind taking part. The reactions become "unnatural" to the same extent as we insist on observing ourselves, or in other words, to the same extent as we let the action become conscious.

Regularity can be measured, rhythm must be felt. Anyone who is not completely uncontrolled can produce a handwriting with regularity. It may be necessary to do it slowly and with a strong effort, but it can be done. But no one can produce a rhythmic writing artificially no matter how much effort he might exert.

Disturbed rhythm can be very serious, providing we are dealing with the writing of a mature person, a person with sufficient writing skill.

If the willpower is the character quality that cannot produce rhythm, or rather is disturbing to rhythm, it means that handwritings showing any of the three major indicators of willpower, namely regularity, angular connections, or pressure, are unlikely to produce rhythm. If, for instance, rhythm appears in a writing with strong pressure, the manifestation of rhythm becomes more significant for this particular person.

If we have just said that a rhythmic writing is unlikely to show a strong regularity, we are also saying that the quality of irregularity may be the first and simplest prerequisite for a rhythmic writing. It is important, however, that the manifestation of irregularity should not be disturbing to the eye. These irregularities should rather serve to enliven and enrich the writing picture. It is therefore necessary to watch if the changes in middle zone height, the changes of the slant and the changes of middle zone width are part of a rhythmic pattern, or simply without rhyme or reason, breaking up the handwriting.

Now that we have a fair idea about what rhythm really is, it becomes easy to answer the following question. Is the tick-tock of an alarm clock a rhythmic motion, yes or no? From my explanation about beat and rhythm there is no question that it is beat, and too exact and mechanical to be rhythm. The same is true for a body of soldiers marching in step. I am using this example particularly to show you that the motion of human beings can be too mechanical also to be considered rhythmic. Many of you may have heard that enough soldiers marching in step across a bridge can cause the bridge to break up. Does this have anything to do with rhythm? It surely does. A bridge has a natural rhythmic vibration of its own. This vibration increases through the vibration caused by the marching soldiers. The intensity of the vibration becomes too much of a stress to the bridge and it breaks apart.

Many functions of our own body are rhythmic. First, the breathing comes to mind. But also the heartbeat. And don't let the word "beat" mislead you here. When a person sings, the vibrations are really rhythmic patterns. Actually even the viewing of colors has to do with rhythmic light waves of different lengths. The flight of a bird is rhythmic. The flight of an airplane is not rhythmic because, hopefully, there is too much mechanical control. The orbit of a spaceship, however, is rhythmic. This could go on and on. Actually, we are more interested in identifying rhythm in handwriting, although all these other examples must have served to broaden our understanding of the magnitude of rhythm.

When I started to teach I found that the identification of rhythm in a handwriting was almost always the greatest source of difficulty. And isn't it understandable? One is supposed to look at the writing and find something that cannot be seen. None of the available methods in both the English and German graphological literature were of great help. Max Hellmut came closest to finding a teaching method with his textbook written in the form of letters. Also the study of the chapter on rhythm in Mueller-Enskat's GRAPHOLOGISCHE DIAGNOSTIK can give a most enlightening picture of rhythm, although their most difficult language makes the book impractical for teaching. There was, therefore, an absolute need to devise a method that would have a chance of good accuracy, and a chance to be understood by everyone. It was also important to make a clear separation of all the factors contributing to the final judgment of rhythm. For the sake of simplicity the evaluation system of Klages was used. The scale of Klages has a range of 5, whereby number 1 is the highest possible qualification while number 5 is the poorest. I must emphasize, however, that even the poorest of rhythm does not necessarily mean that there is a negative implication as far as the character of the writer is concerned.

Here is my four step method to determine the rhythm of a handwriting.

1. Examination of the Writing Impulses

   What is a writing impulse? Each time we put the writing instrument onto the writing surface a writing impulse begins. The end of the writing impulse occurs when we lift the writing instrument off the writing surface. The length of the writing impulses varies a great deal and this is not a factor in determining rhythm. An "I" dot is a complete writing impulse. A very long word can be written without the removal of the writing instrument. The period of time spent above the writing surface between writing impulses is called impulse pause, or simply pause. The airstrokes so well defined and described by Frank Victor occur in this period of time. The discharge of impulses can be harmonious or disharmonious. To be judged harmonious, the writing impulses do not have to come in an even similar set of intervals. If we follow the writing path of a handwriting, the interchange of writing impulses and pauses should produce a wavy rather than a jerky motion.

To determine this it may be of help to make a graphic test. Take a transparent sheet of paper or clear plastic and put it over the handwriting in question. Use a marking pen and connect the beginning with the end of each individual writing impulse with a straight line. After completing this process for the whole writing sample, remove the transparent paper or plastic sheet and you will have a surprisingly intricate pattern which can be harmonious to varying degrees. The interpretation of the graphic pattern reminds us of the electrocardiogram, although it is not nearly as complicated. The straight lines forming the pattern should in some way comprise a system that can be called harmonious. As there are no two handwritings alike, no two handwriting impulse records could be alike even if the identical text was used.

The test on writing impulses is only one of four observations to be made for the determination of rhythm. It also determines only one-quarter or 25% of the rhythmic value of the handwriting. It is therefore conceivable that a person's handwriting producing the poorest graphic record of the writing impulses can still have a good overall evaluation for rhythm.

2. <u>The Distribution of Space</u>

It is well known that the treatment of space is important for the graphologist. How well we use space, how well we distribute the writing over the available space is also important for the determination of rhythm.

It is disturbing to rhythm if the distribution of space is disharmonious or uneven. The following should be taken into consideration.

- Harmony of margins within themselves

  We do not expect an equal margin on the left and on the right side, in fact this would be highly unusual. But we do expect the margins to show some kind of proportion.

- Harmony of spaces between lines

  Very large spaces between lines and very small ones also do not increase the rhythmic picture. It goes without saying that the size of the writing must be taken into consideration when judging the space between lines.
- Harmony of space between words and letters
- Harmony within all spaces

  Disharmony of space should catch the eye.

3. <u>Examination of Rhythm in the Forms (Letters)</u>

   The letters themselves can reveal a rhythmic or nonrhythmic form. Long upper or lower loops by comparison to the rest of the writing are disturbing to the rhythm of form. Capitals should be proportionate in size to the rest of the writing. Harmony of form is not hard to see.

4. <u>Searching for Extremes in the Handwriting</u>

   The following extremes in handwriting are disturbing to the rhythm.

   - Irregular pressure
   - Predominance of one zone over another
   - Extreme irregularity, that does not permit any pattern at all
   - Extreme differences in size

     The signature is important here also. Many times we find that particularly the signature allows us to conclude the harmony of size.
   - Extreme differences in the slant

     Any extreme in the handwriting speaks against rhythm
   - Extreme regularity.

Klages used rhythm as the basis for finding the intelligence of the writer. He called that test "Formniveau" or in the English translation, "form level" or "style evaluation". The five points determining the style evaluation and intelligence of the writer are:

- Rhythm
- Symmetry

- Creativeness
- Legibility
- Speed

Groundrhythm

In her first work, Rhoda Wieser discovered that the increased lack of elasticity that could be seen even in a single stroke indicated a more severe form of criminality when she examined the handwriting of known criminals. In comparison, the extreme lack of elasticity was found only in a few borderline cases of non-criminal writings. The elasticity and the lack of elasticity do not depend on form, on writing skill, on level of education, etc. The classification of elasticity by itself would be worthless without creating two other polaric observations to either side of elasticity or better, a maximum of elasticity or a maximum of groundrhythm. Partly, the meaning of the expression elasticity must include a never-ending ability for growth in an original pattern.

To understand elasticity within the writing motion it is helpful to sketch a picture. The activated motion of a pendulum through its momentum is both to the left and to the right. The swinging towards the extreme right or left creates a situation whereby the force giving center loses its sphere of influence. There is an imaginary locking device near the extreme left and right. Once the pendulum moves beyond the locking device it is incapable of returning to the center position.

It now becomes obvious that the expression of elasticity becomes worthless without the added dynamic quality, without the possibility of the swinging of the pendulum to either side. Therefore, it is never possible to say from a handwriting that it has perfect elasticity or perfect groundrhythm. The original idea of the elasticity with a polaric pendulum-like dynamic motion towards left (soft elastic) or right (tight elastic) came, according to Dr. Rhoda Wieser, from Margaret Hartge who passed away too soon to realize the full implication of her findings.

No single sign and no combination of signs of the orthodox graphologist can come up with the indicators for elasticity. The method coming closest is Klages' form level.

The stroke is the basis for the whole handwriting. The combination of strokes and their correlations to each other represent the "writing picture" or the writing character or the content of the writing image or the form level. On the other hand, Klages wrote that the "Gestalt" to be found in the complete handwriting must be contained in a single stroke. It becomes important to mention right here that a minimum of parts of letters are necessary to determine groundrhythm. In many cases this is not sufficient. It is necessary to see the trace of the movement, the graduation of the motion, and to find this more writing sample may be necessary in many cases.

The trace of the motion can be seen in the middle zone although not exclusively. This motion release can again be compared to the swinging pendulum. But in order for the pendulum to find its way from one position into the other a medium of dynamic "still" elastic motion must be maintained. Both the motion or rhythm that is too slack or too tense are counter dynamic and will not permit our pendulum to move freely. It is difficult for Rhoda Wieser to determine why she chose the word groundrhythm. The expression appears in Klages' books although he does not specify a particular meaning. The trace of motion through the handwriting must show some form of elasticity to be regarded as rhythmical.

It is quite obvious from what I have said up to now that the elasticity in a handwriting has a lot to do with its groundrhythm. The elasticity of the motion becomes the scale for the ground-rhythm, but only when the tendency of the swinging of the pendulum between soft and tight blends with the general motional release. Each minute locomotive impulse must be a part of the correlation between soft and tight. The strength of the motional elasticity influences the homogeneity of the forms, the homogeneity of the kinetic character and the homogeneity of the treatment of the space. As far as the groundrhythm is concerned, everything depends on the correlation of the swinging of the pendulum between soft and tight on one hand, and the equivalent blending with all other writing criteria on the other hand. The less of the blending process can be detected the more we can speak of weakness of the groundrhythm. It can now be stated that a disturbed rhythm is not the same as a weak groundrhythm. In fact it is incorrect to speak of disturbed groundrhythm.

The interpretation of the groundrhythm does not result from some indicators in the handwriting or from some preferred psychological aspects. It does depend on the above mentioned criteria plus a disposition or indisposition of criminal tendencies and also via the utilization of these correlations according to the expressive scientific theory of the "Gestalt", or as Klages said, the personal "guide image". The groundrhythm does not only have an importance for the handwriting of criminals and their limitations with regards to non-criminals. It also can be revealing with appropriate differentiated application in finding tendencies of flexibility or hardening, or the absence of both.

According to the main diagram it is obvious that there is a direct correlation between the strength and weakness of groundrhythm on the one hand and the criminal and non-criminal disposition on the other. The higher the groundrhythm, the smaller the chance for criminal tendencies. The weaker the groundrhythm the higher is the chance for criminal tendencies.

Now it becomes important to determine what we understand to be a criminal disposition. A criminal disposition exists in the open or latent readiness of a person, capable of responsibility, to cause socially unacceptable impairment of interests of others. It is important to mention here that certain qualities of the character make it more likely to give in to egoistic tendencies such as lack of resistance and irresoluteness. Those two are usually present when the fulfillment of personal desires results in the impairment of interests of others. Another important quality in connection with criminal tendencies is the ability to lie. All these characteristics increase the readiness to disregard the socially accepted limits. There are many combinations of character traits that can perceivably increase criminal tendencies. It is impossible to even come near finding them all because they can change with each case of a criminal personality. These combinations determine the direction of the criminal tendencies.

Coming back to what Klages has called the "guiding image" it seems to have a definite relationship to Rhoda Wieser's idea about the criminal tendencies. This guiding image reminds us of the various character types created by such psychologists as Jung, Spranger or Adler. The guiding image is not really a type. The variety of images is too great to list them all. Klages said: "The guiding image will prevail whenever the latitude of expression in the particular field (of the guiding image) is great." The guiding image can change. It can also be compared to our changing values. What one considers important today may not be so important tomorrow. I use the guiding image idea when I set up an analysis. Once you have the guiding image of a person the rest is easily built around it. The equivalent of Klages' guiding image is Rhoda Wieser's ground-rhythm, that ability to "swing" from soft to tight, the ability not to swing too hard and all this consciously or subconsciously. Groundrhythm is not designed to give an answer to every question a graphologist may have.

When Klages speaks about reducing of "soul qualities" or "soul substance" he is almost prophetic in his writings, and his prophecy is not a good one. Many psychologists have similar ideas. Rhoda Wieser expresses the same idea in a different form. The "soul substance" of Klages becomes the reducing of the I and the increasing of love and not love for one's self but AGAPE love.

It becomes obvious that the rhythm, providing we remain with the same definition, must be very much different depending on the stage of development and disregarding the age of the writer. In Rhoda Wieser's eyes this height of development depends on our ability to disassociate ourselves from our own selfishness.

This will open now horizons for each and every one and these fortunate ones will then perceive what they could not see before. The starting point and the road are different for each person. It is quite clear now that the rhythm of a person in the early stages of development is different from the rhythm of people in later stages of their development. We can call the first one "still-rhythm" and the second one "again-rhythm". The still-rhythm is difficult to see in the handwriting and if at all it can be found in the maze of conflicts of personality indirectly, not directly. The again-rhythm is a more or less rhythmic flow of the handwriting where ethical motives can be detected as well. Wherever there should be "again-rhythm" it represents an actual value.

Although the starting point for the development of groundrhythm was a criminal psychological one, it became a general psychological phenomenon. The criminal part of it remained as the point of origin but it became more and more a fringe area. In order to realize the full value of groundrhythm it is necessary to acknowledge three statements in order to be able to judge as Rhoda Wieser did.

1. To acknowledge that it is more important to learn to outgrow selfish tendencies rather than to increase them or to remain status quo.
2. A human being, observant in the general sense of the word can, if he wishes, take a judging view of his own doings, his own omissions, his own desires, his own thoughts, his own feelings, etc. as though he were confronted with another person. The accuracy and the ability to remain objective is different in every case. Many, many psychological aspects have a hand in this process. Therapeutic psychology fully recognizes this. The use of this fact seems to be highly successful. The statement that the possibility of self judgment exists cannot be denied.
3. It is almost impossible to be objective in all aspects of human relations. This becomes even more difficult when we avoid the establishment of definite values of personality. The fact remains that no description of a character exists without a label of value.

There is no word in any of the major languages to signify the type of love that, beyond any personal relationship, can give and not lose the identity. Only Greek has two separate words; one is "eros" and the other is "agape". The meaning of the two words is so different that one could never exchange one word for the other. The word agape was used by theologians, but Rhoda Wieser did not use this word in connection with any religion at all.

Now the question arises whether it is possible to use agape as a scale of value, as a measure for all other measures. Rhoda Wieser says yes. Here she gives a fitting example, a comparison well worth mentioning. There is only one sun in the heavens providing light and heat to us humans. The same sun, the same light, the same heat and the variety of living patterns is enormous. There is, within the sphere of the human mind and the human soul, only one sun. A sun which makes it possible for man to shine from within. This sun also provides light and warmth when he should be his own guide in the human pattern of growth. This sun represents a love directed to the "you" and all the others, to want for others and to share the feelings of others. This sun earns the name of agape, or the desire for the agape.

It all started with the description of the handwriting of criminals. It was shown that there was a definite relationship between the severity of the crime and the decreasing of the ground-rhythm. Increasing lack of elasticity in the stroke formation gave us this negative picture. Now we are ready to show the positive side of groundrhythm, that thinking and wishing for love that we have called agape. Some people may say, how can you build something positive on a psychological theory that starts with a violent criminal? This would be justified, providing agape would be a simple character trait. But it is not. Nobody is born with agape. It is a development, a maturing process. Agape changes the values from one human being to another even in a violent criminal. Where is the starting point? It is a step-by-step process and each and every one starts on a different step. Relatively speaking this is true for the upright citizen as it is for the criminal. The first step for the one who never thinks about anything getting him in conflict with the law will be in seemingly unimportant things of everyday life. To name a few; attitudes at the table, entering the home, in the subway, driving a car, on the job, being with friends, being open with people, being understanding and last but not least, increased consciousness. In a way all these possible changes are the same as if a thief would try not to steal or the attempt of a drinker to give up drinking. It is understandable that the upright citizen may feel insulted when compared in this way with a criminal. It may occur to you that we are not responsible for being born without criminal tendencies.

Now we can ask a different question. Can we use this scale of agape on teenagers or do we have to limit this valuable tool to grownups? It is important to know that groundrhythm can only be seen from the age of approximately 14 years on. There are variations in the age depending on the maturity of the child and other factors, but it cannot be much before that time for two good reasons. The completion of the coordination of the muscles responsible for the writing act is usually not before this age. Also, the young ones only start to feel as real individuals within their surroundings at this time. There are steps in front of each youngster. One wants to grow up, the other does not. There are such differences.

Only slowly the individuality finds its relationship to their own capabilities and to their own surroundings. But we should not underestimate the powers of the mind and the soul in the growing youngster. The avoidance of the "locking device" at the end poles of the pendulum is already in him. He already has the power to remain in the middle. This means that the growing process must be taken very seriously. The serious youngster wants to be taken seriously. You cannot ask if agape can only be found in a mature person. The word maturing indicates in itself that there is never an end to it. There is no question that there are many mature youngsters and many immature grown-ups. So the growing process of agape applies to the young ones as well. A well known biologist Adolf Partmann in the periodical "Universitas" (January 1962, Stuttgart) wrote, "May the young people who choose the middle road for their pattern of growth, and the ones who teach them, never lose sight of the intricate mosaic pattern called the deeds of our lives; I mean the great gift of knowing love." Isn't agape knowing love?

When we talk about performance in connection with the agape we must differentiate between the performance for a third party and the performance for one's self. The performance for a third party starting from the unskilled laborer, to the highest government official, needs the swinging of the pendulum to the middle to some extent. Only then is there an assurance of some form of loyalty and reliability. It is different with people that are self employed. A man who understands his trade and who will keep his promises fairly well will be called back again even if it may be possible to get someone else for a little less money. It becomes very much more complicated to evaluate the performance of say, a doctor or an artist in connection with agape. Even when we talk about a tradesman, the talent for his particular field may get into the foreground. This is even more important with the liberal professions. There are many practicing and (what is more important) productive artists who do not show a strong groundrhythm in their handwriting. Their work does not depend on the importance of groundrhythm. Many times an artist produces as a result of his own suffering.

Groundrhythm does not replace graphology. We can use groundrhythm with any method at our command. The stroke in itself can reveal the groundrhythm. To learn to see the stroke will help greatly in analyzing the handwritings of persons with little education. It will also help distinguish between routine movement and genuine elasticity.

Directional Pressure

Now we have learned that much of the judgment of groundrhythm depends on the elasticity of the stroke. We also have learned that on the one extreme side of the pendulum we find rigidity and on the other end slackness. It follows that the group of people belonging to the left side of the pendulum will react differently than the group on the right side, even though the circumstances are exactly the same. This simple deduction was the starting point for developing something entirely new, something beyond groundrhythm. The original observation leading to my discovery was made in the concentration camps Dachau and Buchenwald.

It was interesting to observe that the people with strong rigidity had the least chance for survival. One had to be very flexible to adjust quickly to the ever-changing situations. It is therefore not surprising that the vast majority of the surviving inmates in concentration camp were flexible. The ones without strong flexibility simply did not survive.

Many times on Sunday, after completing my chores I would go around and ask for samples of handwriting. I observed that nearly all inmates showed a change from a supposedly straight downstroke to a curved one. The strange part was that, for instance, in the small letter "f" the downstroke always curved to the left. One day I had the idea that this might have something to do with the fact that the writers were all in concentration camp. I then remembered Pulver's theory about the different directions and their symbolic values as described in my translation and condensation of his standard work Symbolism in Handwriting. According to Dr. Max Pulver's teaching, the right side is the future. Any pressure coming from the right would have the effect of curving a straight downstroke towards—the left. Here we are dealing with the pressure emanating from the symbolic right and changing the direction.

I called this phenomenon DIRECTIONAL PRESSURE. This is not the type of pressure we are accustomed to discussing. It is an invisible pressure coming out of one of the four symbolic directions of the writing field, a pressure always of a negative nature and always having the effect of changing a straight line into a curved one. Not every person will react to this kind of pressure the same way. As I mentioned in the beginning, a person lacking flexibility will be less likely to show directional pressure. This method of interpretation of directional pressure was developed more than 30 years ago and tested on about 1,000 samples with surprising results. Ten years ago I adopted this method into my curriculum and it is being used widely by my pupils. The article on directional pressure was published in German in the Graphologische Schriftenreihe, June 1967. This organization was the first one to publish it in the English version. And now, I will show you how it can help you.

Right directional pressure—We have said that a pressure from the right (←) can change any straight downstroke into a curved one towards the left. (/-(, f - f). This is called right pressure or pressure from the right, or right directional pressure. The indications for right directional pressure are:

- Fear or anxiety of the future
- Possibility of difficulty with or from the father
- Possibility of fear of our fellow man.

Left directional pressure—Comes out of the symbolic field of the past. The small letter "f" will curve towards the right. (/-), f - f). The indications for left directional pressure are:

- Fear of the past due to unresolved events, possibly influence future decisions
- Maternal pressure

Upper directional pressure—Pressure from above changes a straight horizontal line into a curved one towards the direction down. The most likely letter to be affected is the "t" and particularly the "t" stroke. (t - t). The interpretation for upper directional pressure is:

- Influence from the intellectual field
- Influence from beliefs
- Pressure from people who are considered our superior in intelligence
- An avoidance of such people may also be indicated

Lower directional pressure—Pressure from below will change a straight horizontal line into a curved one towards up. Again, the "t" stroke is the most likely to be affected (t - t). The indications for the lower directional pressure are:

- Influence from the body
- Influence from the financial field
- Influence from the sexual zone
- Pressure from people of lower intelligence
- Pressure of everyday life

An important limitation would be when a strong garland writing would show also directional pressure from above. The probability exists that the pressure from above is simply a continuation of the garland motion. The possibility of a compulsive personality must be taken into consideration.

Bibliography

Hellmut, Max — *Menschenkenntnis aus der Handschrift* (Waldemar Hoffman Verlag, Berlin, 1934.)

Klages, Ludwig — *Handschrift und Charakter* (Johann Ambrosius Barth, Leipzig, 1929.)

Klein, Felix — *Der Richtungsdruck in der Handschrift* (Graph. Schriftenreihe, Juni 1967.)

Mueller-Enskat — *Graphologische Diagnostik* (Verlag Hans Huber, Bern und Stuttgart, 1961.)

Pulver, Max — *Symbolik in der Handschrift* (Orell Fuessli Verlag, Zuerich und Leipzig, 1931.)

Wieser, Rhoda — *Der Verbrecher und seine Handschrift* (Altdorfer Verlag, Stuttgart, 1952.)

Persoenlichkeit und Handschrift (Ernst Reinhardt Verlag, Muenchen, Basel, 1956.)

Mensch und Leistung (Ernst Reinhardt Verlag, Muenchen, Basel, 1960.)

Human Character Types of Erich Fromm

Felix Klein

Human Character Types of Erich Fromm

Why should we graphologists even bother to look for types? The answer is simple. Once we have established a person as a certain character type through his handwriting, all we then must do is look for the variation of the particular person we are analyzing from the type. The analysis thus produced will be quite accurate and really easily and quickly done. Any of the types to be discussed will automatically give you the guiding image, by the name and characteristics of the character type.

Erich Fromm, a remarkable psychologist, established these types for psychological purposes. They can be very helpful to graphologists. A person fitting one type or the other does not have to "remain" this type. As a matter of fact, it is the aim of psychologists to get people to grow "out" of their types, particularly when they belong to a type that we may consider as negative.

The positive type person will grow because it is a characteristic of this type to grow through productivity.

HUMAN CHARACTER
Productive Character Types

In order to understand what a productive human character is, we must begin with a working definition of the mature[1] character structure.

One of the basic criterion for maintenance of the well-being of the mature character is its need to produce. This means not only to produce material things, but it includes a person's mode of relatedness in all realms of human experience. Productiveness as used here, is a person's ability to use his powers and to realize the potentialities inherent in himself. This kind of productiveness is an attitude which every human being is capable of unless he is mentally and/or emotionally crippled.

A brief example of how this mental or emotional incapacitation works might be the nonproductive activity of a person under hypnosis. He may, while in a deep trance, have his eyes open, walk, talk and do things, in other words, he "acts." The general definition of activity, i.e. "productiveness" would apply to him since energy is spent and some change brought about. But a closer look tells us it is not really the hypnotized person who is the actor, but the hypnotist who, by means of suggestion, acts through him. It is very much in this manner that we are sometimes controlled by subconscious compulsions, fears end anxieties, and by experiences so long past that we cannot even consciously remember them. This is a characteristic example of a situation in which a person can be active, and yet not be the true actor, but his activity results from compelling forces over which he has no control.

Just as our example character was a type of nonproductive activity, so are those reactions to anxiety, either conscious or unconscious, which consume much of our energies, also examples of nonproductlve activities.

In the concept of productiveness we are not concerned with activity which necessarily leads to practical results, but our concern is with an ATTITUDE, a mode of reaction and orientation to the world, to oneself, and to others in life. We are concerned, in other words, with man's character, not with his outward success.

Productiveness is man's realization of his own potentialities and the use of these potentialities. This requires his whole life time and the effort never stops in the truly productive character.

---

1 Mature in this context means mental and emotional maturity, not physical maturity.

We mentioned that productiveness is man's relatedness to the world and to other people. But how, one might ask, is man related to the world when he uses his powers productively? There are two basic ways.

I. REPRODUCTIVELY

This is to perceive the world, life and actuality in the same fashion as a film makes a literal record of things photographed. It is the mere recognition of things as they are, or as one's culture maintains them to be. These people are the perfect "realists." They see all there is to be seen of the surface features of life, but are quite incapable of penetrating below the surface to the essential, of visualizing what is not yet apparent. Reality to them is the sum total of only what has already materialized. The extreme degree of this kind of character not only is unproductive, but it is sick. These people's view of reality is distorted because of its lack of depth and perspective. They are apt to err when more than manipulation of immediately given data and short-range aims are involved. EXTREME REALISM SEEMS TO BE THE VERY OPPOSITE OF INSANITY, AND YET IT IS ONLY ITS COMPLEMENT.

II. GENERATIVELY

This is a person's conceiving the world by enlivening and re-creating this new material through the spontaneous activity of one's own mental and emotional powers. The extreme degree of this mode of relatedness is a person who has lost completely his ability to perceive actuality. Just as the extreme degree of the Reproductive mode of relatedness is sick, so is the extreme degree of the Generative mode of relatedness. These people are the psychotic and paranoid extremes who have built up the world of reality completely within themselves. The common factors of reality as perceived by all others are unreal to them. They are unable to relate productively.

THE PRODUCTIVE ORIENTATION IS THE BALANCE BETWEEN THESE TWO TYPES, OR MODES OF RELATEDNESS. IT IS THE OPPOSITE OF THEIR EXTREMES. The well-adjusted, or mature human being is capable of relating himself to the world simultaneously by perceiving it as it is and by conceiving it enlivened and enriched by his own powers. The presence of both Reproductive and Generative capacities is a precondition for productiveness. Productiveness is that something new which springs from the dynamic interaction of these opposite poles.

We have described productiveness as a mode of relatedness to the world. Now the question arises, what does the productive person produce? The most important objective of productiveness is man himself. We will now discuss the types of productiveness involved in the specific activities of man.

I. PRODUCTIVE LOVE AND THINKING

The concept of productive love is very different from what is frequently called "love." It has nothing to do with the possessive dependence of one who has "fallen for" another. While every human being has a capacity for love, ITS REALIZATION IS ONE OF THE MOST DIFFICULT ACHIEVEMENTS AND MUST CONSTANTLY BE WORKED FOR. Productive love can be said to include three types:

A. Love of mother for the child

B. Brotherly love, or love of fellow man

C. Erotic love, or love between members of the opposite sex

Regardless of what type we speak about, there are four components which must be present before the love can be considered a productive one. They are:

(1) Care

(2) Responsibility

(3) Respect

(4) Knowledge

Motherly love is the most readily understood instance of productive love which embodies the components of (1) Care, and (2) Responsibility. The mother's body must labor for the birth of the child, and after birth her love consists of her effort to care for the child and make it grow. Her love does not depend on conditions which the child must fulfill in order to be loved; it is unconditional, based only upon the child's request and the mother's response.

In instances of individual love we often believe that to fall in love is the culmination of love, while actually it is the beginning, and only the opportunity for the actual achievement of love. One's own power to love produces love, just as being interested makes one interesting. To love a person productively is to care and feel responsible for his life, not only for his physical existence, but for the growth and development of all his human powers. To love productively is incompatible with being passive, with merely being an onlooker at the loved person's life. It implies labor and care and the responsibility for his growth.

To love one person productively also means to be related to his core, to him as representing mankind. Productive love for one individual cannot be separated from love of mankind. If love for one individual is divorced from love of mankind in the mind of the individual, it remains superficial, shallow, and is often not love at all, but a dependency.

We have seen how care and responsibility are vital elements of productive love, but without respect for, and knowledge of the beloved person, love deteriorates into domination and possessiveness. Respect is the ability to see a person as he is, to be aware of his uniqueness without wanting to change it, only to cultivate it. And to respect a person is not possible without knowing him, without being thoroughly acquainted with his individuality. Love is the productive form of relatedness to others, and also to oneself.

It implies responsibility, care, respect and knowledge, and the wish for the other person or persons to grow and to develop. It is the expression of intimacy between two human beings under the condition of the preservation of each other's integrity.

II. PRODUCTIVE WORK

For the last few centuries Western man has been obsessed by the idea of work, by the need for constant activity. He is almost incapable of being immobile for any length of time. However, one must keep in mind here that laziness and compulsive activity are not opposites, but are components of the disturbance of man's proper productive functioning. The inability to enjoy ease and repose is just as neurotic as the inability to work.

Productive work, like productive love, implies fruitful pursuit of those activities which give a person pleasure and without any sense on his part of exploitation of the productiveness of others. A protection of the integrity and productiveness of those with whom we work, and on whom we depend in our work.

III. PRODUCTIVE REASONING (THINKING)

We must first examine the diference between reason and intelligence to best understand productive reasoning.

Intelligence is man's tool for attaining practical goals with the aim of discovering those aspects of things in order to manipulate them. This particular quality of intelligence can be seen clearly in an extreme case, and that is the paranoid person. His premise, for instance, that all people are in conspiracy against him, is irrational and false, but his thought processes built upon this premise can, in themselves, show a remarkable amount of intelligence. In his attempt to prove his paranoid thesis he connects observations and makes logical constructions which are often so intelligent that it is difficult to prove the irrationality of his premises.

Reason involves another dimension, that of depth, which reaches to the essence of things. While reason is not divorced from the practical aims of life, it is not a mere tool for immediate action. Its function is to know, to understand, to relate oneself to things by comprehending them. It penetrates through the surface of things in order to discover their essence, their hidden relationships and deeper meanings, their "reason." It grasps all dimensions, not only the practically relevant ones. Being concerned with the essence of things means to be concerned with the essential, the universal traits of phenomena, freed from their superficial and accidental aspects.

To further recognize the existence of productive thinking, one must be able to see certain characteristics. Some of these are:

A. The person is not indifferent to his object, but is affected and concerned by it. It is this very interest and relationship to the object which first stimulates his interest.

B. Productive thinking is characterized by objectivity, by his ability to perceive things and objects as they are, and not as he wishes them to be. He is subjectively related, but there is a balance maintained between subjective involvement and objectivity of perception.

C. Another aspect of productive thinking about living and non-living objects is that of seeing the totality of a phenomenon. If the observer isolates one aspect of the object without seeing the gestalt, he will not understand even the one aspect he studies. One must get a whole or consistent picture, and see what the structure of the whole requires to give meaning to the parts.

Objectivity does not mean detachment, it means respect; that is the ability not to distort and falsify things, persons and oneself. Because, if we think productively, we respect the things we observe, we are capable of seeing them in their uniqueness and thelr own interconnectedness WITHOUT HAVING THE INTRINSIC DESIRE TO CHANGE THEM, OR MOLD THEM TO OUR OWN FORM.

Erich Fromm, MAN FOR HIMSELF, Fawcett Publications, Inc., 1947.

HUMAN CHARACTER
Non-productive Character Types

RECEPTIVE ORIENTATION (ACCEPTING)

In the receptive orientation a person feels "the source of all good" to be outside, and he believes that the only way to get what he wants—be it something material, be it affection, love, knowledge, pleasure—is to receive it from that outside source. In this orientation the problem of love is almost exclusively that of "being loved" and not that of loving. Such people tend to be indiscriminate in the choice of their love objects, because being loved by anybody is such an overwhelming experience for them that they "fall for" anybody who gives them love or what looks like love. They are exceedingly sensitive to any withdrawal or rebuff they experience on the part of the loved person. Their orientation is the same in the sphere of thinking: If intelligent, they make the best listeners, since their orientation is one of receiving, not of producing ideas; left to themselves they feel paralyzed. It is characteristic of these people that their first thought is to find somebody else to give them needed information rather than to make even the smallest effort of their own.

If religious, these persons have a concept of God in which they expect everything from God and nothing from their own activity. If not religious, their relationship to persons or institutions is very much the same; they are always in search of a "magic helper." They show a particular kind of loyalty, at the bottom of which is the gratitude for the hand that feeds them and the fear of ever losing it. Since they need many hands to feel secure, they have to be loyal to numerous people. It is difficult for them to say "no," and they are easily caught between conflicting loyalties and promises. Since they cannot say "no," they love to say "yes" to everything and everybody, and the resulting paralysis of their critical abilities makes them increasingly dependent on others.

They are dependent not only on authorities for knowledge and help but on people in general for any kind of support. They feel lost when alone because they feel that they cannot do anything without help. This helplessness is especially important with regard to those acts which by their very nature can only be done alone—making decisions and taking responsibility. In personal relationships, for instance, they ask advice from the very person with regard to whom they have to make a decision.

This receptive type has great fondness for food and drink. These persons tend to overcome anxiety and depression by eating or drinking. The mouth is an especially prominent feature, often the most expressive one; the lips tend to be open, as if in a state of continuous expectation of being fed. In their dreams being fed is a frequent symbol of being loved; being starved, an expression of frustration or disappointment.

By and large, the outlook of people of this receptive orientation is optimistic and friendly; they have a certain confidence in life and its gifts, but they become anxious and distraught when their "source of supply" is threatened. They often have a genuine warmth and a wish to help others, but doing things for others also assumes the function of securing their favor.

EXPLOITATIVE ORIENTATION (TAKING)

The exploitative orientation, like the receptive, has as its basic premise the feeling that the source of all good is outside, that whatever one wants to get must be sought there, and that one cannot produce anything oneself. The difference between the two, however, is that the exploitative type does not expect to receive things from others as gifts, but to take them away from others by force or cunning. This orientation extends to all spheres of activity.

In the realm of love and affection these people tend to grab and steal. They feel attracted only to people whom they can take away from somebody else. Attractiveness to them is conditioned by a person's attachment to somebody else; they tend not to fall in love with an unattached person.

We find the same attitude with regard to thinking and intellectual pursuits. Such people will tend not to produce ideas but to steal them. This may be done directly in the form of plagiarism or more subtly by repeating in different phraseology the ideas voiced by others and insising they are new and their own. It is a striking fact that frequently people with great intelligence proceed in this way, although if they relied on their own gifts they might well be able to have ideas of their own. The lack of original ideas or independent production in otherwise gifted people often has its explanation in this character orientation, rather than on any innate lack of originality. The same statement holds true with regard to their orientation to material things. Things which they can take away from others always seem better to them than anything they can produce themselves. They use and exploit anybody and anything from whom or from which they can squeeze something. Their motto is: "Stolen fruits are sweetest." Because they want to use and exploit people, they "love" those who, explicitly or implicitly, are promising objects of exploitation, and get "fed up" with persons whom they have squeezed out. An extreme example is the kleptomaniac who enjoys things only if he can steal them, although he has the money to buy them.

This orientation seems to be symbolized by the biting mouth which is often a prominent feature in such people. It is not a play upon words to point out that they often make "biting" remarks about others. Their attitude is colored by a mixture of hostility and manipulation. Everyone is an object of exploitation and is judged according to his usefulness. Instead of the confidence and optimism which characterizes the receptive type, one finds here suspicion and cynicism, envy and jealousy. Since they are satisfied only with things they can take away from others, they tend to overrate what others have and underrate what is theirs.

HOARDING ORIENTATION (PRESERVING)

While the receptive and exploitative types are similar inasmuch as both expect to get things from the outside world, the hoarding orientation is essentially different. This orientation makes people have little faith in anything new they might get from the outside world; their security is based upon hoarding and saving, while spending is felt to be a threat. They have surrounded themselves, as it were, by a protective wall, and their main aim is to bring as much as possible into this fortified position and to let as little as possible out of it. Their miserliness refers to money and material things as well as to feelings and thoughts. Love is essentially a possession; they do not give love but try to get it by possessing the "beloved." The hoarding person often shows a particular kind of faithfulness toward people and even toward memories. Their sentimentality makes the past appear as golden; they hold on to it and indulge in the memories of bygone feelings and experiences. They know everything but are sterile and incapable of productive thinking.

One can recognize these people too by facial expressions and gestures. Theirs is the tightlipped mouth: their gestures are characteristic of their withdrawn attitude. While those of the receptive type are inviting and round, as it were, and the gestures of the expoitative type are aggressive and pointed, those of the hoarding type are angular, as if they wanted to emphasize the frontiers between themselves and the outside world. Another characteristic element in this attitude is pedantic orderliness. The hoarder will be orderly with things, thoughts, or feelings, but again, as with memory, his orderliness is sterile and rigid. He cannot endure things out of place and will automatically rearrange them. To him the outside world threatens to break into his fortified position; orderliness signifies mastering the world outside by putting it, and keeping it, in its proper place in order to avoid the danger of intrusion. His compulsive cleanliness is another expression of his need to undo contact with the outside world. Things beyond his own frontiers are felt to be dangerous and "unclean"; he annuls the menacing contact by compulsive washing, similar to a religious washing ritual prescribed after contact wlth unclean things or people. Things have to be put not only in their proper place, but also into their proper time; obsessive punctuality is characteristic of the hoarding type; it is another form of mastering the outside world. If the outside world is experienced as a threat to one's fortified position, obstinacy is a logical reaction. A constant "no" is the almost automatic defense against intrusion; sitting tight, the answer to the danger of being pushed. These people tend to feel that they possess only a fixed quantity of strength, energy, or mental capacity, and that this stock is diminished or exhausted by use and can never be replenished. They cannot understand the self-replenishing function of all living substance and that activity and the use of one's powers increase strength while stagnation paralyzes; to them, death and destruction have more reality than life and growth. The act of creation is a miracle of which they hear but in which they do not believe. Their highest values are order and security; their motto: "There is nothing new under the sun." In their relationship to others intimacy is a threat; either remoteness or possession of a person means security. The hoarder tends to be suspicious and to have a particular sense of justice which in effect says: "Mine is mine and yours is yours."

MARKETING ORIENTATION (EXCHANGING)

The marketing orientation developed as a dominant one only in the modern era. The modern market-place is no longer a meeting place but a mechanism characterized by abstract and impersonal demand. One produces for this market, not for a known circle of customers; its verdict is based on laws of supply and demand; and it determines whether the commodity can be sold and at what price. No matter what the USE VALUE of a pair of shoes may be, for instance, if the supply is greater than the demand, some shoes will be sentenced to economic death; they might as well not have been produced at all. The market day is the "day of judgment" as far as the EXCHANGE VALUE of commodities is concerned.

The regulatory function of the market has been, and still is, predominant enough to have a profound influence on the character formation of the urban middle class and, through the latter's social and cultural influence, on the whole population. The market concept of value, the emphasis on exchange value rather than on use value, has led to a similar concept of value with regard to people, and particularly to oneself. The character orientation which is rooted in the experience of oneself as a commodity and of one's value as exchange value I call the marketing orientation. In our time the marketing orientation has been growing rapidly, together with the development of a new market that is a phenomenon of the last decades—the "personality market." Clerks and salesmen, business executives and doctors, lawyers and artists all appear on this market. It is true that their legal status and economic positions are different. Some are independent, charging for their services; others are employed, receiving salaries. But all are dependent for their material success on a personal acceptance by those who need their services or who employ them.

The fact that in order to have success it is not sufficient to have the skill and equipment for performing a given task but that one must be able to "put across" one's personality in competition with many others shapes the attitude toward oneself. If it were enough for the purpose of making a living to rely on what one knows and what one can do, one's self-esteem would be in proportion to one's capacities, that is, to one's use value; but since success depends largely on how one sells one's personality, one experiences oneself as a commodity or rather simultaneously as the seller AND the commodity to be sold. A person is not concerned with his life and happiness, but with becoming salable. This feeling might be compared to that of a commodity, of handbags on a counter, for instance, could they feel and think. Each one would try to make itself as "attractive" as possible in order to attract customers and to look as expensive as possible in order to obtain a higher price than its rivals. The handbag sold for the highest price would feel elated, since that would mean it was the most "valuable" one; the one which was not sold would feel sad and convinced of its own worthlessness. Like the handbag, one has to be in "fashion" on the personality market.

But the problem is not only that of self-evaluation and self-esteem but of one's experience of oneself as an independent entity, of one's IDENTITY WITH ONESELF. As we shall see later, the mature and productive individual derives his feeling of identity from the experience of himself as the agent who is one with his powers; this feeling of self can be briefly expressed as meaning "I am what I do." In the marketing orientation man encounters his own powers as commodities alienated from him. He is not one with them but they are masked from him because what matters is not his self-realization in the process of using them, but his success in the process of selling them. Thus his feeling of identity becomes as shaky as his self-esteem; it is constituted by the sum total of roles one can play: "I am as you desire me."

The receptive, exploitative, and hoarding orientations have one thing in common: Each is one form of human relatedness which, if dominant in a person, is specific of him and characterizes him. The marketing orientation, however, does not develop something which is potentially in the person; its very nature is that no specific and permanent kind of relatedness is developed, but that the very changeability of attitudes is the only permanent quality of such orientation. In this orientation, those qualities are developed which can best be sold.

Erich Fromm, MAN FOR HIMSELF, Fawcett Publications, Inc., 1947.

HUMAN CHARACTER
Some Dynamic Concepts Expressed in Productive Character Types

THE PRODUCTIVE HUMAN CHARACTER TYPE

A. Maturity

Strong Need to Produce

Use of Personal Powers

Realization of Potentialities

FUNCTIONS OF PRODUCTIVE CHARACTER TYPE

A. Constructive Modes of Life-Relatedness

Logical Perceptions of Reality

Spontaneity of Mental Powers

Constructive Relatedness to the World and Life

B. Productive Love and Thinking

Care of the Individual

Responsibility for the Individual

Respect for the Individual

Knowledge of the Individual

Expansiveness of Love for Humanity

C. Productive Work

Creative use of Leisure

Creative use of Special Talents

Protection of Co-Workers' Integrity

Protection of Co-Workers' Productiveness

D. Productive Reasoning (Thinking)

Use of Intelligence to Attain Practical Goals

Use of Reason for Penetration to Essentials

Personal Concern for Life-Objects

Objectivity for Reality

Observance of the Gestalt

(1) Objects

(2) Happenings

(3) Circumstances

HUMAN CHARACTER
Some Dynamic Concepts Expressed in Non-Productive Character Types

RECEPTIVE ORIENTATION (ACCEPTING)

Positive Aspect	Negative Aspect
Accepting	Passive, without initiative
Responsive	Opinionless, characterless
Devoted	Submissive
Modest	Without pride
Charming	Parasitical
Adaptable	Unprincipled
Socially adjusted	Servile, no self-confidence
Idealistic	Unrealistic
Sensitive	Cowardly
Polite	Spineless
Optimistic	Wishful thinking
Trusting	Gullible
Tender	Sentimental

EXPLOITATIVE ORIENTATION (TAKING)

Positive Aspect	Negative Aspect
Active	Exploitative
Able to take initiative	Aggressive
Able to make claims	Egocentric
Proud	Conceited
Impulsive	Rash

Self-confident	Arrogant
Captivating	Seducing

HOARDING ORIENTATION (PRESERVING)

Positive Aspect	Negative Aspect
Practical	Unimaginative
Economical	Stingy
Careful	Suspicious
Reserved	Cold
Patient	Lethargic
Cautious	Anxious
Steadfast, tenacious	Stubborn
Imperturbable	Indolent
Composed under stress	Inert
Orderly	Pedantic
Methodical	Obsessional
Loyal	Possessive

MARKETING ORIENTATION (EXCHANGING)

Positive Aspect	Negative Aspect
Purposeful	Opportunistic
Able to change	Inconsistent
Youthful	Childish
Forward-looking	Without a future or a past
Open-minded	Without principle and values
Social	Unable to be alone

Experimenting	Aimless
Undogmatic	Relativistic
Efficient	Overactive
Curious	Tactless
Intelligent	Intellectualistic
Adaptable	Undiscriminating
Tolerant	Indifferent
Witty	Silly
Generous	Wasteful

It must be noted here that the positive and negative aspects are not two separate classes of syndromes. Each of these traits can be described as a point on a continuum which is determined by the degree of the productive orientation which prevails. The different orientations may operate in different strength in the material, emotional, or intellectual spheres of activity, respectively.

Erich Fromm, MAN FOR HIMSELF, Greenwich, Connecticut; Fawcett Publications, Inc., 1947.

ERICH FROMM
GONZALEZ COSIO NO. 15
MEXICO 12, D. F.
TELEPHONE 23-04-19

1. I. 1959

Dear Stanley Plastrik,

I just received your letter and thank you very much for writing me so much in detail. I don't think we disagree too much. I shall answer more another time. Right now I have only a moment and want to send off the article on the Disarmament. I would greatly appreciate it if you would let me know as soon as possible if and when you plan to publish it.

With warm wishes for a Happy New Year

Yours E. Fromm

Productive Character Type

PS. Don't bother about the Rembrandt if it is quite impractical. I wondered whether you join and then immediately cancel? Please don't let yourself in for anything you don't want.

J.

Generatively

Later.

I've just been given a new italic pen. It has much more 'bite' to it than the first one I used, so my writing is much crisper. If its smaller that's probably because I'm freezing!!!

JR.

They had only invited me & the other member of [illegible] because I had offered help (and they were under the influence and I had provided it). Wonder whether they had expected more than it, and I certainly should be one of the bigger contributors. I hope I was/made them feel it. I [illegible] modestly.

August 20, 1968

I had not expected to be on the move again so quickly. Only [illegible] since I returned from Cornwall. It was a pleasant and interesting trip. We saw a few [illegible]. There was really not much to see. I was not overwhelmingly impressed with the [illegible] position. I don't think the [illegible] Park really benefits much from it. I was cross that they did not [illegible] my [illegible]

Reproductively

Refuse containers for disposal of trash only. Items such as cups, trays, knives, forks and spoons are to be returned to proper buffet storage locations. Too many pieces of equipment are lost on all flights!

Receptive Positive

Christina

admirers.

Discussing the need for busy people to have a hobby and that "to be really safe and happy, one ought to have at least two or three"! - Mr Churchill begins with his reflections on work and leisure

Receptive Negative

so I may not be able to attend unless you say I am your guest? Either way, I hope to meet you, please call 265-1735.

Your book, dated Dec. 11, finally arrived, and was well-worth the waiting, as all good things are.

Looking forward to hearing you, at least.

Best Wishes
Patricio J.

Exploitive Positive

November 17, 1968

I do not mind if Mr. Klein Keeps this sample of my handwriting

Elizabeth [illegible]

Exploitive Negative

Hoarding Positive

This is a sample of my handwriting.
Today was such a beautiful day after the
exciting northeaster we had last night
I am very anxious to hear what you have to
say about my character and future potential.

Marcia L

things you say, baby your eyes tell
love story... in their magic way...
your embrace is likened to the touch
of spring... giving me a purpose..
causing my heart to sing.. no other
alone could thrill me the way you
always do... your are as soft as
milkweed down... they made my
dream come true... so I'll nestle
in your arms... close to your heart to heart... baby I'm happy
when you hold me... blue when
we have to part.
God,... peace, love, communications,
friendship be unto you.
Henry Leroy Jr.

Hoarding Negative

Marketing Positive

This is the handwriting of a conventional, dependable, straightforward person. She has a flair for organization and a good business sense. She is systematic efficient whatever she undertakes will be done well. She would make a good efficiency expert.

She has a clear logical mind about average intelligence. A careful person, she might be successful in business or profession but is apt to miss opportunities because she doesn't like to take chances. Will not make up her mind i…

Hello Mr Klein

Glad to see you again and looking so well. I tell everyone I never forgot how impressed I was by you and what a genuine person you are

Sincerely
Hortense Saron

Marketing Negative

The Receptive Type

Positive		Negative	
Accepting	Clear middle zone; garland	Passive	Left trend; slow; light pressure
Responsive	Extended finals; right slant; garland; light pressure	Opinion-less	Light pressure; irregular; poor spacing
Devoted	Formal regularity; strong pressure	Submissive	Thread; weak garland
Modest	Simple capitals; medium-to-small writing	Lack of Pride	Weak garland; poor upper zone; light pressure; no trend emphasized
Charming	Good use of space; medium primary pressure	Parasitic	Thread; flat arcade
Adaptable	Rounded forms; variety of forms; innovative	Unprincipled	Thread; flat arcade; irregular; no emphasis on any trend
Socially Adjusted	Close word-spacing; narrow right margin; rounded forms; medium size	Servile	Weak garland; double bow
Idealistic	Good upper zone; garland; right slant; right trend	Unrealistic	Thread; overlapping letters; extremes; lines too close
Sensitive	Fine lines; light pressure	Cowardly	Double bow; large right margin; irregular base line
Polite	Good left margin; good spacing; any formality indicators	Spineless	Light pressure; weak down strokes; thread; changing slant
Optimistic	Rising lines; medium pressure	Wishful Thinking	High upper zone; weak t-crossings; no emphasis on trend; narrow lower margin
Trusting	Right slant; garland; right trend	Gullible	Low style evaluation with small, irregular spaces between words
Tender	Right slant; delicate forms	Sentimental	Right slant; garland; narrow lower margin

The Exploitive Type

Positive		Negative	
Active	Speed; right slant; spaces between words small & even	Exploitive	Left trend; angles; arcades; thread; sham garlands
Able to Take Initiative	Right trend; right slant; extended end strokes	Aggressive	Angles; blunt horizontal strokes; widening at end; horizontals go down
Able to Make Claims	Large; left trend; simplification	Egocentric	Left trend; large middle zone; finals reversed
Proud	Exaggerated upper zone; straight down-strokes	Conceited	Large capitals; embellishments
Impulsive	Speed; irregularity; right slant; tapering end strokes	Rash	Right slant; excessive speed; light pressure; neglected forms
Self Confident	Strong pressure; firm down strokes; large	Arrogant	Poor rhythm; large; large capitals; embellished; left slant
Captivating	Rounded; large; right trend; signs of confidence	Seducing	Initiative, regularity, right trend

The Hoarding Type

	Positive		Negative
Practical	Simple forms; good middle zone	Lacking Imagination	Meager forms; rigidity; no empty spaces
Economical	Small spaces between words and lines; narrow margins	Stingy	No margins; very narrow spacing; narrow letters
Careful	Clarity; slow; attention to detail	Suspicious	Widening right margin; signs of insecurity; narrow; angular; wiry
Reserved	Vertical or left slant; narrow; high arcades; large margins	Cold	Rigid; lack of rounded forms
Patient	Deliberate; slow	Lethargic	Pastosity; slow; rounded
Cautious	Vertical or left slant; narrow; larger right margin	Anxious	Not flowing; unbalanced spacing; hesitation; directional pressure; extreme narrowness; extremely small
Steadfast	Regularity; firm t-crossings; firm down strokes; pressure	Stubborn	Poor movement; slow; possible disconnections; some rigidity
Imperturbable	Rigid regularity; firm baseline	Indifferent	Wide spaces between words; rigid; wide right margin
Composed Under Stress	Formal regularity; firm base line	Indolent	Slow; neglected forms; possible looped garlands
Orderly	Good space between lines; neat; regularity; legible; good spacing	Obsessional	Extreme left trend; hooks in lower zone; rigid regularity; compulsive repetitions
Methodical	Same as "Orderly" but more rigid	Pedantic	Rigid regularity; possible angularity
Loyal	Garland; left trend; upper zone extensions; signs of sincerity	Possessive	Return end-strokes; possible claw strokes; roll-ins

The Marketing Type

	Positive		Negative
Purposeful	Right trend; simplified; possible primary pressure	Opportunistic	Thread; speed; form neglected
Able To Change	Rounded forms; fluid; light pressure	Inconsistent	Irregularity; uneven base line; irregular pressure
Youthful	Medium-to-strong pressure; fluid; right trend	Childish	Roll-ins; claw end-strokes; excessive circular movement in middle zone
Forward Looking	Right slant; narrow right margin; movement emphasized	Without Future or Past	Upright slant; de-emphasis on down-strokes
Open Minded	Garland; right slant; elastic; possible open "a" and/or "o"	Without Principles or Values	Neglected upper zone; neglected form
Social	Strong garland; right trend; narrow spaces between words; right slant; space between letters	Unable to Be Alone	Narrow spaces between words; wide; lack of margins
Experimenting	Original forms; thread; narrow right margin; simplified connections, measured fullness of loops	Aimless	Neglect of form combined with irregularity
Not Dogmatic	Original forms; fluid	Relativistic	Thread with little pressure; tapered word-endings; fairly good symmetry
Efficient	Simplified; fluid; sense for space	Overactive	Strong right trend; emphasis on movement; illegible due to speed

Curious	Tapered endings of words; extensions into upper zone; rounded	Tactless	Larger toward word endings; swell-strokes (increased pressure toward end of stroke)
Intelligent	Speed; simplification; clever connections	Intellectualism (Pseudo-intellectual)	Upper zone emphasis in low form level; embellishments; unnecessary use of space
Adaptable	Rounded; right slant; fluid; rhythmic	Undiscriminating	Neglect of form; extreme right slant; poor symmetry
Tolerant	Rounded; tapered word endings; good spacing	Indifferent	Neglect of form; meager forms; roll-ins
Witty	Odd-shaped i-dots with simplification; rounded	Silly	Primitive forms; confused space
Generous	Right trend; large size; wide	Wasteful	Waste of space; speed; unusual extensions in any zone

Male and Female in the Handwriting

Felix Klein

Male and Female in the Handwriting

What Every Graphologist Should Know About the Subject

Male and Female Symbols and their Expressions.

Male or female, that is the question—or is it? Let's start examining the differences. We all know that a man is built differently than a woman. There are functions in the woman's body which are not present in a man and vice-versa. The producing of an offspring may be the most outstanding one. These are commonly known facts, and it is not necessary for us to discuss them any further.

It is interesting that the medical profession has found indications that certain sicknesses, seemingly unrelated to the sexes, seem to be more prevalent in men than in women, or vice-versa. Generally it looks as if women have more protection than men. This may also be the reason women live longer than men. It also has been established that women, during pregnancy, enjoy protection against some diseases that neither men nor even women who are not pregnant enjoy. These are facts that can be proven.

We are very much inclined to believe that character traits and abilities are also predominant in one sex more than the other. It may seem at first that the fact that only one watchmaker out of 5000 is a woman becomes a sure indication that men possess more ability and more character traits conducive to becoming watchmakers. Before we can proceed to prove this theory, we first have to touch on a relative a subject.

It was around 1900 when E. B. Twitmyer, a graduate student of the University of Pennsylvania, made an interesting accidental discovery while experimenting for his dissertation. He was working on the patellar reflex, better known as the knee jerk. He constructed a mechanism consisting of a hammer that would strike the patellar tendon. In order to warn the subject that the hammer was about to strike, he struck a bell. At one time he accidentally struck the bell. The hammer was not activated but patellar reaction, the jerking of the knee, occurred anyway. The subject insisted that the reaction was involuntary. Twitmyer immediately realized that he had stumbled upon a major discovery from the point of the psychology of learning. When he reported his findings to the American Psychological Association in 1904, none of the famous scientists recognized the importance of his discovery, which is known today under the name of Classical or Respondent Conditioning.

Within a year Ivan Pavlov, a Russian psychologist, experimented with dogs. Whenever food is put into the mouth, the flow of saliva starts. This is an unconditional reflex. He used a variety of conditional stimuli, a metronome, a light and a brush. The metronome would stimulate the animal through hearing, the light through seeing and the brush through the feeling. The more often the stimuli were used, the higher the production of saliva became. The appearance of the food was eventually not necessary for the production of saliva.

Now let's go back to the question: Is it true that some or all character traits are to be found more in a man, or in a woman? It is my contention that we all have all character traits. It is only a question of degree. This opinion is shared by most psychologists and it is also shared by most graphologists. "There is a little bit of a murderer in each of us." This should sound like a familiar phrase to most of my readers.

Now we will take this information and proceed, assuming it to be correct. How is it then that there is one woman watchmaker for 5000 men watchmakers. If the distribution of traits and abilities is not divided according to the sexes what is it then that causes such drastic division of the sexes within certain professions.

It all starts in early childhood. We indoctrinate our youngsters "what a boy is supposed to be like," and "what a girl should develop into." How often have you heard, "A boy is not supposed to cry." Why is it that we believe it unmanly to cry? There is no reason why either a man or a woman should have to control the emotions to such an extent. It is important to see how we already guide a boy into understanding of technical things by giving him toys that will train him in mechanical thinking, while the girl will get a doll. There is absolutely no early provision for a girl who is mechanically inclined, or for a boy who has tendencies for doing things we usually classify as "women's work." At the age of seven I was fascinated by things that could be done by hand, particularly needlework. My favorite was crocheting.

There is a school system originated by the German educator and philosopher, Dr. Rudolf Steiner, which teaches boys and girls carpentry, bookbinding, woodcarving, etc. and the boys also learn to knit, to crochet and to sew along with the girls. The interesting experience gained from this is that neither the girls or the boys mind. It is, as we see now, that we are "conditioning" our children at a very early age. We are constantly trying to emphasize the masculine qualities in the boys and the feminine qualities in the girls. When a girl shows many masculine qualities we say, "Oh, she is a tomboy" as though there were something wrong with her. They start to worry about, "How is she ever going to get a husband?" And if a boy plays with dolls, or even cries, "He is a sissy! Whatever kind of a man is he going to be."

There are still highly civilized nations that limit the activities of a woman so much that she really becomes a second class citizen. For instance; a few years ago, when I visited the tropical zone of Colombia, my cousin who lives there, took us out in the evening. We went to a large coffee shop and the place was packed—packed with men. There must have been about 250 men there and 3 women—2 waitresses and my wife. The natives do not look with great respect upon the women who take a job as a waitress. Women are not supposed to go out in the evening at all. These are not conditions that will be found in the U.S. However, we do have a very strong discriminatory attitude towards women. It is a rare incident for a woman to get to a top position in big business. In many fields there are still outright discriminatory policies. The musical field, particularly the major orchestras are often reluctant to employ women. A dear friend of mine who played the viola beautifully had the greatest difficulty getting orchestras to employ her. Because she felt funny to accept unemployment insurance she had an additional difficulty. Eventually she became so discouraged she committed suicide.

So many men want their wives to stay home and take care of the house and the children. There are women who can do that and be happy. I believe they represent a minority. It happens too often that a woman becomes highly dissatisfied with her life once the children start going to school and the things that are to be done in the house are not interesting anymore. Invariably, when I have to do a handwriting analysis in such a situation the major point becomes my advice for the writer to pursue something she has talent for, and of which she usually is completely unaware. It is without a doubt that we cannot afford to stand still in personal growth—either men or women. It is an absolute necessity to continue to develop. Failure to do so will have negative consequences in varying degrees. In fact, I would even go a little further. If we have a talent for anything and we do not use it, we become frustrated. I know this is difficult to prove. But I also know that I have seen many times, a person who is told by a graphologist about an unknown talent. He then pursues it only to become highly elated and many times his life changes entirely. Now it seems quite clear that we have different standards for men and women, and that we are conditioning our children to be masculine or feminine, regardless of their original inclinations; that we are, in many cases doing harm. And when we are doing harm, we send them to a psychiatrist or psychologist.

In an article titled, "Men Drive Women Crazy," Phyllis Chesler writes in the July 1971 issue of PSYCHOLOGY TODAY, "For a number of reasons women 'go crazy' more often than men." The statistics she gathered seem to bear out this fact. She believes that the demands society puts on women are the major cause of female neurosis.

"The fact is, most women are unhappy because they have been trained to be passive and dependent in a world that values activity and strength."

Further in the article she writes, "Women's physical and emotional symptoms of disturbance are different from those of men and these differences are first apparent in childhood. When little boys are referred to child-guidance clinics it is for aggressive, destructive, antisocial and competitive behavior. Little girls come in for such problems as excessive fears and worry, shyness, lack of self-confidence, feelings of inferiority, etc. These differences carry on into adulthood."

Most interesting to us graphologists is the report on a study of Inge Broverman and her colleagues. These investigators presented 79 therapists (46 male and 33 female psychiatrists, psychologists and social workers) with a questionnaire consisting of 122 pairs of traits such as "very subjective—very objective" or "not at all aggressive—very aggressive." Each set of traits was to be rated on a scale from 1–7 and the therapists were to answer where a healthy male, a healthy female or a healthy adult (unspecified sex) should fall.

1.) There was high agreement among the therapists on the traits which characterize men, women and adults.

2.) Both male and female therapists had no major differences in their reports.

3.) The therapists showed similar standards for healthy males and healthy adults. However, healthy women were different from both other groups by being: Submissive, emotional, easily influenced, sensitive to being hurt, excitable, conceited about their appearance, dependent, not very adventurous, less competitive, unaggressive, unobjective and they do dislike math and the sciences.

Phyllis Chesler points out that there is no suggestion she could make to change the present trend quickly. All her suggestions are long ranged.

Actually, we can surely see that we live in a society that does not give equal rights to men and women. In my mind there is no question about that, neither is there a question that we indoctrinate our children with that idea. By constant interjection we also develop their character according to what "the society" will expect of them. We are trying very hard to form the character of a boy for acting "manly" and a girl for acting "feminine." Although this trend is strong today, it must be said that it was much stronger the further we go back in time. The progress is a slow one indeed and it would be unrealistic to effect a sudden change, although with every generation a little gain can be registered. I am thinking of the fact that both India and Israel have women at the helm of their governments.

If we cannot expect a drastic change so very soon, can we expect a parent to bring up his children as if there were to be a sudden change? Can a parent expect to find a perfect balance between male and female, let's say in fifteen years? The answer must be NO, although I feel it is the personal obligation of each of us to work toward that goal.

Whenever we talk about bringing up children we think about ways of getting them prepared for the circumstances to come. A difficult task indeed. Is it then necessary to insist that a boy do only things that society deems masculine? Or for a girl to follow society-oriented feminine activities? The answer should be No! We are slowly learning to understand that each person, each child must be treated as an individual. For one boy a lot of "masculine activities" may be the right thing. For another boy, his abilities may point to a different approach in his upbringing. It may not be possible to predict the exact standing of the society either boy will find when he grows up, but it is absolutely sure that he will be better prepared to meet the world if his natural leanings were taken into consideration. Nothing is worse than giving a child a stereotype education. We graphologists know that no two handwritings are alike and no two people are alike—why then treat two people the same way?

In handwriting analysis we first learn to sift out. I never forgot watching a diamond dealer sifting out small diamonds. He had small sifters similar to the ordinary kitchen utensil. Each sifter had smaller holes allowing only the smaller stones to go through. Whatever did not go through was of a particular weight. Actually, we do the same thing in graphology. We sift. We say that the writer is a garland writer—this sifts out all the other connections. A strong right trend sifts out the left trend, etc. We also use typology. We group writings according to their predominance and we achieve by doing this a faster determination of what I call the guiding image. The more experienced you are, the quicker you will find the guiding image. It is not only appropriate to ask for the sex of the writer, but it is very helpful to consider male and female as types.

Already Klages in his book HANDWRITING AND CHARACTER has said that people starting out in graphology believe it is possible always to judge the sex of a person through the handwriting. According to his estimate in 15% of all cases you will be wrong. My own estimate is even higher. A survey conducted in 1964 by the City College of New York revealed that in only 55% the answers to the sex of the writers were correct. The surprising finding was that the handwriting experts and the graphologists did not do any better than the students who participated in the test. However, I did not consider their findings valid because the test was done with insufficient writing samples.

Klages wanted to establish typical male and female characteristics so that it would be easier for the graphologist to determine the sex from the handwritings This will explain why Klages considers a 15% failure of guessing the sex as average.

Klages' Table

MASCULINITY OF THE CHARACTER

(Differentiation)

	+	-
1.	Systematically arranged	Dissension
2.	Ability for enthusiasm (Love for facts)	Sense for illusions (To see reality as we believe it is)
3.	Imagination	Lack of fantasy
4.	Sense of decisiveness Sense of activity, initiative	Restlessness
5.	Energy	Rigidity
6.	Power of conviction	Principles for the sake of principles, obstinacy
7.	Wide range of vision and versatility	Lack of ease, inability for happiness
8.	Objectivity and ability for abstract thinking	Lack of personal susceptibility
9.	Dignity	Unbearable need for importance (intellectual vanity in the form of overemphasis of professional occupations, duty, ability, in short, everything that one does at present)

FEMININITY OF THE CHARACTER

(Differentiation)

	+	-
1.	Uniformity, harmony	Judgment depending on instinct
2.	Personal power of submission (Love for the person)	Partisanship and lack of sense for justice
3.	Sense for reality (clear-sightedness for the immediate surroundings)	Lack of farsightedness
4.	Balance	Sensuous dependency (sensuous pliability)
5.	Warmheartedness, empathy	Lack of energy
6.	Instinctual certainty (strong relationship to nature)	Lack of principles
7.	Perseverance (conservatism, faithfulness, toleration)	Narrowness and pettiness
8.	Inventive security in judgement (intuition)	Lack of objectivity (also reduced receptiveness for argumentation)
9.	Veracity (self-admittance of feelings)	Subjectivity (blindness for outer-personal values)

Muller Enskat's Table
MALE AND FEMALE SYMBOLS

I. Psychological Attributes

A. General-Structural Differences

	MALE	FEMALE
1.	Strength and force with little flexibility	Flexibility with little strength
2.	Ability for concentration and directness	Graciousness and attractiveness, flexibility
3.	Danger of stubbornness in opinions	Danger of idleness
4.	Life from inside toward outside (centrifugal)	Life from outside toward inside (centripetal)
5.	Activity as stepping stone and offense	Pathos of experience and endurance
6.	Pressing, restless, roving	Middle course, reposing, collected, clinging
7.	Discovering, renewing, conquering	Passive receptive, receiving, preserving
8.	Danger of a life of adventure	Danger of impediment
9.	Disintegration and openness	Integration and conciseness
10.	Schizothym, unbalanced	Zychlothym, balanced
11.	Cortical accentuation	Endothym accentuated
12.	Differentiated, individualistic, complicated, original, prone to conflicts, contradictory	Homogeneous, undifferentiated, free of conflicts, uncomplicated, little originality
13.	Danger of disunion	Danger of superficiality
14.	Bound to knowledge, action and achievement	Bound to meeting people and occurrences
15.	Outlook on life and motivation through realizations, achievements and purposefulness	Outlook on life and motivation through feelings and impressions

16.	The legitimacy, the predictability, the formed, the conventional will be valued higher than the manifold of impressions and the organic growth	The natural grown, organic and genuine will be valued higher than education, form giving, mental attitude or principles
17.	Relationship to the past and the future is stronger than the relationship to the moment, "to be above the situation"	The action is determined by specific situations, sense for exceptions, present orientation, dependency on situations
18.	Danger of lack of realism toward life, danger of partiality	Danger of lack of principles, danger of unreliability

B. Specific Differences Within Singular Fields of Personality

Desires and Drives

1.	Sexual drive, desire for ecstasy	Need for tenderness and protection
2.	Eager for conquest and combat	Submission, motherliness

Disposition of Emotion

1.	Tendency for passion, patriarchial feeling for responsibility; love for profession and love for factualism, little sensibility and little empathy, bluntness, coldness	Tender temperament, compassion; love for the home and family, understanding empathy, sensible delicacy of feelings, certainty of feeling, imagination, illusions, enthusiasm, subjective dependency to sympathy and antipathy

C. Mode of Apprehension

1.	Certainty of conception, critique, gift for differentiation, objectivity, logic, awareness of problems, power of observation, power of concentration, aimful thinking, inclination toward forming of theories, intellectualism, dogmatism	Perceptive abilities, power of imagination, intuition, richness of ideas, fantasy, memory for impressions, little ability for differentiations and abstractions, erratic, illogic

D. Relationship to the Environment and Interests

1.	Open distant world, factual orientation, "world-power" through interference and domination	Closed surroundings, personal orientation, readiness for social help, to keep and care, practical and "close to life" interests
2.	Technical and specialized interests. To isolate oneself and keep a distance	Environmental symbiosis, ease in social contacts, ease in self expression and ease in associations

E. Ego Structure

1.	Feeling for autocracy, certainty, pride, feeling for honor, ambition for achievement, inclination for power, leaning toward projections and repressions	Modesty, humbleness, fear, insecurity, longing to be pampered and popular, coquetry, leaning toward recognition and self deception

I. Psychological Attributes

A. General-Structural Differences

	MALE	FEMALE
1.	Dynamic, wide ranging urging, demanding, sure, upright, strengthened, definite, self-reliant, clear, regulated, precise, concise, economical, sober, cool, hard, angular, sharp, impetuous, wiry, spasmodic, deliberate, not genuine	Gentle, soft, moved, rounded out, opened, compliant, adoring, tender, passive, clinging, steady, collected, dense, colorful, warm, enveloping, natural, childlike, naive, dependent, ambiguous, confused, languid, contourless

B. Overlapping Findings

1.	Rather emphasis on form, high degree of rigidity, strong rhythm, originality	Rather emphasis on movement, medium degree of rigidity, weaker rhythm, little originality
2.	Lack of uniformity	Uniformity

* * *

Now we come to the point where the graphologist becomes affected by the findings in the handwriting. Every student usually learns that it is necessary to know the sex of the writer before proceeding with an analysis. As a reason we give the fact that an analysis would be different were it written for a man or a woman. It is difficult for anyone to be completely objective writing an analysis first as if this sample were written by a woman; and then as it were written by a man. In order to solve this problem of objectivity, I have given the handwriting of a 35-year-old woman, for whom I did a professional analysis, to one of my colleagues, but giving the sex as male. And here are the results of the two analyses. (Sample of Handwriting on next page.)

together again - yes it sounds like a broken old tea cup and it feels even worse than that.

I went to the office this morning with some hope in my heart and now all is completely shattered and I dont thin I want to try my hand at this anymore, its just too dangerous for me and how many times can I come back. I am not made of iron.

But I dont want you to feel badly after reading this - you have every right to go which way is best for you but, at this time I feel the wound must heal, its a big one, its going to take a long time so I think in all fairness we should not call each other and there will be no more running into each other, I just dont

Doris

Female 35

The first impression I get from this handwriting is that it is very much lacking in rhythm. And this is the guideline to the analysis. Lack of rhythm in a handwriting reflects on the inability of the writer to lead a rhythmic life.

To be more specific, I specify "leading a rhythmic life" as having the ability to do the right things at the right time, Here, in this case, the emphasis must be on the timing. The result of this arrhythmic behavior is a feeling of insecurity, an insecurity which is regressing her ability to act when it seems to be necessary. It also decreases her ability to be sure about her own feelings. She is trying desperately to find some way to judge her feelings, and in this attempt she is constantly looking backwards to previous events for comparison. This, of course, just acts like a crutch. The answer to her question about her feelings can never be fully there for her and this becomes a source of dissatisfaction.

Her strong emotions, her extreme delicacy of feelings bring her into constant conflict with her surroundings, and because of her own emotional insecurity she can never get a fully stabilized relationship with a man. She is very likely to try to find some pseudo-satisfaction in entirely unrelated fields to her sex life.

She is prone to "giving in", taking the easy way out, because of her difficulties. Basically she has a rather high standard of life. She does not go for halfway measures. Things have to be done right. In this person's handwriting there is the mirror image of a long stretch of disappointment. The disappointments in herself must have been joined by unfortunate disappointments from the outside.

Male 35

This writer, because of a basically compliant nature, has been disillusioned by life. His unrealistic expectations of people have caused many, many disappointments. He is reacting to these disappointments by a stubborn rebelliousness and increasing intolerance of people.

Although the intelligence level is above average, the maturity level is low for this age. He likes to give the appearance of independence and élan, sophistication, but is really not truly capable of these qualities of strength and leadership at his present level of rigidity and rebelliousness. There is too much discipline lacking and also a lack of fulfillment (sexual as well as the ability to relate well to others) for these qualities to be present.

Because of the insecurity. lack of confidence and dependence, which in reality does mold his character, he will feel the need for a defiance of authority. This will not be easy for him, because he has a basically "give-in" nature.

His rigidity, his intolerance and his insecurity make it difficult for him to deal with the opposite sex.

* * *

It now becomes evident that we are educated to become male or female as our society prescribes—and not as our original leanings would dictate. Without a doubt the influence to which we are exposed has a great deal to do with the shape of our character later on.

It is in our time that the changes I believe are so necessary are taking place to a certain degree. But realistically speaking at the present time, we still have to consider such a thing as a male character and a female character.

Bibliography

Chesler, Phyllis — *Men Drive Women Crazy*
Psychology Today, July 1971

Klages, Ludwig — *Handschrift und Charakter*
H. Bouvier & Co.; Verlag, Bonn 24. Anflage, 1956

Klein, Felix — *Elementary Graphology Course*

Klein, Felix — *Sex in Handwriting*
Self published, 1971

Mueller-Enskat — *Graphologische Diagnostik*
(Verlag Hans Huber, Bern und Stuttgart, 1961.)

Psychology Today — by Communications Research Machines, Inc.
David A. Dushkin, Publisher, 1970

Combining Graphological Handwriting Indicators

Felix Klein

Combining Graphological Handwriting Indicators

A key to a better handwriting analysis.

Since the beginning of organized graphology many methods have been devised to make it possible for students of graphology to arrive at the same basic result in determining the character of a writer. All these methods have one thing in common. They all observe something in the handwriting and try to translate it into the language of character. In other words: by determining an indicator in the handwriting they then will know what the interpretation is according to the method they are using. Looking at it on a superficial level this seems to be satisfactory, and in practice many things can be done that way. When you begin to go deeper into the subject you will realize that such a method is not sufficient for all cases that you will come across. If you go to a doctor and all you can tell him is that you have a fever, it will be very unlikely that the doctor will be able to give an exact diagnosis of your problem.

Similarly when you look at a sample of a handwriting, the fact alone that the writer is using a garland connection will not tell the story. Even if you find ten or twenty separate indicators the analysis so produced may not come up to the most important qualification, namely, that it should fit this particular person only.

Once we come to this realization we will find a new awareness of the possibilities in combining handwriting indicators and by doing so we may come up with a new interpretation or find more details of the character in question.

To give you an example: You may find a handwriting that has large spaces between words. This, according to my own study guides and many of the standard books, would indicate the writer to be an introvert, a person with deep feelings and convictions. It is not even unlikely that you will find a writing with large and even spaces between words and at the same time the letters of one line interfere with the letters of the next one. According to my study guides, and that of many other teachers this could be an indication of a lack of inhibition and a lack of self-understanding, ergo, a clear contradiction to the interpretation to the large spaces between words. How then, should you proceed? Should you say the person is an introvert with deep feelings and convictions, or should you say that this person lacks inhibitions and does not understand himself? You may tell me that the two do not constitute a direct contradiction but I do think that you have to grant that the description of the person will be different when you use one or the other. If you want to use both your interpretation will read as follows: the original introversion of this writer has caused him to overcompensate, showing lack of inhibition to the outside world, and all this resulting in a lack of self-understanding. Actually, you have gone very much deeper into the personality than if you just add the two indicators.

Now that we have established that two indicators should not necessarily be simply added up but could be used to describe the person more deeply, more intimately, we have to proceed to organize our thinking. We have to realize that there are four possible groups of combinations between handwriting indicators.

I. Contradictory Indicators
II. Reinforcing Indicators
III. Unrelated Indicators
IV. Multiple Indicator Combinations

I. The Contradictory Indicators

It will be most interesting for us to find the interpretations for the contradictory indicators. Many students believe that the life of the graphologist is made more difficult if he finds contradictory indicator combinations. The opposite is true. Generally speaking, the contradictory indicators will give you the friction, the problems, the stresses, the conflicts, the forces that are working against each other in the character of a person. Bernhard Wittlich, the well-known German graphologist, wrote an article in the April issue of the "Zeitschrift fuer Menschenkunde". The title of this article is "Konfliktzeichen in der Handschrift" (Conflict-indicators in the handwriting.) This article represents an introduction to his recently published book "Konfliktzeichen in der Handschrift", Ernst Reinhard Verlag, Muenchen/Basel.

In this article he writes, "We often find contradictory indicators in one handwriting sample because they originate from contradictory impulses of the movement, the form and the space. They are together but they don't belong together. Such indicators are called contradictory indicators."

He also points out that no single indicator, no combination of indicators and no syndrome could conclusively allow one particular interpretation. He finds it necessary to evaluate the degree of the indicator. We are all familiar with this as most of our graphological worksheets allow for the expression of degree values.

In this article he also describes how Sigmund Freud started out by taking notes of all the discussions with his patients. However, he eventually discontinued this practice and replaced it by putting himself into a sort of passive concentration, a "free-flowing attentiveness", which enabled him to take in the information without criticism and without prejudice. This made it possible for him to get the picture of the person and the conflicts also. We graphologists should also "practice" passive concentration and free-flowing attentiveness. This and this only will get us beyond the limitations of the measurable criteria in the handwriting. By taking this attitude, we are not only being critical but we are learning to open ourselves toward the deeper expressiveness in the handwriting. We should learn to "live" with a writing and "in" a writing. This attitude will make it possible for us to realize that rationalization alone does not get us to our ultimate goal which has to be the achievement of an analysis that penetrates into the depths of the personality.

Why then should two or more opposing indicators appear at the same time? The reason for this is never the same. For instance: a person may very well be most extraverted in his business associations and most introverted in his emotional life. This may very well manifest itself in a right trend in the upper zone and no trend (or even left trend) in the lower zone. The following sample of the handwriting of a male, age 35 and right-handed, is a perfect example for such a controversial condition.

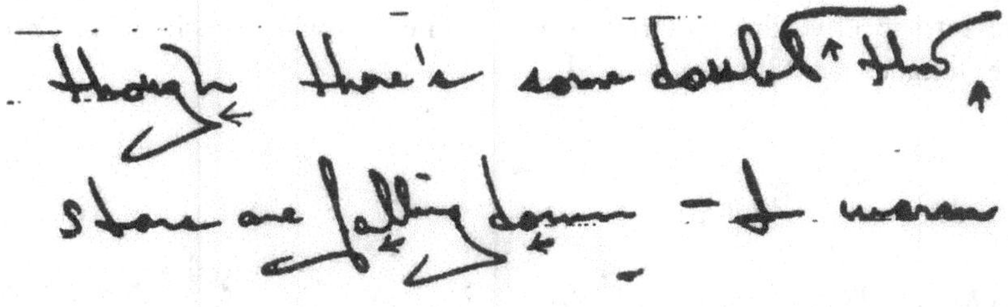

Here the clarification between the areas of introversion and extraversion is achieved by the strict separation of the indicators in the different zones. This, then, seems to be not only logical but also easy to identify as to why there are contradictory indicators (introverted in one area and extraverted in another).

Introversion and extraversion can show through other contradictory indicators (narrowness of the writing with strong right trend). It is important to understand that the narrowness of the writing is the more original, or primary, indicator. It is, therefore, very likely that the writer of the following sample was an originally introverted person and later developed more extraverted qualities.

Why annihilate the
nobility of maturity that
naturally develops with
years by attempting to
burlesque as youth?

Both the left trend and the left slant are contradictory indicators to the garland writer. We associate the garland writer as a warm, outgoing, nature-loving person, a person that also does a lot with his emotions. On the other hand, the backward slant and the leftward trend would indicate a person holding back somewhat, somewhat reserved, even introverted. The garland is the more original of the indicators here in question. So the interpretation would be that this writer whose nature is warm, outgoing, and friendly, became more reserved, more contemplative and introspective due to circumstances. The following specimen is a good example (female, age 28, right-handed).

Dear Sir,
Thank you for your letter
of December 20th, 1969.
I am glad that you could
come.

A marked difference between angularity of the middle zone, small case letters and the roundedness of the capitals would be an indication that the person presents himself in a more pleasant and agreeable way than he really is. Such people are usually capable of hiding their strength and playing the part of a "softy". Every capital represents our feeling about ourself. It is the barometer of our ego. Both samples below show this contradictory indicator.

Great variety in the treatment of space often constitutes a controversial attitude on the part of the writer. A person writing thin and meager letters may be expected to leave little space between letters within one word. An extension of the horizontal strokes connecting the letters would automatically convey a picture of artificiality. The combination of narrow letters and wide spaces between letters would then indicate that the writer finds it necessary to hide an original feeling of inferiority by presenting himself as warm, imaginative, and artistically inclined. Usually it is not too difficult to detect insincerity in the behavior pattern. See the following writing sample.

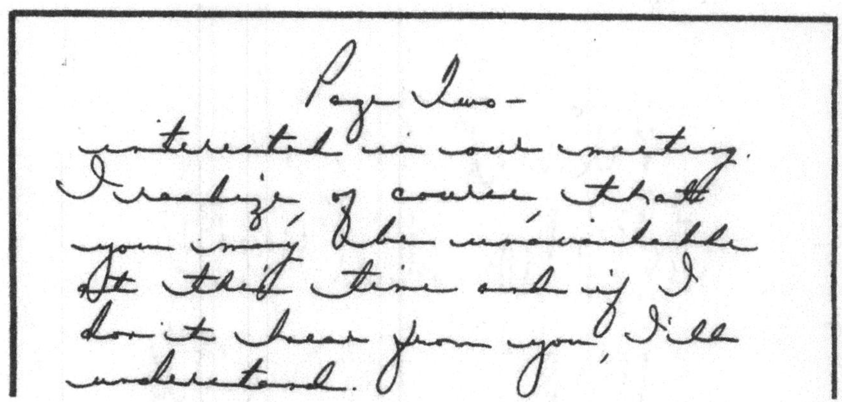

Page Two—
interested in our meeting.
I realize of course that
you may be unavailable
at this time and if I
don't hear from you, I'll
understand.

The signature indicates how we want to appear to the outside world, the writing indicates how we really are. If the signature is very much larger than the rest of the writing it would contradict the true nature of the person and the indication would be that the person wants to make herself "bigger" than she really is. See the sample following—of a woman, right-handed, and aged 42.

Dear Mr. Klein.

Please analyze my writing—

and include a character analysis -

Thank you—

Ruth Wilson

The above sample also shows a contradiction in the garland connection with the wide spaces between the words. The garland again indicates the warmness and the inner feeling, and the wide spaces the inability to get close to people. This would of course, create a frustration pattern where one indicator points towards an entirely different guiding image from the other.

The garland with covering strokes (downstroke covering a large part of the upstroke) would be contradictory also. The garland personality is not the type who hides or pretends. In the sample below the garland is not a genuine garland but a "supported" one.

The sample is also a good illustration for the contradictory combination of the garland with rigid regularity. The rigidity does not conform with the garland personality at all. It would then be indicated that because of the rigidity the garland would be overshadowed by a behavior pattern alien to the garland writer. What this pattern really is would have to be determined by other indicators. The somewhat upright slant in the following sample (that of a woman, right-handed and aged 62) must generally be regarded in contradiction to the right trend. The upward slant is a control position, not allowing a strong movement to the right or to the left. The right trend is then accomplished despite the upward degree of the writing angle. The combination of the two contradictory indicators would suggest a highly active person having difficulty in self-control, and particularly in this writing the indication is strong that there is very much effort given to achieving the necessary control.

Thank you for your long
understanding letter — I often
think of our talks in Chicago
and it helps to know that
you care —
write me please, if you
find a moment —
Give my love to Lie and
the family. Love Marie

A left trend in fast writing is indeed contradictory. Each time the writer moves towards the left he will have to go to the right again resulting in loss of time. This can be compared with swimming against the stream. The speed of writing indicates the speed of thinking rather than the speed of movement. The following sample is that of a forty year old right-handed man, and both the left trend and the speed are easily recognized. A fast thinking person with a reflective tendency will show tension. In this particular writing you can see in addition to the already-mentioned contradictory indicators, the definite right margin which is reinforcing the left trend, and is also contradictory to the high speed of the script. It can be assumed that the right margin is a direct result of the first-mentioned contradictory indicator.

Another set of contradictory indicators is the right slant and the left trend. Leaning towards the future and being strongly governed by the past, is like being pulled from two opposite sides. Fortunately for the young lady of 22 (right-handed), whose handwriting is shown below, her temperament is a slow one. This is the reason why the conflict created by the contradictory indicators does not present a problem to her.

Right now I am downtown with my mother,
my grandparents and my brother. I am down
here just because I wanted to come. Anyhow
there was nothing better to do! I have to go to
the doctor's tomorrow, and his office is quite
near here so my mom brought me along.
So far I think it is all terribly interesting.
I have been listening to my grandmother
talk about the meetings she has been to so
far.

II. Reinforcing Indicators.

The graphologist is quite aware of the indicators in the handwriting that will convince him that his interpretation is correct. It is easy to see that when two indicators have roughly the same meaning they will confirm each other. It is indeed wise to look for reinforcing or confirming indicators before a definite interpretation of character quality should be made. The more confirming indicators found in a handwriting sample, the higher will be the degree of particular character quality.

III. Unrelated Indicators

It is understood that unrelated indicators cannot be combined and must be handled separately.

IV. Multiple Indicator Combination

When more than two indicators are looked at in a combining fashion, they can represent contradictions or reinforcements of one or more character qualities. Many times the observance of multiple combinations of indicators will result in the finding of the "Guiding Image", described by the German graphologist Klages as the "inner core" of the character of a person. Grouping of indicators will result in setting up of character types. This process is often reversed, and a psychological type is analyzed into the forming components and then "translated" into graphological terms by grouping of the related indicators.

Contradictory Indicators	
Indicators	**Interpretations**
1. a) Large spaces between words b) Overlapping lines	The original introversion of this writer has caused him to overcompensate, showing lack of inhibition to the outside world, and all this resulting in a lack of self-understanding.
2. a) Right trend, upper zone b) No trend (or left trend) in the lower zone	Extraverted in areas of endeavors. Introverted in private life and in the establishment of emotional relationships.
3. a) Narrowness b) Right trend	Originally introverted, developed more extraverted qualities.
4. a) Garland b) Left trend (or left slant)	Warm, outgoing person became more reserved more contemplative and more introspective due to outside circumstances.
5. a) Angular middle zone letters b) Capitals rounded	Usually strong, sometimes unbending, presents a "soft" person.
6. a) Narrow letters b) Large spaces between letters (within one word)	Feeling of inferiority hidden by showing self to be imaginative, warm, artistically inclined.
7. a) Small writing b) Large signature	A modest and unassuming person presents herself in a "bigger" way.
8. a) Large spaces between words b) Garland	A person with a warm inner feeling finds it difficult to get close to people, creating frustration.
9. a) Garland b) Covering strokes	Garland interpretation does not apply; indications of hiding, pretending, possible cause: insecurity.
10. a) Garland b) Rigid regularity	Rigid behavior pattern not like garland writer.

Contradictory Indicators	
Indicators	**Interpretations**
11. a) Upright slant b) Right trend	Any self-control is difficult for this highly active person.
12. a) Left trend b) Fast writing	Fast thinker strongly influenced by reflective attitude.
13. a) Right slant b) Left trend	Highly active person strongly past-oriented.
14. a) Right trend b) Right margin wide	Need for activities cannot be consummated due to outside circumstances or inner difficulties.
15. a) Narrow right margin b) Narrowing left margin	This active and outgoing person falls back to the previous overcautious ways.

There are many more contradictory combinations of handwriting indicators possible.

Bibliography

Heiss, Robert — *Die Deutung der Handschrift*
(Hamburg, 1943.)

Klages, Ludwig — *Handschrift und Charakter*
(Johann Ambrosius Barth, Leipzig, 1929.)

Klein, Felix — *Initial Taped Course*

Link, Betty — *Graphology, A Tool for Personnel Selection*
(Paul S. Amidon & Ass., Inc., 1972.)

Mueller-Enskat — *Graphologische Diagnostik*
(Verlag Hans Huber, Bern und Stuttgart, 1961.)

Pulver, Max — *Symbolik in der Handschrift*
(Orell Fuessli Verlag, Zuerich und Leipzig, 1931.)

Wieser, Roda — *Grundriss der Graphologie*
(Ernst Reinhard Verlag, Muenchen, Basel, 1969.)

Wittlich, Bernhard — *Konfliktzeichen in der Handschrift*
(Zeitschrift fuer Menschenkunde, 36/1, 1972.)

Research for this lecture was done by the Master Class of 1971/72.

Eva Boyce
Wilm E. Donath
Helene Eliat van de Velde, Ph.D.
Alice Lake
Roger Rubin
Carole Schuler
Arlene Sheer
Gisela Skutnik

I would like to express my gratitude for their patience, freshness of insight, and dedication to accuracy which helped to make this paper possible. Also, my special thanks to Jo Baxter for her creative stimulation and persistent interest in this project.

Character Structure of Neuroses

Felix Klein

Character Structure of Neuroses

Dr. Bernhard Wittlich, a German graphologist, had the idea to investigate the possibility of establishing the character structure of neuroses through the handwriting. In order to do that he employed two German psychologists, Horst Flebrand, Elga Wessely-Bogner, who developed four basic character combinations for the four neuroses to be investigated. The four neuroses were:

1.) Depressive

2.) Compulsive

3.) Hysteric

4.) Schizoid

On the basis of the findings of the two German psychologists Wittlich created a very complicated graphological method to determine the character structure of the four neuroses from the handwriting. This method was published: "Neurosestructuren und Handschrift", Dipa-Verlag Frankfurt/Main, 1968.

In order to be of practical value the need for a simplification of the method became apparent. However, the new method had to provide results as close as possible to the results from the original method.

Dr. Helene Eliat van de Velde assisted me in establishing the simplified method. Her twenty-eight patients, to whom she had administered a battery of tests, were also examined with the new graphological method. The diagnosis of the graphological analyses was exactly the same as the one established by the battery of psychological tests.

In addition I sent a copy of my method and a sample of my diagram to Renate Kuemmell, the daughter of Dr. Wittlich, with a particular handwriting. Mrs. Kuemmell analyzed the handwriting with the help of the method of her father and wrote an enthusiastic report about the similarity of the two results.

It has been established that difficulties in the oral period will result in the development of the schizoid character structure if the child is highly sensitive. Under the same condition and during the same developmental period a less sensitive child will develop into depressive character structure. Difficulties during the anal period will result in the formation of the compulsive character structure.

Problems during the phallic period will result in the development of the hysteric character structure.

Psychologists that were consulted by Dr. Bernhard Wittlich, the originator of this method in the original version, establised certain character structures of the four types of neuroses. The version of this particular test which will be discussed in this lesson was simplified and translated by myself.

Depressive Character Structure

Desire for nearness
Desire for submission
Incapable of genuine partnership
Lack of ego power
Feeling of being at the mercy of others
Feeling of being asked to do too much
(causing resignation)
No desire for planning
No courage
Guilt feelings

Subordination
Seemingly unassuming
Fear of self-development
Fear of isolation
Fear of losses
but also:
Empathic
Helpful
Devoted
Grateful

Compulsive Character Structure

Cannot tolerate changes
Safeguarding
Obstinacy
Pedantry
Intolerance
Dogmatism
Tendency toward principles
Pondering
Cautious
Retains prejudice

Attachment to tradition
Fear of change of conduct
Fear of the transitory
but also:
Ambitious
Diligent
Sense for duty
Perseverance
Firmness
Seriousness

Hysterical Character Structure

No acknowledgment of order and rules
No relationship to outside world
Rejection of responsibility
Infantile
No self-criticism
No endurance
No concentration
Lack of patience
Looking for admiration
Curious
Spontaneity
Lives in a pseudo-world

Short attention span
Refuses to recognize obligation
More initiative than persistence
Enemy of tradition
Fear of reality and necessity
Seeking artificial nearness
but also:
- Readiness to take chances
- Flexible
- Impulsive
- Optimistic

Schizoid Character Structure

Strives toward self-development
Egocentric attitude
Autism
Rationalism
Emphasis on intellect rather than emotions
Fear of obligations
Few social contacts
Rejecting
Distrustful, skeptical, cynical
Abrupt change of reactions

Chooses between over-/under-estimation of self
Fear of nearness
Fear of submission and adaptation
(will be regarded as loss of identity)
Fear of each new start
but also:
- Independence, objectivity, self-criticism
- No traditions
- No sentimentality
- Uncompromising

It now becomes evident that indicators in the handwriting can be classified to reveal the character structure of the four types. Determination of a character structure of a particular handwriting must be made between opposite indicators, as listed below.

Picture of Movement

1. Rhythm of movement
   a. elastic .... rigid
   b. swinging.......... slack
   c. smooth.......... disturbed
2. Uninterrupted (fast).......... interrupted (slow)
3. Hasty.......... not hasty
4. Curvy.......... linear
5. Strong pressure.......... weak pressure
6. Pastose.......... sharp
7. Connected.......... disconnected
8. Right trend.......... left trend
9. Circular movement counter-clockwise.......... circular movement clockwise
10. Regular.......... irregular
11. Centrifugal, away from center.......... centripetal, toward center

Picture of Form

12. Formrhythm strong.......... formrhythm weak
13. Fullness.......... meagerness
14. To-and-fro movement.......... singular movement
15. Enriched.......... simplified
16. Garland.......... arcade
17. Thread.......... angle
18. Stylish.......... schooltype
19. Uniformity.......... lack of uniformity
20. Cleverly joined.......... clumsily joined

Picture of Space

21. Space distribution rhythmic.......... space distribution arrhythmic
22. Vertical expansion large.......... vertical expansion small
23. Emphasis on upper zone.......... emphasis on lower zone

24. Middle zone high.. middle zone low
25. Wide letters .... narrow letters
26. Distance between letters wide .... distance between letters narrow
27. Emphasis on beginning of word.................. neglect on beginning of word
28. Emphasis on end of word....................................neglect on end of word
29. Large in comparison to format...................small in comparison to format
30. Right slant. .... upright and left slant
31. Distance between words large .... distance between words small
32. Distance between lines large......................... distance between lines small

In the interest of clarity, a few terms may need to be explained:

1a.	Elastic	Rigid	Elastic vs. rigid may not always be considered as opposites, but for this test such designation is appropriate.
1b.	Swinging	Slack	Swinging vs. slack may not always be considered as opposites, but for this test such designation is appropriate.
2.	Uninterrupted (fast)	Interrupted (slow)	Fast-slow is less important than uninterrupted—interrupted. Interruptions should be chiefly considered whenever an interruption is unwarranted. A proper interruption would be a stop for a t-bar or i-dot, etc.
3.	Hasty	Not hasty	Hasty and not hasty do not mean speedy as opposed to slow. Hasty writing must be faster than the writer's personal rhythm. Hasty writing usually shows some neglect of form.
4.	Curvy	Linear	Curvy writing should not only have curves in the middle zone, but upper and lower zone loops should be wider than school model. Linear writing is usually narrow while having upper and lower loops narrower than the school model.

9.	Counter-clockwise circular movement	Clockwise circular movement	An example of counter-clockwise movement is the garland. A typical example of clockwise movement is the arcade. Any letter moving in the opposite direction from the school model is significant for the determination of clockwise and counter-clockwise.
11.	Centrifugal (away from center)	Centripetal (toward center)	Any stroke having a tendency to go away from the center into the upper or lower zone will fit the centrifugal designation. Things having a tendency to remain in the middle zone represent centripetal movement.
14.	To-and-fro movement	Singular movement	This concept refers to development of the writing. Singular movement is not only slow writing, but also shows few variations from the school model. Singular movement usually does not show sense for form; in fact, it is possible that form will be neglected. In all areas of singular movement one gets a sense of awkwardness, of laboring to produce movement.
15.	Enriched	Simplified	Any addition to the school model would produce an enriched writing. Any reduction from the school model, without loss of legibility, would be simplification.
19.	Uniformity	Lack of uniformity	Accurately-repeated letter formations are called uniformity; the opposite is lack of uniformity.
20.	Cleverly joined	Clumsily joined	Good examples of cleverly-joined letters are a t-bar connected to the following letter, and an i-dot connected as such: bill boll
26.	Wide distances between letters	Narrow distances between letters	It is possible for a handwriting to be narrow but with wide connecting strokes between letters.
31.	Large distances between words	Narrow distances between words	The medium distance between two words is the width of the lowercase "m" in that particular handwriting.

The following tables are designed to show you how the character structure of each neurosis can be seen in the handwriting.

TABLE I. DEPRESSIVE

	+ (plus side)	- (minus side)		
		Picture of Movement		
1.	Rhythm of movement			
a.	elastic	rigid		------------------------------------
b.	swinging	slack	-	feeble, aimless, emotionally unstable
c.	smooth	disturbed	- -	hesitating, discouraged
2.	Uninterrupted/fast	interrupted/slow	-	inactive, distrust, no will power
3.	Hasty	not hasty	+ -	unbalanced, aimless
4.	Curvy	linear		------------------------------------
5.	Strong pressure	weak	- -	fearful, tires easily, no initiative
6.	Pastose	sharp	-	no sense for reality
7.	Connected	disconnected	+	blind to facts, unrealistic, melancholy
8.	Right trend	left	-	guilt feelings, distrust
9.	Circular movement counterclockwise	clockwise	+	touchiness, delicacy of feelings
10.	Regular	irregular	-	weak will power, emotionally unstable
11.	Centrifugal	centripetal	-	lack of inner security
		Picture of Form		
12.	Formrhythm strong	weak	-	immature, lazy
13.	Fullness	meagerness		------------------------------------
14.	To-and-fro movement	singular	-	rigid
15.	Enriched	simplified		------------------------------------
16.	Garland	arcade	+	dependent, melancholic

17. Thread	angle	+	weakness
18. Stylish	school type	-	discouraged, narrow outlook
19. Uniformity	not uniform	+ +	dependence on authority; lacks initiative; overly restricted by conscience
20. Joined cleverly	joined clumsily		------------------------------------

Picture of Space

21. Space distribution rhythmic	arrhythmic	-	helplessness
22. Vertical expansion large	small	-	apathetic
23. Emphasis on upper zone	lower zone	- - -	easily disheartened, sluggish
24. Middle zone high	low	+ -	changing demands, disturbed self esteem
25. Wide letters	narrow letters	-	fear of life
26. Distance between letters wide	narrow		------------------------------------
27. Emphasis: beginning of word	neglect: begin. wd.	- -	self doubt, timidity
28. Emphasis: end of word	neglect: end wd.	-	feeble, insecure, fearful
29. Large compared to format	small	+ - or -	disturbed self-confidence, passivity, unproductive
30. Right slant	upright and left		------------------------------------
31. Distance between words: large	small		------------------------------------
32. Distance between lines: large	small	+ +	danger of neurosis

TABLE II. COMPULSIVE

	+ (plus side)	- (minus side)		
	Picture of Movement			
1.	Rhythm of movement			
a.	elastic	rigid	- -	rigidity
b.	swinging	slack		----------------------------------
c.	smooth	disturbed	-	sensitive
2.	Uninterrupted/fast	interrupted/slow	- -	indecisive, obstinate, pessimistic, rigid
3.	Hasty	not hasty	-	fearful, obstinate, inhibited
4.	Curvy	linear	-	pedantry, rigidity
5.	Strong pressure	weak	+	inhibited, fanatical
6.	Pastose	sharp	-	self-tormenting
7.	Connected	disconnected	-	obstinate, intolerant, greedy, unadaptable
8.	Right trend	left		----------------------------------
9.	Circular movement counterclockwise	clockwise	+	obsessive
10.	Regular	irregular	+ +	principles, unadaptable
11.	Centrifugal	centripetal	-	reclusive, pedantic
	Picture of Form			
12.	Formrhythm strong	weak	-	dogmatic
13.	Fullness	meagerness	-	one-sided, abstract
14.	To-and-fro movement	singular	-	artificial
15.	Enriched	simplified		----------------------------------
16.	Garland	arcade	-	formal, defensive, distrustful
17.	Thread	angle	-	obstinate, inhibited, uncooperative

18. Stylish	school type	- - -	stereotyped
19. Uniformity	not uniform	+ +	fear of everything, indecisive, pedantic
20. Joined cleverly	joined clumsily	-	obstinate, narrow outlook

Picture of Space

21. Space distribution rhythmic	arrhythmic	- -	stubborn, asocial
22. Vertical expansion large	small		------------------------------------
23. Emphasis on upper zone	lower zone	-	pedantic, apathetic
24. Middle zone high	low	-	indecisive, cautious
25. Wide letters	narrow letters	- - -	fear of life
26. Distance between letters wide	narrow	-	pedantic, egoist, cautious
27. Emphasis: beginning of word	neglect: begin. wd.		------------------------------------
28. Emphasis: end of word	neglect: end wd.		------------------------------------
29. Large compared to format	small		------------------------------------
30. Right slant	upright and left	- -	defensive, inhibited
31. Distance between words: large	small	+	thinking agility
32. Distance between lines: large	small	-	unclear judgment

TABLE III. HYSTERIC

	+ (plus side)	- (minus side)		
	Picture of Movement			
1.	Rhythm of movement			
a.	elastic	rigid	-	intolerant
b.	swinging	slack		------------------------------------
c.	smooth	disturbed	-	delicate
2.	Uninterrupted/fast	interrupted/slow	+	superficial, conceited
3.	Hasty	not hasty	+	restless, distractible, excitable
4.	Curvy	linear	+	needs to lean on somebody, false nearness
5.	Strong pressure	weak	-	sensitive, unworldly
6.	Pastose	sharp	+	corruptible, love of variety, unstable
7.	Connected	disconnected	+ -	capricious
8.	Right trend	left		------------------------------------
9.	Circular movement counterclockwise	clockwise	+	lets oneself go
10.	Regular	irregular	-	unstable, emotional, tends to exaggerate
11.	Centrifugal	centripetal	+	unstable
	Picture of Form			
12.	Formrhythm strong	weak	-	no self-criticism, no sense for order
13.	Fullness	meagerness	+ +	busy-body and given to exaggeration
14.	To-and-fro movement	singular	+	primitive, uninhibited
15.	Enriched	simplified	+ +	desire for self-assertion
16.	Garland	arcade	- or + + -	formal, defensive, distrustful

17.	Thread	angle	+ + +	not genuine; a sensationalist
18.	Stylish	school type	- - -	on-and-off self confidence
19.	Uniformity	not uniform	- - -	fantasy lies, emotionally changeable
20.	Joined cleverly	joined clumsily	+ + -	"shining intellectualism"

Picture of Space

21.	Space distribution rhythmic	arrhythmic	-	artificial nearness
22.	Vertical expansion large	small	+ +	desire for self-assertion
23.	Emphasis on upper zone	lower zone	+	unsure of one's own instincts
24.	Middle zone high	low		------------------------------------
25.	Wide letters	narrow letters	+ + -	ambivalence about own self-image
26.	Distance between letters wide	narrow	+	irritable, uninhibited, a busybody
27.	Emphasis: beginning of word	neglect: begin. wd.	+ + -	desire for self-assertion, artificial attitudes, play-acting
28.	Emphasis: end of word	neglect: end wd.		------------------------------------
29.	Large compared to format	small	+ - or +	no sense for reality, wish to be important, uninhibited, labile
30.	Right slant	upright and left	+ + -	moody, changeable
31.	Distance between words: large	small	- - -	subjective, unrealistic, dependent, experiences not genuine
32.	Distance between lines: large	small	- - -	experiences not genuine

TABLE IV. SCHIZOID

	+ (plus side)	- (minus side)		
	Picture of Movement			
1.	Rhythm of movement			
a.	elastic	rigid	-	split personality
b.	swinging	slack		----------------------------------
c.	smooth	disturbed	-	irritable
2.	Uninterrupted/fast	interrupted/slow		----------------------------------
3.	Hasty	not hasty	+ -	unbalanced
4.	Curvy	linear	-	stubborn, inadequate
5.	Strong pressure	weak	+ -	pretentiousness, social inadequacy
6.	Pastose	sharp		----------------------------------
7.	Connected	disconnected	- -	no contact, asocial
8.	Right trend	left	+ + -	split personality, problematic
9.	Circular movement counterclockwise	clockwise		----------------------------------
10.	Regular	irregular	-	asocial, ambivalent
11.	Centrifugal	centripetal	-	disturbed self-confidence, immature
	Picture of Form			
12.	Formrhythm strong	weak	+	egocentric, rationalistic
13.	Fullness	meagerness	-	inhibited
14.	To-and-fro movement	singular		----------------------------------
15.	Enriched	simplified	+	wanting to exceed one's limitations
16.	Garland	arcade	-	no contact, closed up
17.	Thread	angle	+	conflicted nature, apathetic

18. Stylish	school type	+	artificial, ambivalent, not genuine
19. Uniformity	not uniform	- - -	inner strife, poor self control
20. Joined cleverly	joined clumsily	-	incapable of adapting

Picture of Space

21. Space distribution rhythmic	arrhythmic	- -	no personal contacts
22. Vertical expansion large	small	+ + -	changeable emotional reactions
23. Emphasis on upper zone	lower zone	+ -	dual personality
24. Middle zone high	low	- -	self-doubt, fearful
25. Wide letters	narrow letters	-	prejudices
26. Distance between letters wide	narrow	-	distrustful, fearful
27. Emphasis: beginning of word	neglect: begin. wd.	+	arrogant
28. Emphasis: end of word	neglect: end wd.	+	opinionated
29. Large compared to format	small	+ -	inhibited
30. Right slant	upright and left	+ - or - -	inhibited, unsure of impulses
31. Distance between words: large	small	+ +	no contact, isolated
32. Distance between lines: large	small	- -	lacking in proper reserve & respect for others

SCORE SHEET FOR CHARACTER STRUCTURE NEUROSES TEST

✓ = confirms standard
X = doesn't confirm standard

Name: ______ Sex: ______
Hand: ______ Age: ______

Indicators			Depressive			Compulsive			Hysteric			Schizoid		
Line	+	-	Indicators	✓	X	Indicators	✓	X	Indicators	✓	X	Indicators	✓	X
	Picture of Movement													
1a	Rhythm of movement, elastic	Rigid	0			- -			-			-		
1b	Rhythm of movement, swinging	Slack	-			0			0			0		
1c	Rhythm of movement, smooth	Disturbed	- -			-			-			-		
2	Uninterrupted (fast)	Interrupted (slow)	-			- -			+			0		
3	Hasty	Not hasty	+ -			-			+			+ -		
4	Curvy	Linear	0			-			+			-		
5	Strong pressure	Weak pressure	- -			+			-			+ -		
6	Pastose	Sharp	-			-			+			0		
7	Connected	Disconnected	+			-			+ -			- -		
8	Right trend	Left trend	-			0			0			+ + -		
9	Circular movement, counterclockwise	Circular movement, clockwise	+			+			+			0		
10	Regular	Irregular	-			+ +			-			-		
11	Centrifugal (away from center)	Centripetal (toward center)	-			-			+			-		
	Picture of Form													
12	Formrhythm, strong	Formrhythm, weak	-			-			-			+		
13	Fullness	Meagerness	0			-			+ +			-		
14	To and fro-movement	Singular movement	-			-			+			0		
15	Enriched	Simplified	0			0			+ +			+		
16	Garland	Arcade	+			-			- or + + -			-		
17	Thread	Angle	+			-			+ + +			+		
18	Stylish	Schooltype	-			- - -			- - -			+		
19	Uniformity	Lack of uniformity	+ +			+ +			- - -			- - -		
20	Cleverly joined	Clumsily joined	0			-			+ + -			-		
	Picture of Space													
21	Space distribution, rhythmic	Arrhythmic	-			- -			-			- -		
22	Vertical expansion, large	Small	-			0			+ +			+ + -		
23	Emphasis on upper zone	Emphasis on lower zone	- - -			-			+			+ -		
24	Middle zone, high	Low	+ -			-			0			- -		
25	Wide letters	Narrow letters	-			- - -			+ + -			-		
26	Distance between letters, wide	Narrow	0			-			+			-		
27	Emphasis beginning of word	Neglect beginning of word	- -			0			+ + -			+		
28	Emphasis end of word	Neglect end of word	-			0			0			+		
29	Large, in comparison to format	Small	+ - or -			0			+ - or +			+ -		
30	Right slant	Upright or left slant	0			- -			+ + -			+ - or - -		
31	Distance between words, large	Small	0			+			- - -			+ +		
32	Distance between lines, large	Small	+ +			-			- - -			- -		
		Totals:													

Depressive character structure: ✓ ____ X = ____
Compulsive character structure: ✓ ____ X = ____
Hysteric character structure: ✓ ____ X = ____
Schizoid character structure: ✓ ____ X = ____

\+ = use indicators in first column
\- = use indicators in second column
0 = does not apply

The sergeant allows his men time because he considers it necessary to maintain their cooperative spirit for work, and the work cannot be accomplished without willing workers. He knows his men demand absolute privacy when they are in quest of vice information or conducting surveillances; this means nothing can be said over the air that reveals what they are doing.

Kathleen McDonald

SCORE SHEET FOR CHARACTER STRUCTURE NEUROSES TEST

✓ = confirms standard
X = doesn't confirm standard

Name: C.McD. Sex: F
Hand: R Age: 31

Indicators			Depressive			Compulsive			Hysteric			Schizoid		
Line	+	-	Indicators	✓	X	Indicators	✓	X	Indicators	✓	X	Indicators	✓	X
Picture of Movement														
1a	Rhythm of movement, elastic	Rigid	0			- -		X	-	✓		-	✓	
1b	Rhythm of movement, swinging	Slack	-	✓		0			0			0		
1c	Rhythm of movement, smooth	Disturbed	- -	✓		-	✓		-	✓		-	✓	
2	Uninterrupted (fast)	Interrupted (slow)	-	✓		- -		X	+		X	0		
3	Hasty	Not hasty	+ -	✓		-	✓		+		X	+ -	✓	
4	Curvy	Linear	0			-		X	+	✓		-		X
5	Strong pressure	Weak pressure	- -		X	+		X	-	✓		+ -		X
6	Pastose	Sharp	-	✓		-	✓		+		X	0		
7	Connected	Disconnected	+		X	-	✓		+ -		X	- -		X
8	Right trend	Left trend	-	✓		0			0			+ + -		X
9	Circular movement, counterclockwise	Circular movement, clockwise	+	✓		+	✓		+	✓		0		
10	Regular	Irregular	-		X	+ +		X	-		X	-		X
11	Centrifugal (away from center)	Centripetal (toward center)	-	✓		-	✓		+		X	-	✓	
Picture of Form														
12	Formrhythm, strong	Formrhythm, weak	-	✓		-	✓		-	✓		+		X
13	Fullness	Meagerness	0			-	✓		+ +		X	-	✓	
14	To and fro-movement	Singular movement	-	✓		-	✓		+		X	0		
15	Enriched	Simplified	0			0			+ +		X	+		X
16	Garland	Arcade	+	✓		-		X	- or + + -		X	-		X
17	Thread	Angle	+		X	-	✓		+ + +		X	+		X
18	Stylish	Schooltype	-	✓		- - -		X	- - -		X	+		X
19	Uniformity	Lack of uniformity	+ +		X	+ +		X	- - -		X	- - -		X
20	Cleverly joined	Clumsily joined	0			-	✓		+ + -		X	-	✓	
Picture of Space														
21	Space distribution, rhythmic	Arrhythmic	-	✓		- -		X	-	✓		- -		X
22	Vertical expansion, large	Small	-	✓		0			+ +		X	+ + -		X
23	Emphasis on upper zone	Emphasis on lower zone	- - -		X	-	✓		+		X	+ -		X
24	Middle zone, high	Low	+ -	✓		-	✓		0			- -		X
25	Wide letters	Narrow letters	-		X	- - -		X	+ + -		X	-		X
26	Distance between letters, wide	Narrow	0			-		X	+	✓		-		X
27	Emphasis beginning of word	Neglect beginning of word	- -	✓		0			+ + -		X	+		X
28	Emphasis end of word	Neglect end of word	-		X	0			0			+	✓	
29	Large, in comparison to format	Small	+ - or -	✓		0			+ - or +		X	+ -		X
30	Right slant	Upright or left slant	0			- -	✓		+ + -		X	+ - or - -	✓	
31	Distance between words, large	Small	0			+	✓		- - -		X	+ +		X
32	Distance between lines, large	Small	+ +		X	-	✓		- - -		X	- -		X
		Totals:		17	9		16	11		8	22		8	21

Depressive character structure: 17 ✓ 9 X = 8 ✓
Compulsive character structure: 16 ✓ 11 X = 5 ✓
Hysteric character structure: 8 ✓ 22 X = 14 X
Schizoid character structure: 8 ✓ 21 X = 13 X

+ = use indicators in first column
- = use indicators in second column
0 = does not apply

Extremes in Graphology

Felix Klein

Extremes in Graphology

If we want to talk about extremes in handwriting analysis we have to be clear that we know what we call an extreme. For the various indicators an extreme will have to be defined according to the criteria conducive to the indicator.

The Webster's Dictionary defines the word extreme as follows: "existing in the highest or greatest degree." "Going to great or exaggerated length." "Exceeding the ordinary, usual or expected." "Situated at the farthest possible point from a center."

For the purpose of Graphology the best definition of an extreme would be: "Exceeding the usual or expected to an exaggerated degree.

General Guidelines for the Interpretation of Extremes in Handwriting

In practically all cases, where an extreme is found in a writing sample the eyes of the observer are drawn to this particular criteria. In so many instances it becomes almost impossible to separate the one item from the rest of the writing. However, for the sake of producing an objective analysis it is advisable to observe all criteria of the sample before attempting to interpret the extreme. In that fashion it becomes more likely that the general impression so achieved will provide a picture of the Gestalt of the writer. It is then possible to match the extreme to the Gestalt. It is essential to fit the extreme into the maze of the personality. If this should meet with difficulties it is far better to disregard the existence of the extreme altogether.

There are several rules for the interpretation of extremes:

1. Extremes in the handwriting usually refer to unusual and/or unrealistic behavior patterns of the writer.
2. Extremes may or may not be the Guiding Image[2] of the handwriting.

---

2 For a better understanding read:
The Guiding Image by Felix Klein.

3. Extremes have a tendency to disturb the rhythm.[3]
4. Extremes have a tendency to lower the judgment of the intellect of the writer.
5. Extremes usually are the breeding ground for contradictory indicators.[4]
6. Extremes should not be interpreted by putting emphasis or additional value to the conventional indicator.

Major areas of extremes

We can list seven major areas of extremes:

1. Slant
   a) Right
   b) Left
   c) Upright (rigidly)
   d) Changing (extremely)

2. Size
   a) Large
   b) Small

3. Zones
   a) Ratio of zones
   b) Zonal interference
   c) Zonal neglect

---

3 Additional information on Rhythm:
Style Evaluation, by Jo Baxter
Rhythm, Groundrhythm and Beyond, by Felix Klein
Roda Wieser's Basic Rhythm by Felix Klein.

4 Further information on indicators:
Combining Indicators by Felix Klein.

4. Trend
   a) Left (extreme)
   b) Right (extreme)

5. Rhythm
   a) Slack (extreme)
   b) Rigid (extreme)
   c) Impulse pattern (extremely poor)

6. Space
   a) Margins
   b) Distance between words
   c) Distance between lines
   d) Direction of lines

7. Form
   a) Neglect of form (due to illegibility)
   b) Neglect of form (due to excessive speed)
   c) Overdone forms

Slant.

Extreme Right.—Generally we consider the right slant from the angle formed between the down stroke and the base line and when this angle measures between 55 and 85 degrees. Any right slant measuring less than 55° would have to be considered an extreme right slant. The ordinary methods of interpretation of the right slant do not apply to the extreme. Symbolically the extreme right slant can be compared to the extreme leaning forward at a subway station in order to see the oncoming train. We all know that this practice is dangerous and may lead to serious consequences. The attitude portrayed by the practice of extreme right slant may indeed lead to serious consequences. Ill. 1 originated from the hand of a seventeen year old right-handed girl. This will give a strong impression of imbalance. There are strong indications that the writer will not be able to handle her problems realistically. The girl was brought up in a very strict home where self-expression was not practiced. Shortly, after this sample was produced she left home in the company of a young man without letting her parents know where she went!

Ill. 1

<u>Extreme Left Slant.</u>—Left slant comprises slants measuring 95 to 125 degrees. Any handwriting with a slant measuring 125° or more would have to be considered as an extreme left slant. As it is a practice of many private schools to teach their pupils to write left slant it is necessary to establish the genuineness of the left slant by finding reinforcing indicators. Symbolically the extreme left slant could be compared with a person leaning backward when shaking hands with another person. Tendency toward isolation is the indicator for this extreme. Ill. 2 was written by a 45 year old woman (right-handed!). The tendency toward isolation is strongly confirmed by the large distance between words and lines, also separations of letters within words. Her attitude makes her self-centered (curved, returning end strokes). Her problem originated early in life. (Directional pressure from the past seen in the *f* of the word "*often*"). The strong right trend (t-bars in "*difficult*" and "*present*") would indicate frustration!

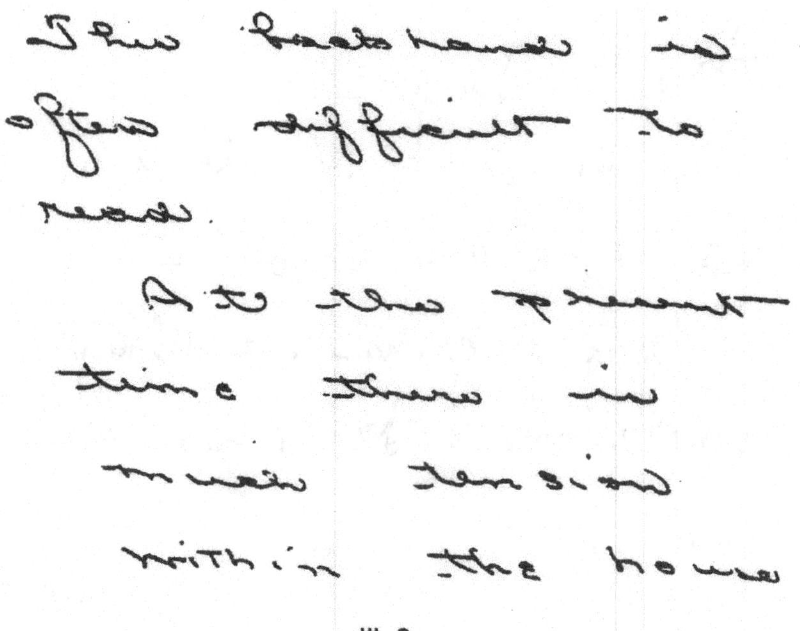

Ill. 2

Upright (Rigidly).—Generally the upright position would indicate a present oriented person with good control and possible lack of emotional qualities. Whenever this position is rigidly maintained the rigidity is the guideline for the interpretation. Ill. 3 is the handwriting of a 45 year old woman right-handed (F45R). The handwriting gives the impression of artificiality. The contradictory indicators will allow the interpretation that her way of life is dictated by her surroundings and although she is keeping rigid control over her emotions, she is capable of high emotional attitudes. Although there are indications of frustration her level of tolerance is high. She gives the appearance of self-confidence. However, her achievement level will be low, due to a poor self image.

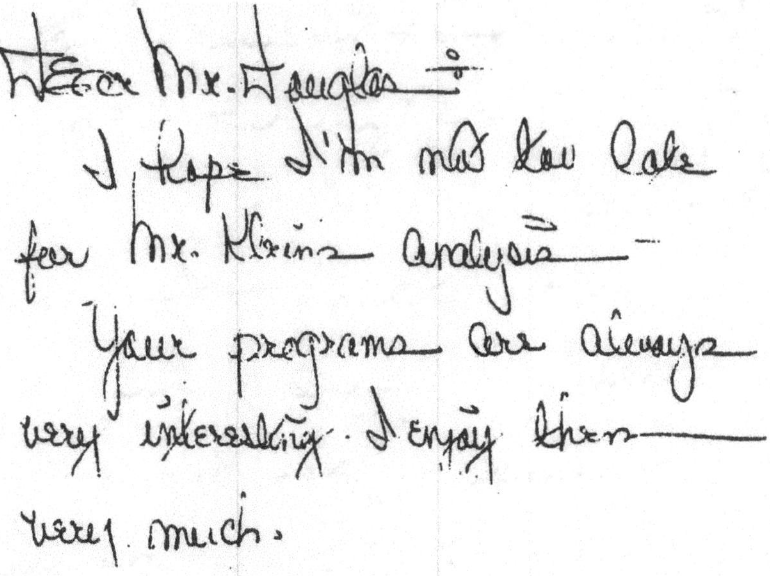

Ill. 3

Changing Slant (Extremely).—The changing slant implicates lack of control due to strong emotional tendencies. When the change of slant becomes extreme the lack of control becomes extreme and this indicator must be classified as a danger signal both for mental balance and for neuromuscular control. In Ill. 4 (F35R) the writing gives a definite impression that there is something wrong. The indications point to severe difficulties in physical control due to lack of motor control. (Pallidical). Although the handicap is severe, other indicators allow the conclusion that functioning on a daily routine basis is possible.

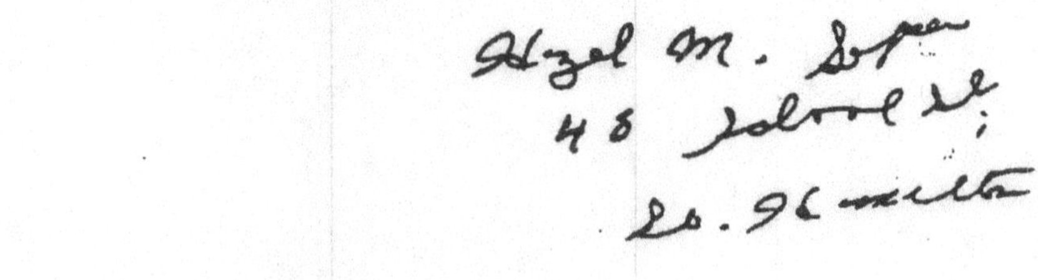

Ill. 4

Size.

Large (Extremely).—Large writing generally portray people that have no intentions to be overlooked. In extreme cases there is a tendency to emphasize the outside appearance with distinct possibilities of an ego problem. The extreme size in Ill. 5 (F44R) portrays a woman in great need of recognition particularly in the area of appearance. Her ego powers are overemphasized although she really does not believe in herself to the extent she shows it in the handwriting.

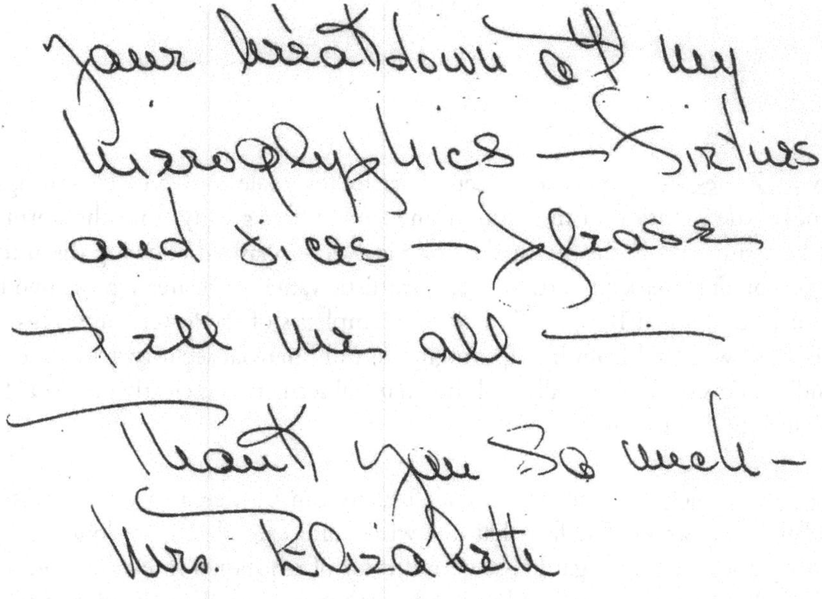

Ill. 5

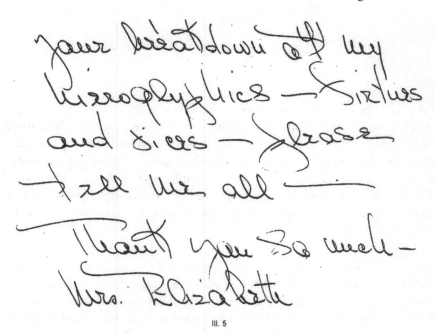

Small (Extremely).—Small writings in high style value often indicate leanings to the abstract and detail. In low style value and/or signs of poor vitality and introversion carries an interpretation of self-denial and isolation. Ill. 6 (F28R) shows a person that did not have a chance to mature emotionally. Self-denial was the accepted norm and her self-confidence in the area of her feelings is extremely poor. In addition she has a poor male image due to the difficulty with her father.

go smoothly, I'm planning to call yo
to visit you, provided you have time,
I still have Elizabeth's book,

Ill. 6

Zones.

Ratio of Zones.—There is an accepted ratio for male and female writings.[5] Whenever the variation of the ratio of one zone differs greatly from the norm it must be assumed that this particular zone is overemphasized allowing the interpretation of an increased or artificial or unrealistic value of the area represented by that zone. Looking at Ill. 1 we find such an emphasis of the lower zone. This 17 year old girl was used from her upbringing to full financial security. Nevertheless she did not develop emotionally and the financial security was clearly put aside for the chance to develop on her own.

Zonal Interference.—Zonal interference usually can be a sign of unclearness in any of the three areas. The fact that one writes into extended lower loops in the following lines must be regarded as an indicator of emotional insecurity and disturbance. Whenever we are faced with an extreme it must be assumed that there are severe difficulties in the value system of the writer. Ill. 7 (F32?R) shows an extreme interference of the lower zone due to extreme length. Unrealistic values in that area is the interpretation.

---

5 Jo Baxter's Style Evaluation, Page 5.(Symmetry).

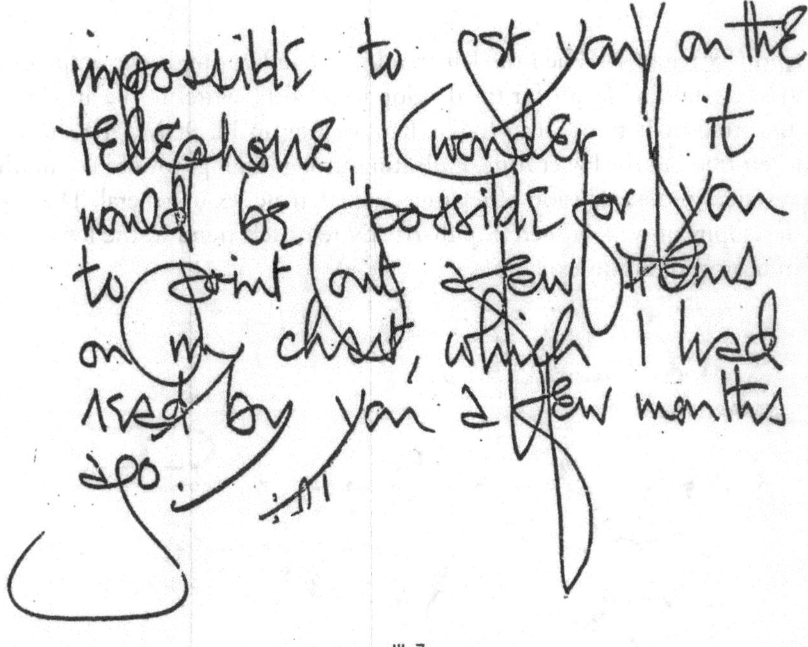

Ill. 7

Zonal Neglect.—The most likely zone to be neglected is the middle zone. Neglect of any zone indicate a difficulty in that area. The neglect of the middle zone usually refers to the ego power or rather the lack of it. Ill. 8 (F38R) shows a neglect of the middle zone. The writer has a very poor self image, only self-confidence in areas she is very familiar with. Her reaction to this is to shut herself off as much as possible indicated by the strong backward slant. The backward slant is genuine.

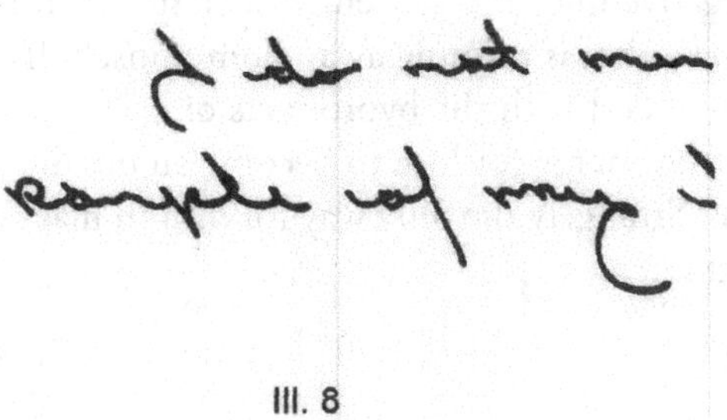

Ill. 8

Trend.

Left Trend (Extreme).—When the left trend in a handwriting is overemphasized it has to be a retarding factor for the development of the writer in the area (zone) where the strong left trend occurs. The handwriting in Ill. 9 (M35R) shows an extreme left trend in the lower zone, indicating strong leanings toward the mother which resulted in the exclusion of relating to the female sex in general. The emotional development was arrested in puberty. Extreme left trend in the lower zone is one indicator for homosexuality.

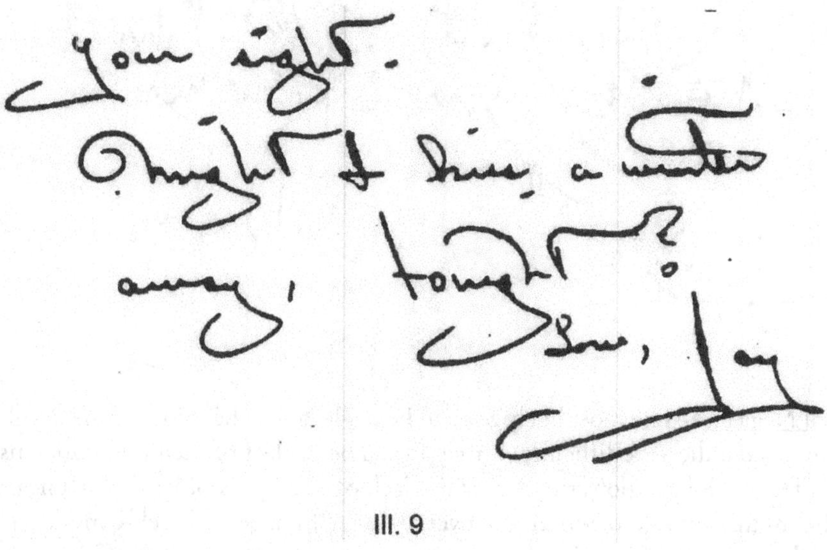

Ill. 9

Right Trend (Extreme).—Our natural feeling to move on which is to the right becomes highly negative once the movement is faster than the personal rhythm. We then say that the writer is running away from himself. Ill. 10 (M35R) demonstrates extreme right trend with the byproducts of excessive speed and neglect of form. It needed all the energy for him to become an ordained Rabbi and then all the problems began. Strangely the only way for him to make a living was to teach small children religion.

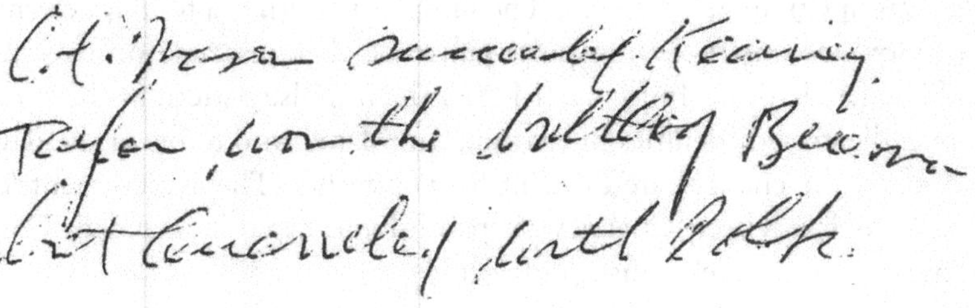

Ill. 10

Rhythm.

Slack (Extreme).—In graphology the word slack means a reduction of movement, contraction and an overemphasis on release. Extreme slack would indicate that the writer is incapable of resisting temptation. This is one of the two extremes which Roda Wieser takes as the basis for criminal leanings. Ill. 4 is a perfect example for this.

Rigid (Extreme).—Although rigidity is the counterpart of slackness, there is also a reduction of free movement. Often we find extreme angularity together with the extreme rigidity. The higher the degree of rigidity the higher the possibility of criminal tendencies according to Roda Wieser. The rigidity in Ill. 11 (M19R) is extremely high giving rise to fear for the ability to function in society. The possibility of getting into a pattern of crime is also very high. The extreme narrowness only serves as a confirming factor. Also the extreme neglect of form plays a part in the above interpretation.

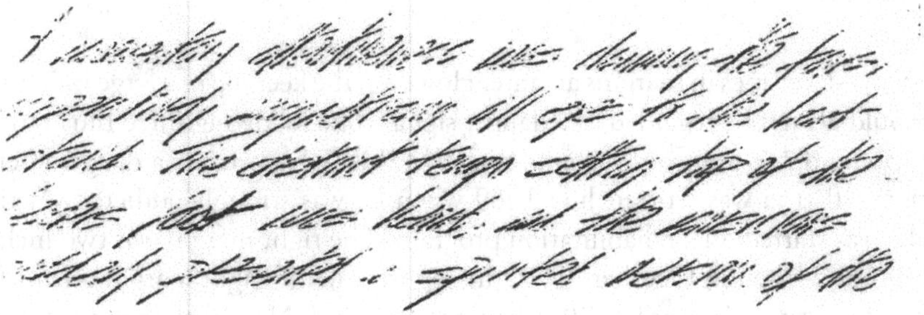

Ill. 11

Impulse Pattern (Extremely Poor).—The impulse pattern is a tool in determining rhythm. (How to construct an impulse pattern is demonstrated on page 2 of Jo Baxter's Style Evaluation.) In Ill. 12 (M28R) the impulse pattern of this writing is very poor indicating difficulties in rhythm. Translated into terms of the daily life it would mean the changes are difficult for this writer. The achievement level is high due to high intellect. Changes are painful and carefully avoided. Constant tension makes personal relationships difficult.

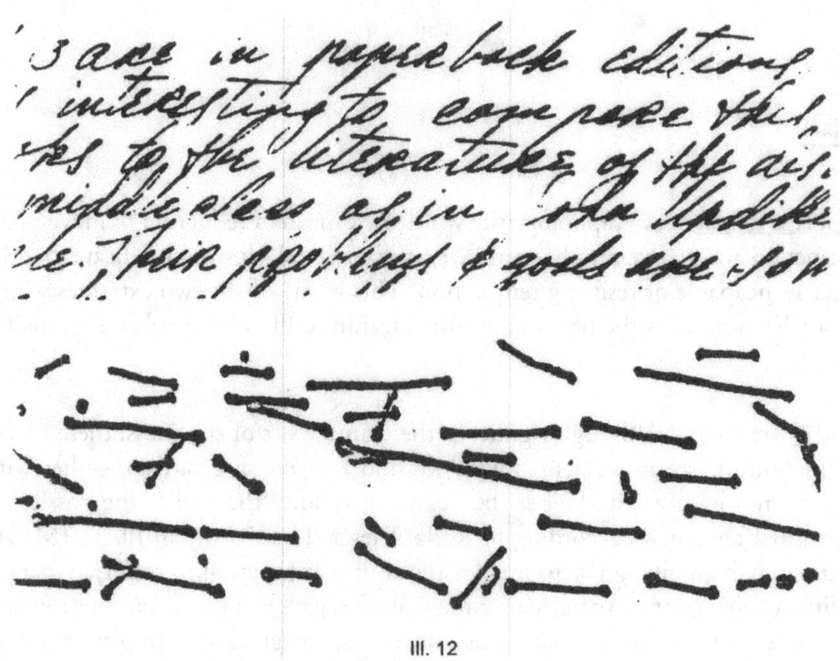

Ill. 12

Space.

Margins.—Extremes in margins are rare. However, the keeping of a large right margin should always be regarded as a danger signal. The following three Illustrations 13a, 13b, and 13c are from a young male (M21R) who became a drug addict in Vietnam. Ill. 13a was written July 1969 when he was strongly addicted. At that time he was started on a rehabilitation program. The right margin was two inches. Ill. 13b was written in October 1969, during treatment. Right margin one inch. Ill. 13c was written in April 1970, when he was cured. No right margin.

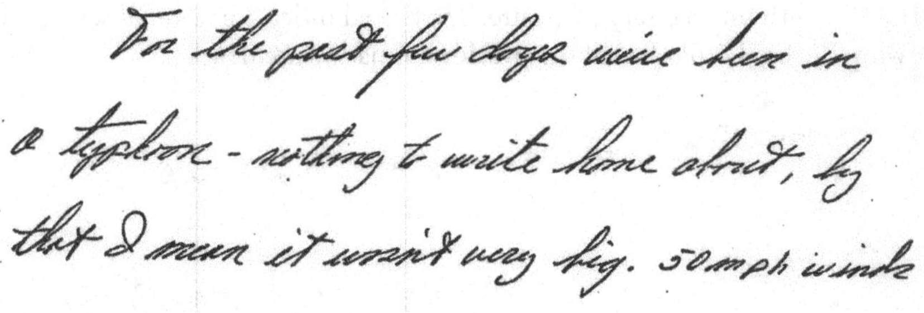

Ill. 13a

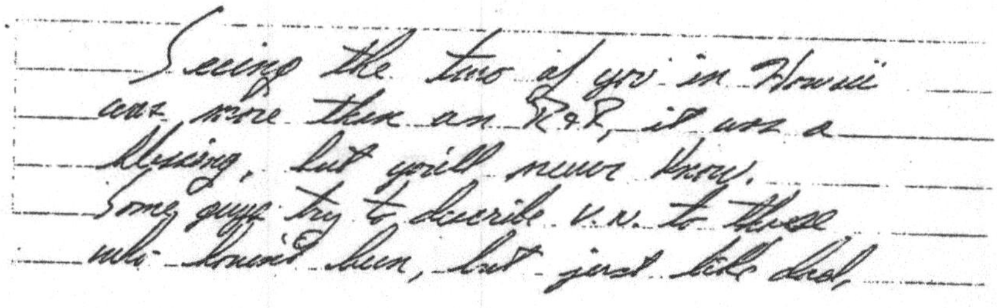

Ill. 13b

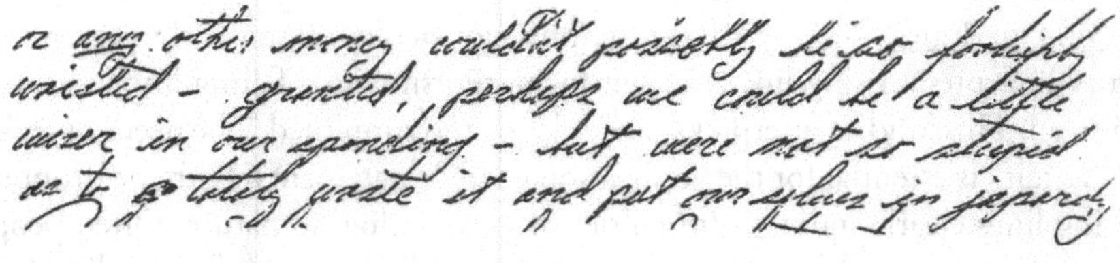

Ill. 13c

<u>Distance Between Words.</u>—Rarely do we find excessive distance between words. The normal distance between two words is the width of the letter *m* of the particular sample. Anything wider is a large distance between words. The distance between words is the distance from one person to the other at the time one shakes hands. When the distance is larger than the letter *m* we find it likely that "rivers" are formed. These are passageways all through the script. The larger the distance between words the easier it is for "rivers" to form. It is my opinion that the large distance between words already indicates a form of isolation without looking for "rivers."

<u>Distance Between Lines.</u>—People that keep large distance between lines are usually quite introverted. But they also need "Lebensraum". They don't clutter their

apartments with unnecessary furniture. They need order. They are observers. The following Ill. 14 (F26R) fits all the previously made statements.

compare to my feeling of gratification and security in
learning a person such as you really exists. Now that I
know spirits like yours are real, my hard times are less and
my good days are more. I look forward to seeing you again.

Frances

Ill. 14

<u>Direction of Lines.</u>—Many of the graphology books of the early part of the century interpret a rising line as a sign for optimism and a falling line indicating pessimism. This kind of interpretation is clearly too simplified. The need for seeing the "Gestalt" is essential for the verification of such statements. Extreme dropping or rising lines clearly indicate difficulties of a psychological nature. Often people under the influence of drugs will loose control of the keeping of a base line. Also excessive use of alcohol will have the same effect on a writing. Ill. 4 shows psychological difficulties partly because of the incapability of staying on an even keel.

Form.

<u>Neglect of Form (Illegibility).</u>—Simplification is a positive indicator. The person that simplifies the script without the loss of legibility shows clearly the achievement in the process of learning and experiencing. Whenever the legibility is sacrificed the interpretation must become negative. The basic purpose of handwriting is communication. An illegible writing then becomes neglect of form. Form is our sense for self-expression and when you write illegibly you cease to express yourself.

Neglect of Form (Speed).—When a person writes too fast he sacrifices expression for action. He sacrifices quantity over quality, See Ill. 10.

Overdone Forms.—Whenever the forms are overdone the interpretation must be negative also. Overdone forms show a problem in the area where these forms are prevalent. In Ill. 15 (F28L) the overdone forms here clearly indicate the need for recognition. There is great confusion between mind and feeling which in turn creates havoc with the value system.

(EXCUSE MY POOR WRITING, I'M LEFT HANDED)
Gail, I didn't receive the books as yet, and hope there is some way to stop Judith Stevens from sending them, since I do not know whether I will stay here or not.

Ill. 15

* * *

In a way any contradictory indicator has a flavor of an extreme. Whenever right and left trend appears in the same zone it is like pulling a person in two directions. Not only is this unproductive but it also wastes energy.

Many other extremes can be discussed.

Comparison Between the Thematic Apperception Test (TAT) and Graphology

A study conducted at Hunter College, N.Y., complete with a reprint from the magazine *Perceptual and Motor Skills*, 1973, and 10 analyses by Felix Klein

Perceptual and Motor Skills, 1973, 36, 703–706.

ACCURACY OF MATCHING TAT AND GRAPHOLOGICAL PERSONALITY PROFILES

THERESA LOMONACO AND ROSS HARRISON

Hunter College, City University of New York

AND FELIX KLEIN

New York City

Summary.—85 students matched 10 *Ss* for personality descriptions independently derived from analyses by a TAT specialist and a professional graphologist. Two sets of material were employed, one obtained from 5 male *Ss* and the other obtained from 5 female *Ss*. Chi-square tests indicated that the judges were able to match the personality descriptions ($p = .001$) for both sets. While the results demonstrate nothing about the validity of the two approaches, they support the conclusion that under suitable conditions the TAT and graphology can yield consistent personality profiles.

One of the persistent problems in personality research is the degree of congruence between different approaches, either to the measurement of personality variables or their evaluation by holistic methods. The results of personality research are determined by the specificity of the measuring or evaluative techniques and cannot legitimately be generalized by reason of this very specificity. The present study attempted to discover the amount of consistency between personality descriptions based on two commonly employed techniques—TAT and graphology—both of which have considerable validation literature.

Although the TAT validity research contains contradictions, most of the evidence is favorable, particularly when methods of analysis and validity criteria are adequate (Harrison, 1965). The TAT, however, is not a unitary, standardized test but consists of a variety of techniques for scoring or interpretation. "TAT validity can be discussed meaningfully only when defined operationally in terms of a particular interpreter using particular evaluative techniques with a particular population in a particular design against specific criteria" (Harrison, 1965, pp. 592-593).

The situation is similar regarding graphology where validity is a function of the graphological method and the skill of the individual interpreter as well as the reliability and adequacy of the validity criterion. Even conclusions about the value of graphology depend on the particular review, but the most comprehensive reviews of early studies (Allport & Vernon, 1933) and of more recent work (Fluckiger, Tripp, & Weinberg, 1961) are for the most part favorable to handwriting as an index to personality.

If the TAT and graphology possess some degree of validity and have some areas of information in common, they might be expected to yield consistent personality profiles. This was the hypothesis on which the present research was based. Secord (1949) in a study which served as the immediate impetus for the present investigation (LoMonaco, 1972) had college students match handwriting samples with unanalyzed TAT stories produced by the same *Ss*. The results turned out negatively. Secord suggested that the unfavorable findings could be explained by the many inherent difficulties in the matching method. More probably the negative results could be attributed to the fact that the students were untrained in either graphology or TAT interpretation. The current study required students match TAT and graphological personality descriptions, but in both instances the descriptions were written by specialists.

Method

Subjects

Ss whose personalities were studied were 5 males and 5 females of diverse ages, marital status, and education. They were for the most part young and college educated. The judges were 85 in number, 39 graduate students and 46 undergraduates.

Procedure

The 13-card TAT was administered to *Ss* by the investigator (TL), and the protocols were then interpreted by a TAT specialist (RH). The latter drew up a personality sketch for each *S* based on his TAT stories. The profile took into consideration four variables: intellect, affect, traits, adjustment and diagnosis. *Ss* were required to submit a handwriting sample of neutral content which was then analyzed by a professional graphologist (FK). He was asked to draw up a personality sketch from the handwriting samples, focusing on the same personality dimensions. Both the TAT specialist and the graphologist did their analyses independently without any contact with each other or with *Ss*.

The problem of homogeneity and heterogeneity of one's sample of *Ss* is a crucial one in a matching investigation, since an extremely homogeneous sample may make the matching task too difficult while an extremely heterogeneous sample may make the task too easy. Random selection of *Ss* is the solution of choice. This solution proved to be infeasible because the experimental task required *Ss* to donate a good deal of their time, and it was difficult to persuade a sufficient number of volunteers to cooperate. The investigator therefore drew upon her circle of friends, family, and acquaintances for *Ss*. In this way it was possible to select a sample that was not extremely skewed in either direction on the homogeneity-heterogeneity scale.

Two sets of five TAT profiles and corresponding graphological analyses were assembled. Set I was made up exclusively of males, and Set II was made up exclusively of females. The procedure was intended to control for the possibility that the judges might be able to distinguish between *Ss* solely on sex differences.

The matching task consisted of two 5:5 sets. This design was decided upon on the basis of how much material the judges could handle. A set larger than 5:5 appeared to be too unwieldy. In order to settle the issue of whether a 5:5 set could be handled without a great deal of discomfort on the part of the judges, a small pilot study was done with several judges who were not included in the study proper. The judges were able to handle the task successfully, although there were some complaints about the length of time required to complete the assignment.

The judges were undergraduate psychology majors and graduate students in psychology. An attempt was made to distribute materials from Set I to one-half of each participating class and materials from Set II to the other half. Thus there were four groups of judges: (1) undergraduates matching protocols from Set I, (2) undergraduates matching protocols from Set II, (3) graduate students matching protocols from Set I, and (4) graduate students matching protocols from Set II. It was expected that random and approximately equal-sized groups would be formed. Twenty-one graduate students and 24 undergraduate students served as judges for Set I, and 18 graduate students and 22 undergraduate students served as judges for Set II.

The judges were asked to match the TAT profile, each denoted by a letter, and the graphological analysis, each denoted by a Roman numeral, which referred to the same *S*. The two sets of analyses were labeled in scrambled order. Matches were made without any possibility of contaminating information between the two sets of profiles. The judges were told that, if they matched all five pairs of writeups correctly, they would be awarded a five dollar bonus. The bonus was used to motivate the judges to perform the task conscientiously, since the task was somewhat tedious.

Results and Discussion

A chi-square test was carried out to determine if matching of personality profiles derived from the TAT and from graphology was performed beyond chance level of success. This was done for both the data from Set I and the data from Set II. The data obtained from graduate and undergraduate judges were pooled for the χ^2 test. The observed frequencies of correct matches were 19, 28, 19, 26, and 16 where 9 was the number of correct matches expected by chance ($N = 45$). The observed frequencies for Set II were 17, 11, 16, 10, and 10 where 8 was the number of correct matches expected by chance ($N = 40$). For Set I χ^2 was significant ($\chi^2 = 99$, $df = 4$, $p < .001$) and also for Set II ($\chi^2 = 20.2$, $df = 4$, $p < .001$). Hence, there was only one chance in 1000 that the results were obtained by the operation of chance factors alone.

The mean number of correct matches for Set I was compared with the mean number of correct matches for Set II, combining the data for graduate and undergraduate judges. The results were not statistically significant ($t = .61$, *df* = 83), indicating that the results for both sets were comparable. Also, the mean number of correct matches was compared for graduate and undergraduate judges. This was done for the data from both sets. The results indicated that the graduate judges made more accurate judgments than the undergraduate judges used in Set I (protocols for men; $t = 3.57$, $df = 43$, $p < .001$). The results of the t test comparing the accuracy of the graduate and undergraduate judges used in Set II (protocols for women) indicated that there was no significant difference between their performances ($t = .03$, $df = 38$).

These positive results and the lack of success in the Secord study can most plausibly be explained in terms of the qualifications of the assessors of stories and script. In the one case, untrained college students were exposed to a matching task that they could not reasonably be expected to handle successfully, since they did not have the requisite knowledge of the two techniques. In the present study pains were taken in the choice of the two specialists who participated in the research. Both had many years of professional experience in their disciplines. The TAT specialist had contributed frequently to the TAT literature, while the graphologist at the time of the study was national president of the American Association of Handwriting Analysts.

One barrier to successful matching present in the current investigation was that each technique sometimes yielded personality information for which there was no coverage in the other. Another difficulty for the judges was that the two sets of descriptions were not strictly comparable in form. The TAT writeups followed the pattern of separate identified paragraphs for intellect, affect, traits, adjustment and diagnosis. The graphologist found this format uncongenial and did not follow it, although a common structured format had been a part of the original plan. Finally, although the two approaches yielded significant congruence, this finding does not necessarily validate either the TAT or graphology, since there is no assurance that there was not considerable error in the commonality. However, the predominantly favorable validity literature for both approaches makes this contingency unlikely.

References

ALLPORT, G. W., & VERNON, P. E. *Studies in expressive movement.* New York: Macmillan, 1933.

FLUCKIGER, F. A., TRIPP, C. A., & WEINBERG, G. W. A review of experimental research in graphology, 1933-1960. *Perceptual and Motor Skills,* 1961, 12, 67-90.

HARRISON, R. Thematic apperceptive methods. In B. B. Wolman (Ed.), *Handbook of clinical psychology.* New York: McGraw-Hill, 1965. Pp. 562-620.

LOMONACO, T. The accuracy of matching personality profiles derived from TAT and graphological analyses. Unpublished Master's thesis, Hunter College, City Univer. of New York, 1972.

SECORD, P. F. Studies in the relationship of handwriting to personality. *Journal of Personality,* 1949, 17, 430-448.

Accepted January 22, 1973.

Thomas F. Hopkins
I am twenty-seven years old, Lefthanded
Male,
Five feet ten and one-half inches,
and one-hundred and seventy-five pounds

I.

In my opinion, the greatest innovation in the development of mankind was the establishment in the ancient Greek world of a tradition of intellectual inquiry. Earlier cultures from pre-historic onwards clearly indicate that individual men exercised this mode of interacting with life but the Greeks formally established this behavior as a <u>value</u> in their culture. This tradition of intellectual inquiry has had a tremendous impact upon man's cultural evolution. Man's interaction with his environment displays the clearest indication of the effect of the inductive-deductive approach upon civilization through the history of technological progress. An intellectual approach has also strongly affected much of man's interaction with each other. The social sciences, & many aspects of government are now feeling the influence of the extension of this approach to problem-solving. The greatest problems facing man are those involving his living with himself and others. Socrates gave philosophy an ethical orientation as opposed to the "natural world" orientation of the pre-Socratics. The ultimate test of intellectualism will be the extent to which it is instrumental in aiding man to resolve the conflict within a man and between men.

A

TAT

I

Intellect

The stories are original, quite succinct with no waste of words, reflect a superior vocabulary level, and there is one reference to a high quality play. Despite all this, there are a couple of misspellings. He is of superior intelligence, probably above 130 IQ, has a sharp analytical mind, and is well educated. While there is perceptual and ideational originality, there was no indication of marked esthetic qualities.

Affect

Mr. A has little warmth or real affection for people. Narrative characters display a lack of relativeness and are not particularly likable. Sometimes they are unpleasant; at other times merely neutral. He is not very people-involved and is emotionally isolated. Mr. A is tightly controlled with an underlying vein of hostility. He has a cold, rather cynical outlook on the world with more than the usual amount of aggression which may find expression in the form of being critical or irritable.

Traits, other characteristics

The uniqueness of the stories suggests that he is independent-minded and idiosyncratic. He is nevertheless not settled in his views; he is trying to find himself and work out values he can live with. He is skeptical and often questions whatever may be presented to him. On the surface, he may be cooperative, but there is an underlying resistance. Thus for the blank card, for which he was supposed to imagine a picture, his response was: "The card is blank & ∴ the story is blank." He is not putting himself out more than he has to. He is not a generous or giving person. He is also impatient with details. His approach is usually lean, hard, masculine, and unsentimental.

Adjustment

The parent-child area is neglected; perhaps he was not close to his parents. Stories about man-woman relations show a clear heterosexual orientation with men being in the ascendancy. There are suggestions that he may have problems in his relations with women. At the same time he fantasizes about a peaceful, rewarding marriage. The imports or morals of the stories are usually negative. There are a number of indications that he has unresolved conflicts. From this inference, together with the evidence of coldness and hostility, he must be judged as somewhat maladjusted though not severely so. Although his brightness and ambitiousness may allow him to present a socially acceptable facade, basically he is a person who wears a concealed armor to protect himself and fend off intimacy with others.

I.

The intelligence of this writer is above average in the range of 65-70%. However, there are emotional difficulties which are preventing him from making full use of it. The most outstanding way in which this will manifest itself will be in the area of judging realistically. The danger also exists of getting too much involved in details. He is the type of person to get very much "attached" to a subject because he originally decided to go into it.

As to the emotional difficulties, the depth of the problem starts with the relationship to the mother. This, in turn, creates a problem with the relationship to the female sex in general. As a result of this problem he will have insufficient emotional release and there will be a tendency of overcompensation in other areas. It will also direct his strongest efforts into realms that seem to be unrealistic for him. His willpower is quite strong and therefore he will be able to overcome difficulties of a lighter nature by substituting with strong efforts.

He is not ready to face the future head-on. He rather shows a hesitancy which really goes beyond the expression of introversion. His interests are not in the practical area. He will be much more likely to establish a place in the intellectual world, possibly trying so hard for it that he may even overshoot the expected height he could reach. He should not be termed as immature because the level of maturity he can reach entirely depends on his ability to solve his emotional imbalance.

Antonio Aromando
age - 59 years old
sex - Male
Height 5 3
Weight 167
Handedness Righty

II

Radio is the best invention
because I could hear my
favorite sports news and
singer.

I wanted to know how
those little tubes could
bring all this entertainment
and now the television, I
remember one time how the
police would teletype the
bad characters now I
see all the belly dancers
how great it to be alive
and enjoy all this greatness

TAT

II

B

Intellect

This collection of wild and incredible stories full of crime, violence, improbabilities, and illogic must come from a man of rather idiosyncratic mentality—a "character." While he shows some imagination, the originality is poor in quality, and the intelligence is not better than average. He is not well educated, though he puts stock in education as a way of getting ahead in the world. From the milieus of stories, social class would not seem to be higher than lower middle class.

Affect

The excessive amount of narrative violence implies hostility, though it is interesting that the would-be perpetrators of violence are always restrained by some one more in control. Some of his aggression may be fantasy rather than acting out. He is impulsive, emotional, and probably irascible. Mr. B seems never to have grown up emotionally or for that matter intellectually; while worldly, he manifests a rather simplistic, unsophisticated outlook.

Traits, other characteristics

His great concern is with acquiring money and material success. His achievement need has not been too well satisfied and has become a preoccupation. He is unrealistically optimistic about schemes for making money. One story suggests a passion for gambling. In the stories crime does not pay, yet at the same time crime fascinates him; how much is fantasy and how much is reality is hard to say. His characters have little or no conscience, and it is likely that he has few scruples and may be irresponsible. He is selfish and ungenuine, giving only lip service to conventional mores.

Adjustment

In the sexual area, he would appear to be a sensuous man with a history of affairs and infidelities. Women are manipulated or used, and there is no real feeling of affection. The same is true of other human relations, such as those involving parents and children. The world to Mr. B is a tough place, and one has to be tough and even unethical to cope with it. There is a lack of persistence when there are obstacles or frustrations. The basic attitudes expressed in the stories indicate that he has not evolved a mature philosophy or set of values. The combination of such traits as egocentricity, impulsiveness, lack of social feeling, and antisocial impulses points to a character disorder, probably of the sociopathic type.

II.

The intelligence of this man is below average and it must be regarded in the range of 35-40%. He is not aware of this. He feels that he is outstanding in many areas and there are fields of practical endeavor where he will perform quite satisfactorily. He is conscious of the fact that his education is insufficient. His reaction toward others is one of a defensive nature. He can also be aggressive in order to avoid to be on the defensive continuously. He does show signs of mental aberrations and the tendency would be toward schizophrenia. His emotional release is uneven and as a rule he is unpredictable. He seems to have an intuitive understanding of things for which he was not trained. There are strong indications for body deficiencies, creating anxiety and a fear of death. He must be regarded as insecure. Because of all the problems, he relates strongly to the past in areas that are unrelated to future decisions. His emotional maturity did not exceed the age of puberty.

Sex - Male III.
Age - 29
Height - 6'1"
Weight - 180
Handedness - Left
Signature - Nicholas C. Zonca

The greatest discovery was that of the telegraph. The telegraph which is the father of the sophisticated machine which we call today the telephone.

I feel this was the greatest discovery because is was a link between two people and by forcing two people to talk or communicat it will bring a better understanding and maybe eventually a better world to live in. A world where truth and understanding may overcome and squash fears, hatreds and prejudice in man.

C

TAT
III

Intellect

The stories are compact, concise, and are well-organized. They also show imagination and more than an average amount of originality. Summary impression is that Mr. C is an educated man of superior intelligence.

Affect

The feelings and emotions in the stories are almost all unpleasant (unhappiness, hurt, fear, shame, anguish, boredom, and emptiness). While he is not a contented person neither is he overwhelmed by depression, and he continues to conform to social expectation. There is a lack of warmth and real friendliness and in their place a feeling of emptiness and considerable hostility which expresses itself by his being critical and impatient.

Traits, other characteristics

Scant attention is paid to parent-child relations. What little he contributes suggests parental domination and reactive rebellion on his part. Psychosexuality, in contrast, is an area of greater concern with several stories about husbands and wives. In marriage he is the dominant partner. While he has a clear heterosexual orientation, there is suggestive evidence that all is not well in this area. Thus one story deals with impotence. He is psychologically masculine but feels he has to constantly prove his virility. He may feel entrapped in the cocoon of domestic life and the day-to-day routine of work. He daydreams of escape but will not because of the strong hold of convention. Charactero-logically he is dominant and forceful, realistic and pragmatic, manifests some decisiveness and strength despite the underlying problem of coming to terms with his world. Mr. C has need for achievement, yet questions the value of the ends sought. Despite one story with a humorous twist, he moralizes and philosophizes a lot in the interpretations and is basically serious and even meditative.

Adjustment

Fundamentally Mr. C is a somewhat disillusioned pessimist. Life is hard, imperfect, even tragic. There is fear of failure, and he is in conflict. He does not find his life satisfying and fulfilling, and although he may present the appearance of normal adaptation on the surface, in actuality he is maladjusted and insecure. He nevertheless continues the daily struggle.

III.

The intelligence of this man is slightly above average, The range is between 50-55% and there are indications that he is able to use his intelligence productively. The application of his intelligence is limited by two factors. 1.) The lack of sufficient will-power. 2.) He is getting too much absorbed in secondary subjects. Clear indications point to an interest in intellectual subjects, even to the extent of being unrealistic in comparison to the amount of intelligence he has. On the other hand he is not the type to go overboard anyway and this will result in a process of compromise. The ability to compromise, at least in this area, is probably the most positive quality in this writing.

This is a person with strong emotions. However, there are indications of a difficulty in the sexual area. A latent homosexuality, not too strong, does influence him in his relationship to the opposite sex. The basis can be found in the amount of feminine qualities, resulting in an unresolved mother image.

He will be functioning in most areas well with the exception of his relationship to the opposite sex. He will have difficulties in establishing a "permanency" in such a relationship.

Charles Milisenda
Age - 58 .
Male
Height 5'2"
Weight 135 lbs
Right Handed

IV.

I invented the Photo Stat machine
it makes wonderfull pictures - better than
a zerox machine.
The best invention I like is the Photo Stat machine
it brings the picture bright and clear, everyone
want's to look inside the Close Box door, but it
Cant not be open because the paper inside will
be exposed, that reason why. I have to make
up my own Chemical's at least ten gallons at
a time to be a head, in case of a rush.

TAT

IV

D

Intellect

Mr. D is an uneducated man of average or perhaps less than average mental ability. On a verbal IQ test he might score low average, but this could be a reflection of his lack of education and relatively low socio-economic status. He does have a lively imagination, and his plot constructions are to say the least original. The originality is often poor in form and affected by peculiarities in his rather unique personality.

Affect

There is a gay tone to many of the stories and also a number of unrealistically happy endings. At the same time there are also other stories containing anger, sadness, and crying by both men and women. All characters are emotionally expressive as he is. Mr. D is excitable, impulsive, volatile, and labile, changing his ideas and feelings rapidly from one time to another.

Traits, other characteristics

His stories about parents and children mostly mirror his values which may be the values of his culture. Children owe obedience and respect to their parents and even though there may be family friction there is also family loyalty, and children should strive to advance their status by education and hard work. College education is an open sesame to success. The relations between the sexes concern him much more and show romantic fantasies about love in contrast to the reality of his unhappy marriage. Despite talk of ideal love he is more a sensuous and hedonistic man than a person capable of deep attachment. He is extroverted and socially dependent for approval, may be expansive and exhibitionistic as outlets for his vanity. Although shallow he may present a social facade of sentimentality. Some humor of a childish and stereotyped nature was evident in one story.

Adjustment

Even though he is not deeply disturbed Mr. D has a flawed and limited character structure. He is materialistic and not highly scrupulous and operates usually from self-interest, although in one exceptional story the hero is altruistic. Above all he is emotionally immature and rather simple-minded, even naive; his characters do not face up to problems realistically but resort to magical resolutions. His stories portray more of his wishful fantasies than his real life.

IV.

This is a scan of slightly below average intelligence. The range is 40-45%. He could have made more use of his intelligence. The indications in his handwriting are that he did not have a chance. He is able to function in other areas although his lack of self-confidence is constantly holding him back. He bolsters himself up and consequently he is liable to make unrealistic claims of achievements. In order to have a continuous "upholding" of his confidence he is looking for an audience. He has to find people that will listen to him. The writer has a tendency to look back to the past.

This is not a very sensuous person. He can enjoy simple things. He is likely to look for a better world for the ones to come after him. He is proud of his name and what it represents. He is not too clear what he wants or what he wants to achieve. It is always the lack of sufficient training that is holding him back. He is capable of holding his own. He has found a pattern of life that is not really satisfactory to him but which allows him to live a life of at least partial contentment. His relationship to his parents was an uneven one with the emphasis on the mother. The feminine tendencies in this writing are strong.

Donald A. Levy 5'7¼"
Age 19 Sex: Male 150 lbs V
Right-handed

Man, in his seemingly unending quest for peace, happiness, prosperity, and the better mousetrap, has discovered, or invented, war.

With increasing technology, man has been able to wage war incredibly more efficiently than he ever could before. And therefore made his invention a tool for the progress of mankind.

Everything man has ever done, no matter how irrational, has always been functional. The problem lies somewhere here: man has always prided himself on his sense of morality. He is therefore too moral to allow famine and pestilence to desolate the earth. He needs to do it without feeling guilty about violating his inviolate morals.

The solution is simple. One a man becomes your enemy he is no longer a man. He has therefore forfeited not only his rights as a man, but has lost the feeling and compassion man reserves for his fellow man. An enemy is a thing and therefore can be wiped from the face of the earth without as much thought that one reserves for a fly.

TAT

E

V

Intellect

The narratives are cryptic, quasi-poetic, and show a good deal of imagination and originality. Mr. E possesses superior intelligence and is educated. Considerable esthetic sensitivity, particularly along literary lines, is reflected. He did not relate ordinary stories with plot developments but instead literary cameos and mood pictures. There was a great deal of preoccupation with physical settings and natural elements. He is an intellectualizer but one whose intellectualizing is suffused with feelings.

Affect

Unpleasant emotional states like anger, grief, fear, anguish, and depression predominated. There were no really happy people in the stories. He too is a depressed individual who finds life empty. There are suggestions of emotional deprivation in his family life, especially from his father, and a need for warm and affectionate relations in general which, because of his egocentricity, he would be incapable of reciprocating.

Traits, other characteristics

He tries to create esthetic effects to impress the reader. He is a narcissistic poseur who is introspective and given to psychological analysis. Mr. E shows resentment of convention and the status quo, is irreligious, and may be a campus rebel or at least sympathetic to radical dissent. He craves excitement and novel experience. A thinker rather than a doer, he may be ineffectual in action and impractical. There is a streak of mysticism in him.

Adjustment

There was very little on the parent-child theme. One may surmise that there was a lack of closeness; from minimal cues a generation gap is suspected. Psychosexuality is another problem area; there is not a single satisfying heterosexual relation. Vanity rather than empathy on his part dominate these relationships. The main moral of his stories is that life is a drag. He himself is maladjusted and alienated, at peace with neither himself nor the world. He is complicated, conflicted, hostile, critical, and cynical. Mr. E is a weak person whose characteristic mode of dealing with difficulties is to run away, to break off relationships, to escape. It is hard for him to stick with anything and see things through to a successful conclusion, especially in personal relations.

V.

The intelligence of this person is above average in the range of 75%. However, he is not capable of using his intelligence to the fullest. He is not sure of himself and it is his lack of sufficient reality that causes him to fall back to a lower level. Then, it takes time for him to "recuperate" and continue to grow. He is not strongly masculine and not sensuous. The emphasis is on the spiritual and his happiness depends to a large degree in finding a place in the intellectual world. He is not too practical in his method of finding such a place.

He does show, that just lately he has made progress in getting better organized. He needs a father image, a person, that will guide him through this difficult period of his life.

He is emotionally immature. His maturity in this area has not been able to keep pace with the development of his mind. This, very well could be due to the type of upbringing he had and the relationship to the young people around him. He is not very social minded, except with a very few. He is reluctant to start superficial relationships. This may be due to his fear of not being able to handle himself in any kind of emotional relationship. He is very good-natured. However, his good-naturedness ends whenever he is called upon to defend his ideas. His basic intelligence allows him to pick up things quickly, to be argumentative when it concerns ideas and to obtain a high level of awareness in intellectual matters.

Camille Aromando
Right-handed
Female
Age-23
Height 5'-3" Weight 140 lbs.

VI

I feel a little ridiculous writing about the greatest invention. I am as unqualified to judge the world's greatest invention as I am to judge the world's greatest human being. Enough evasion. If I were to actually decide upon an invention I think I would decide upon the moveable printing press. I might sound patronizing or pedantic, but there is little dispute that this invention is responsible for transforming the development of the society of man.

It is the printing press which made available to great masses of people the printed word. It is the printing press that made the exchange of ideas between men and nations possible. Men were able to share their thoughts on love, beauty, war and hate. Nations were no longer to be isolated and Men were no longer to be ignorant. A free flow of ideas was started which as yet has not ceased.

TAT

VI

F

Intellect

While the stories are short and contain more populars, or common associations to the pictures, than originals, there is some exercise of the imagination in the narrative development. The vocabulary (words like mesmerize and Voila!) implies an educated person. Assuming that she is a student, she would fall in the average range of mental ability for college students or college graduates, which is to say, superior but not very superior.

Affect

There is a considerable amount of emotionality in the stories. She is a "feeling person." Characters are variously described as stunned, startled, upset, angry, hysterical, emotionally exhausted, happy, contented, or impatient. While the emotions cover a wide span, affects are more negative than positive. Nevertheless, she is in the normal range of emotional reaction, and usually her emotions are under pretty good control.

Traits, other characteristics

F is a self-contained, thoughtful, introspective person who is not aggressive or given to decisive or impulsive action. This comes out in the story of an upset friend whom she feels sympathy for but does not actually try to help. Usually she respects people's privacy and keeps her distance. She is probably introverted and passive except when her interests are deeply stirred as in relations with men she cares about. Then she can be possessive. There is a great preoccupation with heterosexual relations and especially with marriage. Her values here are conventional and bourgeois. There is a craving for affection, a concern with love making, and a sentimental feeling for children. In her life, as in 2-3 of the stories, men have the dominant role, and women placate and are submissive to them. Again in the stories women have greater need for men than men for women. Withal she maintains a young girl's romanticism and is idealistic about a fulfilling marriage. Her psychology is definitely feminine—no Women's Liberation here!

Adjustment

While heterosexuality is her main focus of concern, another problem area may be parent-child relations. Children not only rebel against parents but have their way with them. She may feel some rebellion against one or both of her parents and want her emotional independence. Aside from these not unusual problems she is probably no more conflictful than the average young woman of her age and situation. She falls in the normal range of adjustment, leaning a little more toward the side of maladaptation because of unresolved problems.

VI.

The intelligence of this young lady can be characterized as medium, according percentile between 50-55% or slightly above average. Her ability to learn is good although the limitations are definitely set. Her desire to learn may get her to the brink of her capacity and the realization of this may get her to the point of frustration. Within this capacity she can think clearly although her capacity does not allow for abstract thinking in the strongest sense.

She is clearly affectionate and she shows a fine sense for the problems of others. Her original shyness will prevent her from going too enthusiastically into new relationships, although, once she has been able to overcome the original shyness she can be extremely warm and friendly.

Her natural reticence keeps her behind the general flow of her age group. She will be regarded as a conservative by them which, I believe, is due to her background. As far as her elders are concerned, she will be regarded as much too modern. This in itself makes her unclear about herself. It is safe to say that she is not sure of herself although the progress she has made in the last few years must be considered to be remarkable.

Her emotional balance must be classified as a delicate one. On the one hand she has to consider her background and she is not capable of excluding the resulting influences, and on the other hand she has the desire to forge ahead and move with the crowd. To find the appropriate middle road requires a maturity which she has not attained as yet.

Linda Haag   22 years old   Female VII.

Height 5'6"   weight 160 lbs.   right handed

In the days of the cave man the wheel ~~was~~ was invented. The caveman must have found that now it was easier to move objects in a cart. As time passed on they built carriages for there own transportation. They were able to use the wheel to ground flour. They were able to build river boats, trains, cars and hundreds of other things. The man who invent the wheel probly had no idea of all the uses the wheel could be used for. In todays life the wheel is taken for granted. The whell moves the traffic the trains planes, clocks, + machines. Though the wheel was initself a great invention it led to many others. The man who invented the wheel, ~~had~~ unknowly changed the course of history.

TAT
VII

G

Intellect	There is no real indication that she is of more than average intelligence. The frequent misspellings and occasional errors in punctuation suggest that she does not have more than a high school education.
Affect	The stories, for the most part, show a modulated or even bland affect, although there is an under-current of sadness and loneliness. She is not a happy, vivacious sort of person, but neither does she appear to be deeply depressed. In one allegorical story, a man struggles to loosen the hold of mysterious hands that would pull him back into darkness. She too struggles and manages to maintain control over her emotions. She is a self-contained person who does not show her feelings very readily.
Traits, other characteristics	The stories are often about lonely figures given to daydreaming or indecisiveness. She may impress many as a rather strange girl who is quiet and introverted and much given to introspection. Characters are acted upon by outside forces and, like her, are usually passive. G is anything but a strong decisive, articulate individual. Aspiration level is not high; worldly achievement is attributed only to men. She gives some indication of a desire to travel and change of environment. She likes quiet, peace, security, and the beauties of nature.
Adjustment	Psychosexuality is a region of disturbance. There is nothing about marriages, which is unusual for a young woman of her age. Moreover, heterosexual relations in the stories are unhappy. In one case, a man kills a woman for unstated reasons; the sexual implications of the picture are ignored. There is misidentification of gender in a story involving two homosexual males. There is some question about her sex identification; she may have Lesbian tendencies which could be either covert or overt. She craves affection but is afraid she will end up alone and unloved. There are hints of problems in parent-child relations with a suggestion of a communication barrier. In general, there is little satisfaction in her life. She is maladjusted, but not acutely or severely disturbed.

VII.

This person must be regarded as below average intelligence. Because of the poor writing skill it is almost impossible to determine the percentage. My estimate would be in the range of 25-30%. Her very slow temperament does not even allow her to be too anxious to learn.

The activities she seeks are more of an indulging nature. Indulging seems to be contradictory to the tension she operates under and the lack of release seems to be a problem. The tension is a result of an inferiority complex which is partly justified. All this has a strong influence on her emotional life, and problems are indicated in this area also. It must be stated that her maturity is far below the age group she is in, particularly her emotional maturity. Her feeling of insecurity is a result of the different difficulties she encounters.

One of the traits that is of some importance is her openness. She often will come out with statements that are not expected or outright undiplomatic. It is part of her lack of intelligence which prevents her from making the right judgment in such instances. In so many ways she seems to be primitive, if not retarded. Her usefulness must be seen in the light of her severe limitations.

What do you believe to be the best invention and why? VIII

If it weren't for Alexander Graham Bell, it wouldn't be possible for Grandma Jones to tell ~~his~~ her son-in-law who's in the army in Germany that his wife gave birth to a baby boy. The telephone is the best piece of invention of all time. Without it, it wouldn't be possible to ~~spend long weary~~ make up for the long weary hours that pass when one is alone at home.

Long hours are spent talking to the neighbor next door. If the rain is coming down very hard and one does not want to travel across the fence to the neighbor's house to talk, you can just pick up the telephone a few feet away. How often have I spent wasting my free hours on the phone? If it weren't for the telephone, my life would be one complete bore.

Dolores Resignio
Female
5'3", 127 lbs
right-handed
24

TAT

VIII

H

Intellect

The stories are long with full particulars about narrative characters as though H enjoyed the task. They are dramatic, sometimes even melodramatic, and show some originality. She possesses a vivid imagination and is highly verbal. Intelligence is better than average, though not very superior. From the vocabulary, one would judge that she has been exposed to higher education.

Affect

The narratives are jam-packed with emotion, and there is much description of inner feelings. She is very much interested in people's feelings, including her own. H is lively and emotionally expressive. While not immune to depression, she tends to fight dysphoric affect, or unpleasant emotions, and usually maintains an optimistic outlook.

Traits, other characteristics

She is outgoing and sociable. Stories are replete with action, while the characters, who are always dynamic, do not give up in the face of difficulties. She also is persistent and shows evidence of ego strength. H is also very energetic, vigorous, and impulsive. Tempo is rapid, and there may be some impatience with detail. Worldly ambition is attributed only to men; her own goals are traditionally feminine and include a strong desire for marriage. The stories tell of difficulties in getting properly married, including two stories of being jilted, which may have some either direct or indirect autobiographical significance. Nevertheless, matrimony is her main concern, and she maintains idealistic aspirations about a mutually fulfilling union.

Adjustment

Most of the stories have a positive tone. H too has a hopeful, optimistic outlook. Despite some psychological immaturity, she falls in the normal range of adjustment.

VIII.

The intelligence of this person is being judged at 50-55% with an emphasis on the ability to make use of it for the purpose of learning. A considerable learning process has taken place and there are indications of a willingness to learn.

This is a good-natured person with hardly any trace of hostility. She has a good sense for monetary security and she is capable of planning ahead in this respect. Her plans in this area do not always materialize and this may cause her to be frustrated. She likes to be active but her activities are limited to a more conservative range of subjects. Her sense for beauty includes her own outside appearance. She is also affected by the outside appearance of others and she must be considered as slightly vain.

With all the forward move and the activities it is surprising that she is liable to have depressive moods. The cause for this must be deep-seated, most likely in her parent relationship. This had, however, also a positive affect on the writer. She has learned at an early age to rely mostly on herself. It also has helped her in the maturing process. She is capable of accepting responsibilities, however, because of her tendency to depression only a slow increase of responsibilities is advisable.

Rose Lo Moraw

IX

Age - 65 years old

Sex - female

Height - 4 feet 11 inches

Weight - 130 lbs.

Handedness - left-handed

Electricity was the best invention. We have many uses for it. For example, we use it to run machines, to give us light, to cook, + for a great many other things. For instance, to vacuum clean, for television + radio; also many industries depend on electricity for power.

Electricity was invented by Thomas Edison. He was one of our greatest inventors.

I

TAT

IX

Intellect	Stories are short and characterized more by emotional pathology than by plausible logical development. There is originality in picture interpretation, but it is due more to projection of personal problems than to healthy exercise of imagination. She is not better than average in intelligence and, judging from some of the grammar such as double negatives, is not a well educated person.
Affect	The stories are wildly emotional. The feelings expressed are almost all negative such as the characters being stunned, speechless, dazed, dejected, disappointed, shocked, and generally disturbed. Life is pictured in dark, dismal tones. Characters have serious problems which they cannot handle. She also is overwhelmed by life situations which she cannot cope with. There are frequent suicides, usually involving loss of a mate. One wonders whether she is afraid of losing her husband and being left alone and desolate. It is clear that she is unhappy, even suicidal, and probably agitated as well.
Traits, other characteristics	From thematic evidence, she is not a strong person who can solve problems. She pictures herself as an ineffectual parent who cannot help her child and generally as a quitter, one who gives up in the face of difficulties. All of her characters are beaten down and defeated. She is a pessimist. She is also a feeling, intuitive person rather than a thinking, rationally-controlled woman. The personality structure is simple rather than complex. The only light-hearted story is told in the first person and concerns her dog. While she shows a liking for canines, she even presents the dog as slightly frustrated.
Adjustment	Another disaster area is marriage. Husbands in the narratives, who occur frequently, lie, are unfaithful, lose jobs, but she thinks of herself as consoling and helpful. At the same time, she is emotionally dependent and nurses feelings of ambivalence. When a wife or girl friend dies, the husband or boy friend commits suicide. Perhaps this is her way of sayings "you cannot live without me" (or that she cannot live without her husband and is afraid of his dying). At any rate, death is a preoccupation. She is seriously maladjusted, as shown by unresolved conflicts, frictional interpersonal relations, despondency, and suicides. The stories seem to express the attitude that life is full of misery and that she has nothing to live for. She is deeply depressed and needs psychiatric attention.

IX.

The intelligence of this writer must be regarded as average or slightly below, about 45-50%. There are many reasons why she was not able to use her intelligence for the purpose of learning. One of the important ones is her difficulty in making changes. Anything new represents a source for insecurity.

Her insecurity is the result of her emotional immaturity which probably originated as far back as her childhood and was due to the type of upbringing she had. The shyness of a young person has remained with her, particularly in the area of the emotions. There she shows strong frustrations and it is safe to assume that she must have found substitutions to offset the emotional frustrations.

In other areas this writer functions well. I am thinking of her sense for practicality. She is very conscious of cleanliness. She is opinionated beyond her intellectual capacity. She does not have a strong will but once her mind is made up she will have difficulties to change it. She is quite delicate in her feelings and the fact that she is offended easily may present a problem in her relationship to others. She is bound to object to criticism due to her insecurity and lack of self-confidence. She wants to hide the lack of self-confidence. As a result of that she may fall into a pattern of overemphasizing the "good deeds" she has done for others. She is very strong on honesty and truthfulness. It is not easy to gain her confidence. Once established it will remain as long as no disappointing acts by the other party has been committed.

Female
late twenties
5'7
130 lbs
right handed
Ellyse Vitello

X.

The greatest discovery is writing. It is helpful in recording things, remembering things, and communicating them. It also can reveal your personality. Since I have never had my writing interpreted I am particularly eager to know what can be discovered about me from my scrawl. Is it only the writing or the content & word choice that is used?

TAT

X

J

Intellect	For the most part, stories have an abundance of particularized and detailed description, deal with prosaic everyday life situations, and have a quality of immediacy and pettiness that one might suspect that the narrator was a rather limited person. However, this profile has to be modified in the light of the last two stories which deal respectively with a visitation from outer space and an art innovation. These indicate greater imagination and originality and untapped potentialities. Intelligence is average or better with an even higher potential. Judging from the numerous misspellings, often of higher level vocabulary, she is probably not a college graduate, but may have educated herself through reading and personal contacts. At any rate, she is informed about the current New York scene, knowing about such things as drugs and encounter groups.
Affect	The characters have normal feelings without the predominance of any one kind of emotion. J falls into the normal range of emotional responsiveness. Affectivity and interests are definitely feminine.
Traits, other characteristics	J is in her daily life, despite unplumbed depths, matter-of-fact, down-to-earth, and very practical. She is not a soft person but seems to have a certain toughness of fibre which is part of her realism. J is people-oriented and is concerned mainly with marriage and domestic life. She has basically conventional values; the only times her characters come to grief are when the mores are violated. Usually the narrative husbands and wives are considerate of one another, and wives are supportive of their husbands. There was scant attention paid to parent-child relations; they were probably not an area of great conflict.
Adjustment	Themes are diversified, imports or story morals are positive, so presumably she is well adjusted with a minimum of complexes. There is no evidence of unusual amounts of conflicts, anxieties, depression, or hostilities. The heroes and heroines are normal and responsible people who meet their daily problems head-on. She is similar; outgoing, sociable, realistic, a person who can cope. She also seems to be a close and objective observer of what goes on around her.

X.

This writer is highly intelligent with an emphasis on the ability of abstract thinking. On a 100% scale for the maximum of the intelligence I would rate her between 70-75%. It is also the speed of thinking that is of importance here. Her intelligence allows her to pick out the essential and so she is not in danger of getting lost in details. The good order in her thinking processes include both the power of logic and the power of intuition. This combination would enable her to pursue scientific fields.

This person is open to feelings. She is capable of feeling on a large scale although the constant training of her intellectual abilities have a tendency to put her own feelings into the background. It is also the quality of sorting out the details and concentrating on the essential that will have an influence on her emotional life. Although the exclusion of feelings and emotions is desirable in her eyes, she is enough of a woman to have the understanding that emotions play a big role in her life.

The lack of sufficient willpower for the activities she so strongly desires makes it necessary for her to employ substitutes. Her tenacity is being helpful in this respect. Also her sense for "drive". Once she has a goal, the drive that she has will carry her to the conclusion of her endeavors. She has her own sense of values and she does live by them. These values do not differ substantially from the accepted medium.

Although her balance is a delicate one, she is able to function in all areas of life. She has been able to overcome an original shyness in approaching other people, particularly those that she meets for the first time. Even today, it is not too easy for her to talk about her own feelings.

Priorities

Felix Klein

Priorities

A New Typology Based on Alfred Adler[6]

A priority is a precedence established by order of importance or urgency. It is a summary (shorthand) statement about a person's convictions which answers the questions "What is most important to me?"—within my own life style—and "What must I avoid most?" There is an obvious connection between the answers to the first and the second question.

Every person has all of the following four priorities and therefore operates within a hierarchy, that is, one priority first, and then the other three, in decreasing intensity.

Priorities should not serve to label people, since priorities represent only one facet of a person's life style, and do not adequately describe the complexity of a whole human being. However, a priority is like a calling card. It indicates, by a person's relationship with others, what that person values most.

Most Important	To Be Avoided Most
Comfort	Stress
Acceptance (Pleasing)	Rejection
Control	Humiliation
Superiority	Meaninglessness

The following tabulation summarizes the four priorities and their main indicators and relates them to their graphological pointers.

6 Based on concepts of Alfred Adler's Individual Psychology this typology was introduced by Nira Kefir and William L. Pew. See W.L. Pew, The Number One Priority (St. Paul, Minnesota, 1976).

COMFORT

Priority Character Indicators	Graphological Indicators
1. Reluctance to change priorities	Regularity; upright slant; preference for left trend; extreme connectedness
2. Reduced productivity	Looped garland or arcade; fullness; simplification level below form level
3. Predictability	Regularity; upright slant; preference for left trend; extreme connectedness
4. Easy disposition	Rounded; fullness; good middle zone
5. Preference for a comfortable environment	Rounded; fullness; good middle zone
6. Optimism	Rising lines; good rhythm; strong rightward movement
7. Peacemaking inclination	Roundedness; preference for right slant
8. Diplomatic ability	Slightly diminishing ends of words; terminal threading
9. Tendency to mind one's own business	Space between words larger than width of lowercase "m"; upright slant; closed "o" and "a"
10. Minimizes differences	Roundedness; preference for right slant
11. Self containment; lack of aspirations	Under-developed upper zone
12. Modesty	Small writing; low pressure
13. Mellowness	Roundedness
14. Empathy	Well-rounded forms; light pressure; right slant
15. Considerateness	Rounded connections and forms; small and even spaces between words; right trend
16. Flexibility	Garland; fluidity; ease on connecting; thread; right trend; moderate speed
17. Quietness	Steady baseline; slowness; good spatial arrangement

18. Avoidance of extremes and confrontation	Avoidance of extremes in handwriting; no zonal interference
19. Interest in own comfort more than in others' comfort	Left-tending ("turned around") terminals; strong pressure in downstrokes
20. Insistence on own immediate gratification	Excess circularity; left-tending ("turned around") terminal strokes; hasty writing
21. Avoidance of responsibilities and expectations	Secondary thread; possible double-bow connection; neglect of form
22. Retreat from growth-producing conflict	Avoidance of extremes in handwriting; no zonal interference

ACCEPTANCE (PLEASING)

Priority Character Indicators	Graphological Indicators
1. Little self-respect	Under developed middle zone; poor zonal balance; ill-defined forms; poor spacing; imbalance in capital "I"
2. Not expecting respect from others	Under developed middle zone; poor zonal balance; ill-defined forms; poor spacing; imbalance in capital "I"
3. Sociability	Even and small spacing between words; good movement; right trend especially in upper zone; finals extended
4. Tendency to perform	Persona writing
5. Perceptiveness	Original forms; breaks in high style-value writing; good spacing
6. Friendliness	Well-rounded forms; light pressure; right slant
7. Considerateness	Round connections and forms; moderately extended finals; small and even spaces between words; right trend
8. Willingness to volunteer	More slackness than rigidity
9. Flexibility	Garland; fluidity; ease in connection; thread; right trend; moderate speed
10. Avoidance of confrontation	Avoidance of extremes in handwriting; no zonal interference
11. Empathy	Well-rounded forms; light pressure; right slant
12. Tendency to meet others' expectations	Right slant; light pressure; rounded connections; moderate speed; large writing
13. Generosity	Wide distance between letters; right trend; consistency in upper-zone forms
14. Peacemaking inclination	Roundedness; preference for right slant

15. Lack of aggressiveness	Low pressure; roundedness; finals diminishing in size and width
16. Avoidance of risks	Large right margin; narrow writing; no extremes; reduced pressure; writing hugs base line

CONTROL

Priority Character Indicators	Graphological Indicators
1. Distance	Large distance between letters and words; upright or left slant; narrowness
2. Reduced spontaneity	Slowness; rigid regularity; preference for up-and-down movement
3. Reduced creativity	Little development of writing; lack of simplification
4. Leadership ability	Right trend; moderate primary pressure; good legibility
5. Organizational ability	Good spacing; accuracy; attention to details
6. Reliability	Formal regularity; good zonal balance; no extremes
7. Tendency toward being conscious of time and tact	Good sense for space; moderate-to-small size in comparison to format
8. Productivity	Fairly regulated movement
9. Practicability	Good spacing; fairly stable base line; small writing form; accuracy
10. Tendency to abide by the law	No neglect of form; not extremely slack or rigid
11. Persistence	Formal regularity; connectedness; fairly small writing; no neglect of form
12. Assertiveness	Moderately large writing; possible angularity
13. Righteousness	Emphasis on regularity; possible angularity
14. Preciseness	Attention to detail; preference for small writing; accuracy of form
15. Predictability	Regularity (not rigid); fairly stable base line; no extremes
16. Responsibility	Formal regularity; no variation in slant; low pressure; distinctive upper zone

17. Ambition	Right trend; fullness; emphasis on upper or lower zone
18. Industriousness	Moderate speed; right trend; good rhythm; moderately connected
19. Courage	Right slant; right trend; moderate pressure
20. Ability to withdraw	Upright slant; no emphasis on terminal strokes
21. Self-sufficiency	Upright slant; moderately-developed capitals; moderate pressure; proper space between words
22. Bossiness	Moderately large writing; angularity likely; pressure; large capitals
23. Competitiveness	Large capitals; preference for angularity
24. Tendency toward depression	Lower-zone emphasis; weak pressure; disturbed rhythm; large distance between lines

SUPERIORITY

Priority Character Indicators	Graphological Indicators
1. Disposition toward creating one-upmanship relationship with others	Oversized capitals; enriched writing
2. Competence	Good middle zone; good legibility; accuracy of form
3. Persistence	Formal regularity; connectedness; fairly small writing; no neglect of form
4. Idealism	Emphasis on upper zone; right trend
5. Moral sense	Sense for form
6. Willingness to expand oneself for the improvement of society	Right trend; emphasis on finals; right slant; medium-to-small spaces between words
7. Desire to save time	Simplification; moderate speed; right trend
8. Inclination toward: self-assertion, self-glorification, self-advancement	Emphasis on capitals; emphasis on the Personal Pronoun "I"[7]; well-developed movement

---

7 See Jane Nugent Green, *You and Your Private "I"*, (St. Paul, Minnesota, 1975), Felix Klein, *Character Structure of Neuroses* (Wittlich's Method, New York, 1974).

Publications mentioned above are available from Manhattan Handwriting Consultant, 250 West 57th Street, New York, NY 10107.

Priority Type: C O M F O R T

Female, 53, R

However, I have already planned work and a visit to Bristol so I am sorry to say I shall not be able to see you. But as I will be in N.Y in July this won't matter so much. Life is pretty hectic one way or another and I can no longer cope with rushing around etc.

If you phone me (I shall be out Wed. + Thursd. evening till about 10 p.m and leave for Bristol on Sunday appx 10 a.m.) perhaps you

Priority Type: P L E A S I N G

Male, 29, R.

When things go wrong as they sometimes will,
When the road you're trudging seems all up hill,
When the funds are low and the debts are high,
And you want to smile, but you have to sigh;
When care is pressing you down a bit,
Rest if you must, but don't you quit.
Life is queer with its twists and turns,
As everyone of us sometimes learns,
And many a failure turns about
When he might have won had he stuck it out;

Priority Type: C O N T R O L

Male, 31, R.

And so the young lady asked me to write some gibberish so she could investigate my impulsive habits, or whatever this proves to be.

For how long I am suppose to continue this shall be determind by my signature at the end of this page.

Priority Type: S U P E R I O R I T Y

Male, 61, R

I am recuperating - feeling much better. Entered hospital at 119 lbs & am now rapidly becoming a new man in looks & strength - weight now 139 lbs stuffed. The moral is - fasting does not eradicate all conditions & we must always remember

PRIORITY SCORE SHEET by Felix Klein			
COMFORT			
Priority Character Indicators	**Graphological Indicators**	**Yes**	**No**
1. Reluctance to change priorities	Regularity; upright slant; preference for left trend; extreme connectedness		
2. Reduced productivity	Looped garland or arcade; fullness; simplification level below form level		
3. Predictability	Regularity; upright slant; preference for left trend; extreme connectedness		
4. Easy disposition	Rounded; fullness; good middle zone		
5. Preference for a comfortable environment	Rounded; fullness; good middle zone		
6. Optimism	Rising lines; good rhythm; strong rightward movement		
7. Peacemaking inclination	Roundedness; preference for right slant		
8. Diplomatic ability	Slightly diminishing ends of words; terminal threading		
9. Tendency to mind one's own business	Space between words larger than width of lowercase "m"; upright slant; closed "o" and "a"		
10. Minimizes differences	Roundedness; preference for right slant		
11. Self containment; lack of aspirations	Under-developed upper zone		
12. Modesty	Small writing; low pressure		
13. Mellowness	Roundedness		

14. Empathy	Well-rounded forms; light pressure; right slant		
15. Considerateness	Rounded connections and forms; small and even spaces between words; right trend		
16. Flexibility	Garland; fluidity; ease on connecting; thread; right trend; moderate speed		
17. Quietness	Steady baseline; slowness; good spatial arrangement		
18. Avoidance of extremes and confrontation	Avoidance of extremes in handwriting; no zonal interference		
19. Interest in own comfort more than in others' comfort	Left-tending ("turned around") terminals; strong pressure in downstrokes		
20. Insistence on own immediate gratification	Excess circularity; left-tending ("turned around") terminal strokes; hasty writing		
21. Avoidance of responsibilities and expectations	Secondary thread; possible double-bow connection; neglect of form		
22. Retreat from growth-producing conflict	Avoidance of extremes in handwriting; no zonal interference		
	Score		

PRIORITY SCORE SHEET by Felix Klein			
ACCEPTANCE (PLEASING)			
Priority Character Indicators	**Graphological Indicators**	**Yes**	**No**
1. Little self-respect	Under developed middle zone; poor zonal balance; ill-defined forms; poor spacing; imbalance in capital "I"		
2. Not expecting respect from others	Under developed middle zone; poor zonal balance; ill-defined forms; poor spacing; imbalance in capital "I"		
3. Sociability	Even and small spacing between words; good movement; right trend especially in upper zone; finals extended		
4. Tendency to perform	Persona writing		
5. Perceptiveness	Original forms; breaks in high style-value writing; good spacing		
6. Friendliness	Well-rounded forms; light pressure; right slant		
7. Considerateness	Round connections and forms; moderately extended finals; small and even spaces between words; right trend		
8. Willingness to volunteer	More slackness than rigidity		
9. Flexibility	Garland; fluidity; ease in connection; thread; right trend; moderate speed		
10. Avoidance of confrontation	Avoidance of extremes in handwriting; no zonal interference		
11. Empathy	Well-rounded forms; light pressure; right slant		

12. Tendency to meet others' expectations	Right slant; light pressure; rounded connections; moderate speed; large writing		
13. Generosity	Wide distance between letters; right trend; consistency in upper-zone forms		
14. Peacemaking inclination	Roundedness; preference for right slant		
15. Lack of aggressiveness	Low pressure; roundedness; finals diminishing in size and width		
16. Avoidance of risks	Large right margin; narrow writing; no extremes; reduced pressure; writing hugs base line		
	Score		

PRIORITY SCORE SHEET by Felix Klein			
CONTROL			
Priority Character Indicators	**Graphological Indicators**	**Yes**	**No**
1. Distance	Large distance between letters and words; upright or left slant; narrowness		
2. Reduced spontaneity	Slowness; rigid regularity; preference for up-and-down movement		
3. Reduced creativity	Little development of writing; lack of simplification		
4. Leadership ability	Right trend; moderate primary pressure; good legibility		
5. Organizational ability	Good spacing; accuracy; attention to details		
6. Reliability	Formal regularity; good zonal balance; no extremes		
7. Tendency toward being conscious of time and tact	Good sense for space; moderate-to-small size in comparison to format		
8. Productivity	Fairly regulated movement		
9. Practicability	Good spacing; fairly stable base line; small writing form; accuracy		
10. Tendency to abide by the law	No neglect of form; not extremely slack or rigid		
11. Persistence	Formal regularity; connectedness; fairly small writing; no neglect of form		
12. Assertiveness	Moderately large writing; possible angularity		
13. Righteousness	Emphasis on regularity; possible angularity		

14. Preciseness	Attention to detail; preference for small writing; accuracy of form		
15. Predictability	Regularity (not rigid); fairly stable base line; no extremes		
16. Responsibility	Formal regularity; no variation in slant; low pressure; distinctive upper zone		
17. Ambition	Right trend; fullness; emphasis on upper or lower zone		
18. Industriousness	Moderate speed; right trend; good rhythm; moderately connected		
19. Courage	Right slant; right trend; moderate pressure		
20. Ability to withdraw	Upright slant; no emphasis on terminal strokes		
21. Self-sufficiency	Upright slant; moderately-developed capitals; moderate pressure; proper space between words		
22. Bossiness	Moderately large writing; angularity likely; pressure; large capitals		
23. Competitiveness	Large capitals; preference for angularity		
24. Tendency toward depression	Lower-zone emphasis; weak pressure; disturbed rhythm; large distance between lines		
	Score		

PRIORITY SCORE SHEET by Felix Klein			
SUPERIORITY			
Priority Character Indicators	**Graphological Indicators**	**Yes**	**No**
1. Disposition toward creating one-upmanship relationship with others	Oversized capitals; enriched writing		
2. Competence	Good middle zone; good legibility; accuracy of form		
3. Persistence	Formal regularity; connectedness; fairly small writing; no neglect of form		
4. Idealism	Emphasis on upper zone; right trend		
5. Moral sense	Sense for form		
6. Willingness to expand oneself for the improvement of society	Right trend; emphasis on finals; right slant; medium-to-small spaces between words		
7. Desire to save time	Simplification; moderate speed; right trend		
8. Inclination toward self-assertion, self-glorification, self-advancement	Emphasis on capitals; emphasis on the Personal Pronoun "I", well-developed movement		
	Score		

Emotional Release As Seen in Handwriting

Felix Klein

Emotional Release As Seen in Handwriting

In order to understand the subject of emotional release, it is necessary to start with defining what we mean by this expression. The definition of emotional release as given in A Comprehensive Dictionary of Psychological and Psychoanalytical Terms (English and English) is "The outpouring of emotion after a period of attempted suppression."

Checking various books on psychology yielded surprisingly little, if anything, relating to emotional release. As the definition already indicates, in order to have emotional release a temporary resistance to the release must precede it. Very few reactions to an emotion are produced instantaneously, and even a spontaneous reaction to a feeling needs a split second of restraint to make a reaction possible.

There is hardly any character quality which is not in some way involved in furthering or restraining emotional release. It may be a good idea to divide emotional release into two groups. Using Eric Fromm's term "productive," we can say that the two groups consist of productive emotional release and unproductive emotional release. Both groups have one thing in common and that is the reduction of tension. According to Sigmund Freud, even the blinking of an eye reduces tension. Productive emotional release is concerned with the reduction of tension by expressions which seem to be acceptable, at least to the majority of people. Whenever the result of the emotional release is without a doubt negative or even destructive, we must classify this emotional release as unproductive.

This can best be explained by giving at least one example for each of the two groups. Productive emotional release would be the culmination of two people with strong erotic feelings for each other seeking and finding emotional releases. A young person seeking release through vandalism can only be identified as having an unproductive release pattern. The basic emotion in the example for productive emotional release was the feeling of love which may have been mixed with sexual desire. The basic emotion for the unproductive release example (if one can call this an emotion) may be satisfaction of aggressive tendencies, which is produced by the emotion of anger. This doesn't mean that in every case anger can only result in an unproductive emotional release. It is often the case that the failure to reach the productive emotional release may result in a substitution. We all are very familiar with such substitutions. The process can be simply explained this way: a person experiencing an increase in one particular emotion without being able to release his or her emotions produces a great deal of tension which will eventually come to the point where the tension becomes unbearable. For instance, a person who is very much in love with another person and does not find response on the part of the loved one, experiences frustration and tension without an outlet. When the level of frustration becomes too high, the individual will then seek unrelated substitutes to reduce the high degree of tension. This then varies with different people. While one person may turn to overeating, another may get into the consumption of alcohol, while still another may become a "workaholic." We often advise a teenager to substitute emotional release by engaging in sports. A modern way of replacing emotional releases may be the tendency to go jogging, although there one also obtains the by-product of physical fitness.

Because the situations that can be described involving adults are so complex and so difficult to separate, it is necessary for the understanding of emotional release to go back to the child. In Psychology: An Introduction to Behavior Sciences by Smith and Smith, we are told that "Watson's (1924) studies of emotional expression in infants led him to believe that there are three primary inborn emotions: fear, rage, and love. He described the infant's fear response as the catching of the breath, random movements of arms and hands, closing the eyes, and crying; rage, as a typical temper tantrum with stiffening of the body, striking movements, and flushing of the face; and love, as smiling, cooing, gurgling, and cuddling.… Bridges (1932) concluded that newborn infants respond to any highly stimulating condition with generalized excitement that only later becomes differentiated into more specific emotions. Within a month or two reactions of distress and delight can be distinguished, and by the age of two years, affection, delight, elation, excitement, disgust, distress, jealousy, fear, and anger appear.… As children develop more diverse patterns of emotional response, they also start to develop emotional habits that help to mold their individual personalities and structure their patterns of living. Some of the habits based on positive emotional reactions are patterns of love, happiness, loyalty, and enthusiasm. Reactions such as fear and anger help define worry, aggression, timidity, negativism, fantasy, the use of drugs and alcohol, peculiar postures and mannerisms, overactivity, and antisocial patterns of behavior—habits that sometimes lead to the serious behavior problems."

Children react towards pleasantness and unpleasantness by appetites or aversions already present at birth. As a consequence, one child may react to a stimulus in a very positive way while another child may react to the same stimulus by feeling uncomfortable. This particular mode of reaction later on in life makes it possible to relate to more complex emotions. If a child reacts in an early state positively towards other people, that in turn may later on create situations that will make association with others more likely. It gives pleasure to a child when an adult strokes or fondles it, and this positive reaction is the cause for the youngster's attachment to something fuzzy or what we often call "the security blanket."

H. F. Harlow in 1962 conducted tests with monkeys and established that monkeys growing up without the mother and having a substitute mother holding a feeding bottle made out of wire without any fuzzy material covering it, prefer this form of substitute less than a wire mother covered with a soft material, even though this substitute mother does not provide the food.

The laughing of a child is a spontaneous reaction to a stimulus. This reaction is supposedly exclusive with humans. A child reacts with laughter usually before the third month of life, and the stimulus is a social one. The same reaction can be achieved by pets or moving toys. In contrast, adults laugh due to pleasure, exuberance, or excitement, but mostly because of something humorous that has happened. Laughter in adults is not exclusively a reaction to humor. It is often followed by a rage stimulus, fear, or compensatory action which counteracts the stimulus. A person described as having a good sense of humor is usually the one who can readily laugh at himself.

Fear reactions can be elicited by pain, loud sounds, and in some cases by the loss of support. "A reaction that resembles rage or anger," according to Karl U. Smith and Margaret F. Smith, "can be elicited in a very young infant by restricting their body movements. Infants and young children also seem to get angry in some cases when they are hungry, uncomfortable, or over-tired."

Emotional motivation is caused by aroused specific external stimuli which result in characteristic motivational patterns. Fear results in withdrawal or flight, rage comes with threat or fighting, and pleasure becomes approach and further interaction. Reactions to frustrations vary. It has been observed that people who are close to a goal will try harder than people who are not near it. The fact that some people have to perform in comparison to national standards on a particular test causes them to react more positively.

There seems to be a causative reaction between frustration and aggression. It is almost so that one can predict that aggression has a greater chance of developing when frustration is present.

To quote again from Smith and Smith, "A student hurrying to get to class on time who cannot find his notebook may search until he finds it, grab another notebook to use in place of the lost one, or go to class without one. Or he may display unreasonable emotional disturbance and disorganized activity that is unrelated to the original goal of getting to class, such as 'blowing his top,' slamming a book on the table, or flouncing around in disgust. The frustrating situation has aroused him emotionally but the emotional stimulus is not a specific object or event in his perceptual environment on which he can vent his wrath. Rather it is the lack of an object. He has been blocked not by a physical barrier but by a psychological barrier. Frustration often involves a situation that cannot be seen or controlled directly, so that the emotional response tends to be disorganized bodily behavior accompanied by generalized tension and often the vague generalized fear called anxiety."

Some emotional releases require regression. The fact alone that removal of clothes is necessary for sexual intercourse constitutes a form of regression dating back to early childhood.

There is no question that emotional release has a direct effect on the learning process. The conclusion of various tests conducted both with animals and with humans shows that emotional release interferes with learning. The higher the intensity of the emotional release, the less the ability to learn. It might also be assumed that a high intellectual level may have a blocking effect on emotional release. "The tendency of organisms to control their own environmental interactions means that an emotional response is more likely to be pleasant and less likely to be unpleasant if the individual controls its onset and timing." (Smith and Smith).

There is another way of dividing emotional release into sections. Emotional release is greatly dependent on emotional capacity, which in turn is dependent on libido. As defined in A Comprehensive Dictionary of Psychological and Psychoanalytical Terms, libido is "(1). sexual craving. (2). any erotic desire or pleasure. (3). any instinctual manifestation that tends towards life rather than death, integration rather than disintegration.—Syn. Eros, life instinct. (4). any psychic energy, constructive or destructive."

"Freud, who introduced the term, continually changed his usage as well as the concepts for which libido was proposed; and his followers have not in general been more consistent. Common to all uses is the idea of some sort of psychic dynamics or energy, an irrational and instinctual determiner of both conscious and unconscious processes. The sexual impulses are, at the least, the type to which other libidinal manifestations may be compared: in Freud's earlier treatment libido was quite simply a direct or indirect sexual expression; even in usage (4) the connection with sex cannot be severed. Freud later seemed inclined to drop the term libido altogether, but finally chose meaning (4), which is also Jung's usage. This is to introduce—or to increase—confusion between the professional use and the layman's understanding.

The psychoanalytic movement has from the beginning suffered from an ambiguity about sex, if not in the writings of adherents, at least in the minds of those who follow from a distance. Libido is now firmly established as a semi-popular term with a meaning somewhere between (1) and (2). Any other meaning is likely to be misinterpreted. If it is to mean <u>any</u> kind of psychic energy, why not use that phrase or the very closely akin horme? (horme: purpose striving). If it means any constructive instinctual activity, why not life instinct?"

Many people consider vitality to be the same as libido but in order to clarify, I would like again to quote from <u>A Comprehensive Dictionary of Psychological and Psychoanalytical Terms</u>, to make clear what vitality really is. As English and English define it, vitality is "(1). the quality of being alive, (2). the property of an organism of being able to stay alive. (3). biological vigor, energy, endurance, (4). a complex personality pattern manifested by lively gestures and movements and by low threshold for the pleasant emotions."

All of the information given up to now has an influence on emotional release. All the factors concerning personality qualities have indicators in the handwriting. The most basic list of graphological indicators includes those that facilitate emotional release on the one hand, and those that "bind" or retard emotional release, on the other.

<u>BINDING INDICATORS</u>

Upright slant

Left trend

Arcade connection

Angle connection

Uniform connections

Small writing

Big zone extensions

Emphasis on lower length

Regularity

Strong pressure

Disconnectedness

Meagernsss

Slowness

Disproportioned

Arrhythmic

<u>RELEASE (LOOSENING) INDICATORS</u>

Right slant

Wide

Right trend

Garlands

Curves

Thread

Mixed connections

Emphasis on upper length

Large writing

Small zone extensions

Irregularity

Light to moderate pressure

Connectedness

Fullness

Pastosity

Speed

Proportioned

Rhythmic

The following handwriting samples portray writers with some form of difficulty in their emotional release patterns.

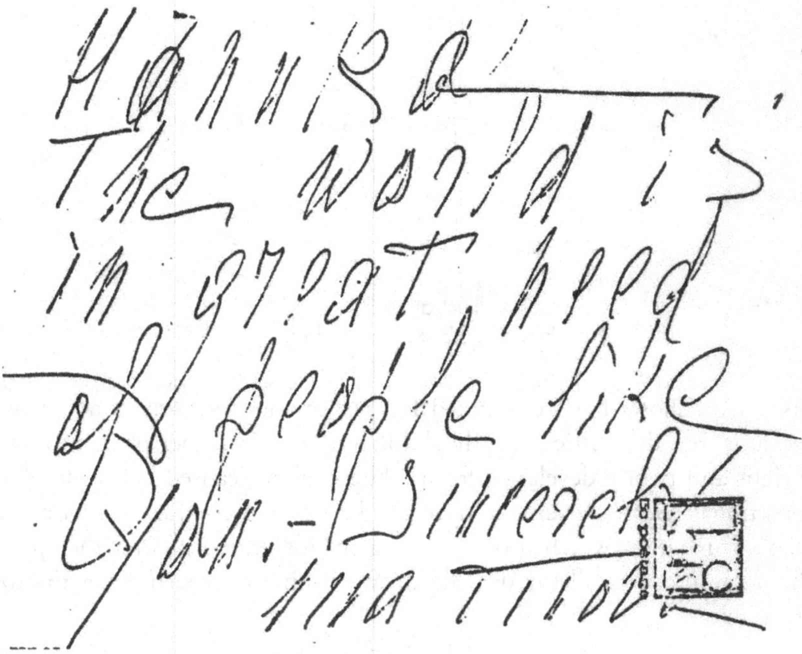

Illustration 1.
Female, 65, Right handed.

The strong separation of letters in combination with a strong movement to the left and to the right horizontally, would indicate, on the one hand, a poor pattern of emotional release, but on the other a great capacity for expression in a non-emotional form. Her expressiveness may evoke emotional responses in other people, while she expresses her emotions only in a purely artistic sense. The writer's life was devoted to performing as a dancer.

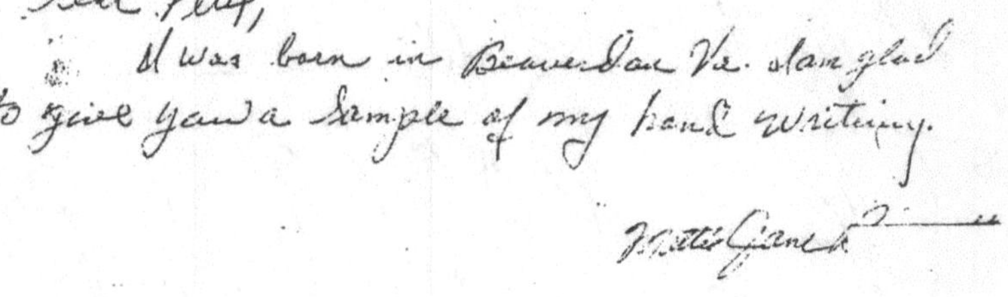

Illustration 2.
Female, 32, Right handed.

This person shows by her rounded letter formations a fairly good capacity for emotions, but difficulties in early childhood, as seen in her poor movement to the right and poorly developed forms. These factors caused her to develop a poor emotional release pattern, resulting in lack of self-confidence and a near-intolerable frustration which drove her to a suicide attempt. After therapy she was able to improve in all the difficult areas, making it easier for her to attain emotional release.

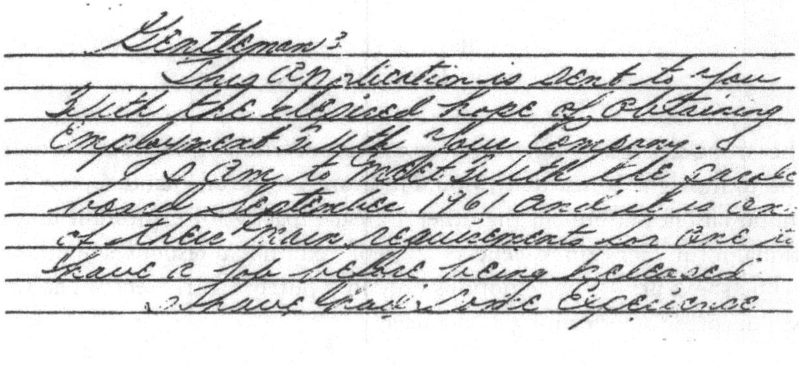

Illustration 3.
Male, 24, Right handed.

This handwriting is highly rigid, and as seen in the second line of the sample the last words "obtaining," shows a lower loop in the "g" that not only is very malformed but also reverses the direction, giving rise to the possibility of homosexual tendencies. The rigidity can be traced back to the anal period, which occurs around the age of three and produced, in this case, an extreme concern with control. Due to the inability to release his feelings and the rigidity, he fell into a criminal pattern.

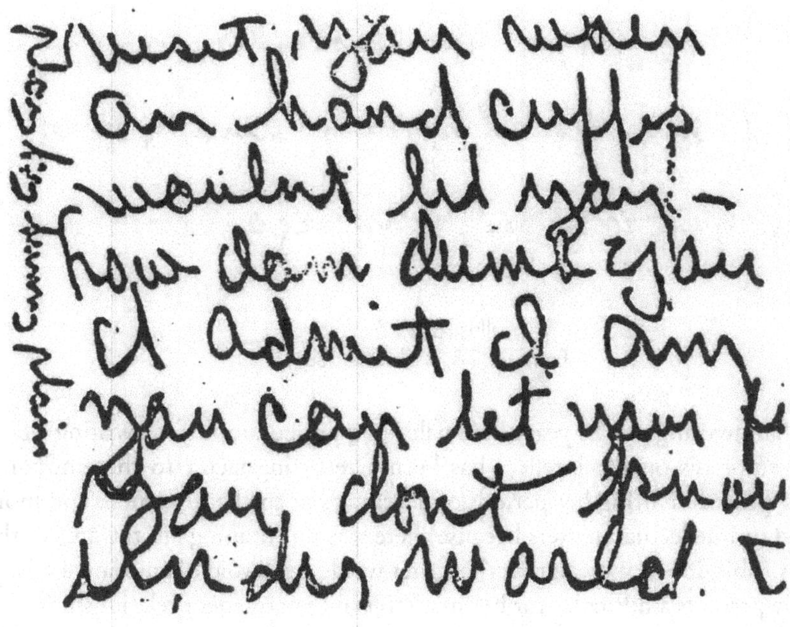

Illustration 4.
Male, 30's, Right handed.
(Charles Manson)

This writing has a truly arrhythmic pattern. There is little in it to indicate emotional capacity. Strong disturbances in the realm of values are seen in the extreme directional pressure in the word "don't," and the t-bar in the next to the last line. Whatever emotional release was achieved was released in a completely negative way.

Dear Mr. Klein,

I hope you remember me. I had my handwriting analyzed by you over a year ago.

Illustration 5.
Female, 28, Right handed.

This handwriting of a 28 year old female is a typical example for a writing where the over-emphasis on the intellect has been a retarding factor to the emotional maturing process. During her periods of development she became more and more interested in intellectual matters because there was no "training" in the area of the emotions. This does not mean that the writer would be devoid of emotional release but surely presents a difficulty for her in establishing permanent relationships.

Illustration 6.
Female, 35, Right handed.

This is a woman with very high emotional capacity but her release pattern is completely blocked, causing her to divert her feelings into unrealistic behavior, and making her nearly incapable of coping. One of her outlets in the emotional area will be persistent talking.

As per your advertisement in the Sunday New York Times, I wish to apply for the position as Sales Manager. I am a young man, thirty three years of age with a College Education from New

Illustration 7.
Male, 30's, Right handed (?).

This writer shows a strong capacity for emotions but because of developments in early childhood he failed to adjust to physical changes in puberty, resulting in a difficulty with the emotional release pattern.

The following writings show a more productive ability to release emotions.

8.6.75

Dear Mr. President,

In the name of your National Society for Graphology you sent me such an understanding letter.

Many thanks and my best wishes for successful getting on.

Yours Grace Wittlein

Illustration 8.
Female, 50's, Right handed.

The fine rhythm and good letter formation with beautifully connected letters in conjunction with well developed lower zone portray a person with highly developed emotional release, although she imposed restrictions on herself because of her strict upbringing.

The image of the morning sun in
a dew drop is not less than the
sun
The reflection of life in your
soul is not less than life.
A dew drop mirrors the
light because it is one with
light

Illustration 9.
Male, 50's, Right handed.
(Kahlil Gibran)

This handwriting may be a near-perfect example for emotional release, in almost all areas, as indicated by excellent rhythms beautifully rounded letter formations, and fine (but not over-emphasized) movement to the right.

The high t-bars are a true indication of his ability to integrate his feelings with his aspirations, in both the philosophical and intellectual areas.

I Know you are an Expert in Genealogy.
Enclosed, 2 Sheets as part of an Extensive
Genealogy Lillian Adams has done of her
family lines. She was stuck as you can
See by the question She raises. Lillian

Illustration 10.
Female, 48, Right handed.

This writer established a good emotional release pattern despite the fact that the father image could not be established in early childhood. As a result of this fact, she married late in life and her partner was twenty years her senior.

* * *

One of the most common indicators for emotional release and/or emotional problems are the lower loops. The proper crossing point for the realization of instinctual drives is the base line. If the crossing point is above or below the base line, the instinctual needs are suppressed or non-existent.

One can go down into the lower zone with forcefulness and without hesitation—or with hesitation, which is seen by shortening of the down-stroke or avoiding making it in a straight line.

If there is no fear of the lower zone, the writer goes down straight and with pressure. Going down into the lower zone reflects your expectancy. The way the writer goes up indicates the realization and fulfillment of the instinctual needs.

If there is any diversion in the way the writer goes down or up, the indication is that there is a diversive tendency in the instinctual needs. If there is a tendency toward the left, the instinctual needs are tied to the mother image. If the right side is emphasized without reaching the middle zone, there is an aversion to going back, and the instinctual needs are not fulfilled. Failure to go to the right can also be interpreted as a failure to move toward the father.

Observe what part of the loops are emphasized or de-emphasized. Movement into the lower zone and from the lower zone can be likened to carrying a bag uphill—it is easier to go down, harder to go up. It is harder to effect emotional release than to become aware of the actual need.

If the loops are crossed above the base line you are over-emphasizing the upward movement, thereby bringing something into the middle zone that is supposed to stay in the lower zone.

Restrictions placed on ourselves are to be expected in the upper zone. All restrictions, however, are not seen in the upper zone. Anything that restricts the normal flow of the lower loops must be considered a restriction of the release of the instincts.

When the instinctual needs do not find the proper release we have a tendency to sublimate or transfer them into different areas (possibly becoming compulsive, as seen in repetitive forms or rigidity). The hysterical type is the most unlikely one to become compulsive.

Bibliography

English, Horace B. and English, Ava C. — *A Comprehensive Dictionary of Psychological and Psychoanalytical Terms* (David McKay, New York, 1958.)

Smith, Karl U. and Smith, Margaret F. — *Psychology: An Introduction to Behavior Science* (Little, Brown and Co., Boston, 1973.)

The Ductus

Felix Klein

The Ductus

The Quality of the Stroke

The famous poet, astronomer and natural scientist, Wolfgang von Goethe, was convinced that many invisible things could be seen through a microscope or telescope. It does not seem necessary to use a microscope to interpret handwriting if, as in this case, some partial enlargements have been made in order to make it easier to recognize details. In this manner details become visible which the naked eye simply could not recognize.

There are books where the author admits not knowing the people whose handwriting he analyzed. Among these is the very well known book of Klages, "Graphological Reader," which in the true sense is a collection of analyses. In no way is there an indication as to the personal dates of the writers, their social position, motivation, connection to the outside world and similar things. It is true that the author was assured that his analysis was correct. The one who is used to verifying his analyses will know that this kind of response is not sufficient. Many receivers of very complimentary analyses will become incapable of recognizing their true character. In order to get to a proper verification it is necessary for the graphologist to collect all psychological material available to him from the writer. Such a method becomes extremely difficult under the circumstances in which we find ourselves as graphologists. A book that gives vital dates and descriptions of cases would be Roda Wieser's "The Criminal and His Handwriting," Stuttgart, 1952. This material was based originally on the criminological and social aspect. Another book which should not be forgotten was Otto Kellner's "Expression in the Handwriting," long out of print (Hamburg, 1952), which describes within the regular teaching plan a lot of individual cases.

The following quotation is from Sonneman's *Handwriting Analysis*, page 142: "A worksheet, such as proposed by some for this purpose, would restrict him unduly in one respect of central importance: the way in which a perceptual field organizes itself, the order of turns in which its 'unity' and its 'multiplicity' prevail under his focus and acquire more and more specific meaning varies from observer to observer, and this variability exists quite independently of the interconsistency among the rounded-out concepts at the end of the investigation—the finished products of graphological analysis conducted by different workers; neither do individual differences in approaching the sample interfere with this interconsistency, nor is this interconsistency ever achieved at the cost of sacrificing that necessary variability of procedure. To a certain extent, of course, the same already holds true for the overall approach just recommended. It is meant to facilitate the student's first practical contacts with samples of handwriting, but once he becomes more spontaneous in his investigation and begins to experience the 'overall' procedure as an impediment rather than an aid, he should disregard it and entirely follow his own way; for the more facility he develops in his graphological training, the more he will be able to perceive and understand the complexities he deals with 'at once,' i.e., in a synoptic rather than syllogistic manner—even though, in verbalizings his findings, he again will have to resort to the discursive approach necessitated by the task of 'describing' his subjects. Against the new background of his own 'synoptic' experiences, the concrete and lively precision which graphological studies of personality can have (and which his own may acquire before long) will no longer astound him then either, for already he will have ceased merely to line up trait names in his analyses. He will have understood personality as the functional unit which it is and which does not allow for mutually inconsistent and arbitrarily aggregated properties but only of specific and definite ones which are determined by the system principle. This means that the recognition of the system principle itself is implied in that of any sector of the configuration. The more of the latter, by way of either direct or 'supplementary' perception, becomes visible, the more limited, from the observer's viewpoint, becomes the scope of possible properties of those parts of the system still out of his immediate perceptual reach. Graphological analysis, therefore, could be defined as a succession of multiple effects of closure, each of them setting the background for the following one and all together tending toward greater and ever greater specificity of the characterological precepts."

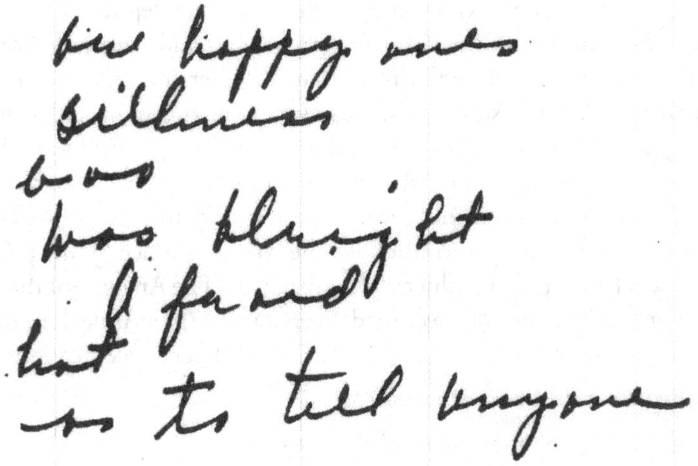

FIG. 126 (7%). On first glance graphological analysis, the writer was diagnosed as a passive homosexual whose personality organization is centered in his need for locomotor action. According to the clinical diagnostician's statement, he is a passive homosexual who has taken up a career in physical education. Notice the low middle zone, the fluctuating upper lengths, the narrowness of the rounded forms, the pressure displacements, and the coincidence of stiffness and impulsivity, inhibition and aggression, in his writing.

One formulation of Sonneman is important: each person organizes his area of recognition in a different way. The mixing of observations and experiences reaches results in a different way. Whoever opens a graphological textbook for the first time will find out that graphology seems to be a science of indicators and combinations thereof. The registration of all indicators and the making of a protocol will often be described as imperative. Even knowledgeable experts in the field still fill out a graphological worksheet. Jacoby finds 500 interpretations for the connections. However, practically for each of the indicators there are dozens of different differentiations which include a great deal of contradictory indicators, which really represents a labyrinth.

It becomes obvious that the analysis of singular signs is most insecure. To work with indicators can only be of help to a very experienced expert and not only because he can make combinations but also because he is extremely experienced at recognizing what he sees. The registration of a graphological worksheet for the purpose of interpretation of handwriting according to all singular signs surely represents a great loss of time. It is more desirable to look at a great deal of handwriting samples. According to the philosopher Hegel, it is better to move from quantity to quality. Originally it is better to recognize the individual picture of the handwriting and to look across the surface than into the depths. Many graphology teachers emphasize working with a few particular handwritings for weeks and even months, which is much less fruitful than the mere observing of thousands of handwritings which transmit to the observer more and more inner workings. "Because physiognomic intuitions are not dug out but are received in flight—that way or not at all." (Wellek, "The Polarity in the Building of Character," p. 263.)

There is, in my estimation, no better way in which to achieve Wellek's ideal than through observing the imprint left on the writing surface by the pen, which is scientifically referred to as the ductus. In my paper "The Analysis of the Stroke," which represents the essence of a lecture delivered in 1973 in Anderson, Indiana, I explained that the ductus can be viewed from five different specifications.

(1) degree of liveliness of the stroke
(2) fluidity of the movement of the stroke
(3) dynamic of the stroke movement
(4) forms of the stroke movement
(5) color of the stroke

1. Degree of Liveliness of the Stroke.

The degree of liveliness of a person finds its expression in his gestures. In a low degree of liveliness, they appear to be more mechanical and unreal. The same is true for the gesture that we call handwriting. The liveliness of the stroke reflects the liveliness of the writer. It shows the extent to which his thinking, his volition, his judging and his feeling originate in the depth of his psyche. A lively stroke, a lively writing expresses an immeasurable amount of vibration which can be present in a writing with regularity as well as in a writing with irregularity. It is a mistake to assume, as some do, that irregularity in a writing is an expression or a measure of emotional animation. So we can, from the liveliness of the stroke, determine the writer's vitality, his emotional status, his ability to imagine, his judgment, his capacity to observe, and his will. Primary pressure, which is the pressure against the point of the writing instrument, would indicate the instinctive will, or drive, while the will power that we acquire by experience is a conscious effort to imitate the unconscious will power, and this is found in the handwriting through regularity.

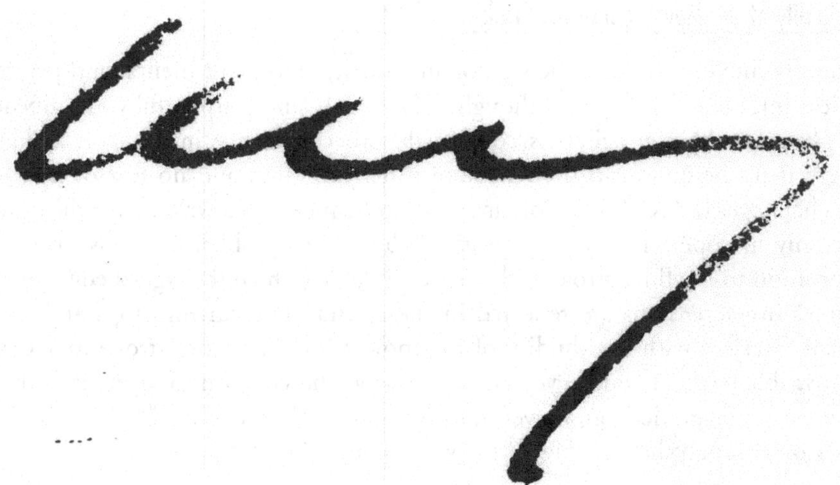

Illustration 1. The lively stroke. (Female, 44 years. Writing enlarged ten times.)

This enlargement was taken from the handwriting shown in Illustration 2. It is quite clear that the stroke already indicates that the writing it was taken from has to be a lively one. As there are so many factors which influence any writing, the handwriting in its normal size will not always be as obvious in its liveliness as the greatly enlarged stroke.

I hereby autorize
handwriting analyst
keep this sample
my writing.

Illustration 2. Same writing as Illustration 1; enlarged twice original size.

2. Fluidity of the Movement of the Stroke.

A fluidly moving stroke is the sign of an effortless release of mental and psychological impulses. The writer's thoughts flow freely and purposefully, unimpeded by obstacles. Mental agility is combined with confidence in decision making. There is no hesitation in the release of inner impulses, and no fear of meeting the challenges of life. The fluidly moving stroke indicates a writer with the power not only to cope but to create positive solutions to problems. Almost in direct opposition to the fluid stroke is the tense stroke, in which the jagged edges of the writer's inner tensions are reflected in the constantly recurring stops and starts which interfere with the fluidity of the movement. The tense stroke may often be invisible to the unaided eye and may deceive the viewer into seeing it as fluid. Under high magnification, however, the sharp points of tension show up, so obviously obstructing the free flow of the writing movement.

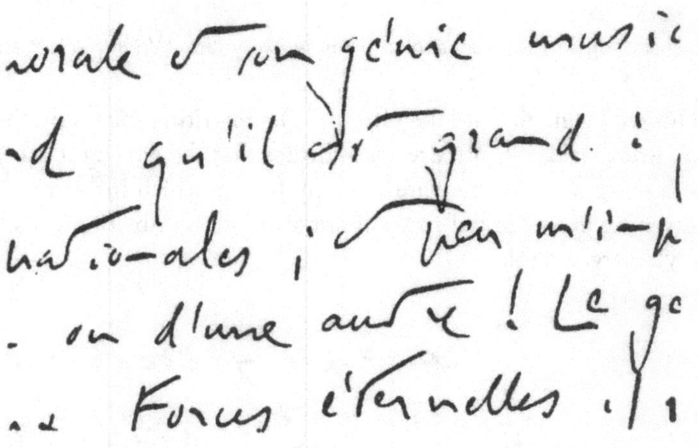

Illustration 3. The fluid stroke.

This is the vigorous script of French author Romain Rolland, which represents a handwriting with extremely fluid and simplified strokes. The t-bars are aggressive and their strong thrust into the upper zone can be interpreted as passion, sincerity and heroic idealism.

Illustration 4. The tense stroke. (American novelist and poet, male, 42 years. Writing enlarged ten times.)

This enlargement shows tremors hardly observable in the original writing (see below). There are, however, many indicators in the unenlarged sample that will confirm the findings so easily visible in this illustration.

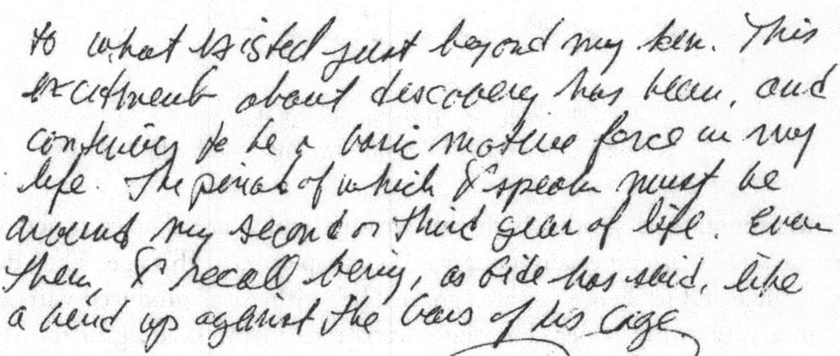

to what existed just beyond my ken. This excitement about discovery has been, and continues to be a basic motive force in my life. The period of which I speak must be around my second or third year of life. Even then, I recall being, as Gide has said, like a bird up against the bars of its cage

Illustration 5. Original of the enlargement above.

In regard to Illustration 5, some of the confirming indicators of the tremors visible in Illustration 4 are here seen in the over-emphasis on circular movement in the middle zone, angle formations, and a capital I showing a poor relationship with the mother.

3. Dynamic of the Stroke Movement.

A stroke can be both lively and dynamic. For the dynamic stroke, the degree of pressure is not important. However, if the pressure becomes too heavy, the extent of dynamism will be gradually reduced. The dynamism in the stroke is a manifestation of the quality of the movement and is related to the goal direction of the writer.

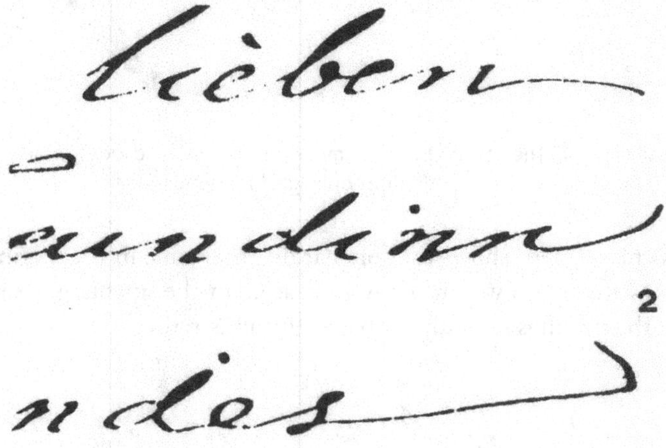

Illustration 6. The dynamic stroke.
(Goethe at the age of 72; handwriting enlarged.)

The strength and steadiness in this writing, which are characteristics of the dynamic stroke, are especially remarkable for a person of this age. They denote perseverance and resilience towards goals. The writing was produced with a steel pen on a very satiny paper. The slight variations in the shading of the strokes are most likely due to technical causes. During the period of Goethe's life when this sample was produced, he was very productive. It is possible to evaluate this writing as a more or less school model writing. The letter formations are precise. However, there are also variations, noted particularly in the treatment of the word endings. While in the first word the end stroke is characterized by delicate pressure and an arcadic curvature, it changes in the second word to a garland type formation. Both words end with the same letter "n" and the end strokes are so different. The second word's end could be compared to a gesture saying "Come on." Finally, in the third word the end stroke is elongated in comparison to the two other words. In fact it is twice as long and with a hook taking a backward direction. This final stroke shows pressure. The return stroke allows an interpretation of a searching quality. The length could indicate a seeking of contact with the surrounding world.

4. Forms of the Stroke Movement.

The form of the ductus depends on whether the stroke continues in the same direction (in other words, in a straight stroke), or, if in changing direction it becomes a curved stroke. A further form of the ductus is established by the stop and go movement, which is reflected in the stroke. This criteria can be observed in an angular formation in the handwriting.

Illustration 7. (German chancellor Conrad Adenauer, at the age of 80. Writing more than twice enlarged.)

Very few handwritings of men of sixty allow an enlargement of this sort without showing a multitude of disturbances of the movement, such as tremors and interruptions. Nothing of this can be observed in Illustration 7. The movement is produced with complete security, and the name was obviously produced in one writing impulse. The cross-bar on the capital letter A was the only thing produced after the completion of the signature. If one observes the distances between the downstrokes in the middle zone or the distribution of the spaces between the A and the d, it is still quite obvious that, despite the appearance of inflexibility, there is still a rhythm pulsating in the script. These strokes are perfect models which can allow the interpretation of a possible vitality of the organism. The regularity of the strokes, which surely do not show arrhythmic changes in pressure, denotes further quite clearly his even temperament. Many of Adenauer's acquaintances reported that aggravations were handled by him in the same smooth way that water flows off a duck's back. Although the initial letter is quite outstanding, it still would not, at least in this case, allow the interpretation of an insecure ego. For the determination of ego-power it is extremely important to establish from the ductus the vitality of the writer and to avoid seeking it through singular signs.

5. Color of the Stroke.

Just as the voice has a "color," so has the handwriting. We can divide the color of the stroke into two groups: the sensitive and the coarse stroke. The sensitive stroke is gentle on touching the paper. It is fine, delicate. There are many variations of the sensitive stroke, generally indicating sensitivity in various areas. The coarse stroke is heavier and indicates a more robust person, psychologically speaking. Pastosity must be regarded as a form of coloring of the writing.

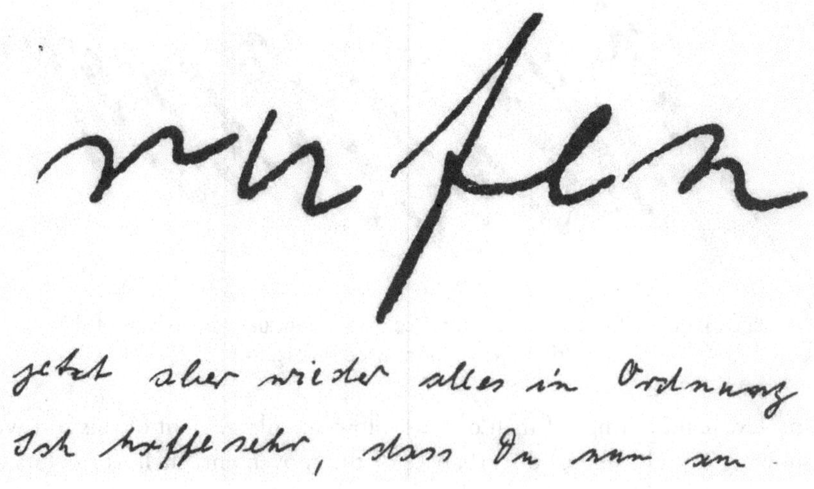

Illustration 8. The gentle stroke. (Female, 40 years, right handed.)

The light pressure, slightly trembling, often interrupted stroke portrays a person of high tension due to an excessive use of vitality. However, this person can not be characterized as a stereotype. The enlargement of the single word seems to give the impression of a light, free and spontaneous movement which is not loaded with dynamism but rather with a sensitive and swinging rhythm. This person had an impoverished youth with many privations and sicknesses. Later she was able to make a living by hard physical labor. Under the political pressure of Hitler's time, she showed a lot of character. She was able to overcome situations which, for other people, would have been only solved by suicide. Her silent tenacity resulted in her succeeding in saving the lives of people who were close to her. She was not able to find any support in her activities and she never asked for it either, although she had the opportunity. Her own faith inspired her to be self-sufficient, which did not eliminate her humor and her willingness to help others. If it is possible to judge her integrity in the face of severe hardships, which never embittered her, then we must say that the measure of her integrity was high indeed. It goes without saying that it was not possible to find out from the writer what she went through. Although she was not given the possibility of educating herself beyond the minimum, she was regarded in art circles as an "original."

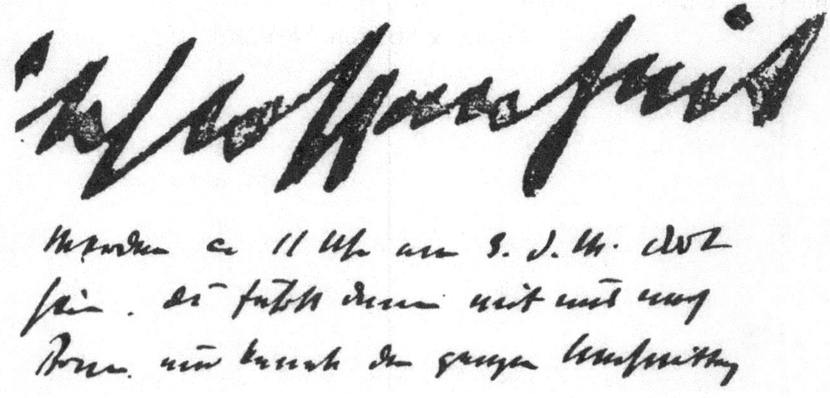

Illustration 9. The coarse stroke. (Male, 40 years.)

This is a perfect example of a handwriting with masculine vitality, strength and perseverance. The surprising fact about this writing is that an extreme primary pressure, in combination with an angle formation, does not make it rigid, as seen by the variations in the height of downstrokes in the middle zone. It is easy to see in the original writing that there is a variation in the baseline. There is no question that this is a person with great will power which, to some extent, makes it impossible for a smooth edge in the enlarged version of the sample.

Bibliography

Klein, Felix — *Elementary Graphology Course*

Klein, Felix — *The Analysis of the Stroke*
(A lecture given in Anderson, Indiana, in 1973.)

Knobloch, Dr., Hans — *Graphologisches Archiv Atlas*
(Wilhel, Braumuller, Wien IX—Stuttgart, 1958.)

Mueller-Enskat — *Graphologische Diagnostik*
(Verlag Hans Huber, Bern und Stuttgart, 1961.)

Sonnemann, Ulrich — *Handwriting Analysis*
(Grune & Stratton, New York, 1950.)

All Roads Lead to Rhythm

Felix Klein

All Roads Lead to Rhythm

We ask first: "What is the difference between regularity and rhythm?" Regularity, as we know, is characterized by the constancy of the slant, the size, the width, the pressure, and the straightness of the lines. Regularity is the same as beat, and in fact originates from the Latin word meaning "to beat."

Rhythm derives from the Greek word for "flowing." Regularity and rhythm have in common the fact that they are both a reflection of the movement. An uninterrupted curve represents the rhythm, while the interrupted line represents the angularity, which does not mean that every angular writing is arrhythmic. However, very narrow, angular, left trended strokes reduce the flow of the movement. It can be assumed that with an increase of the sharpness of the angles a reduction of rhythm will be the consequence. According to Ludwig Wirz[8] "The theory of the rhythm is probably the most controversial subject in German graphology. The same theory has hardly been incorporated into French graphology."

Discussions on the subject of rhythm were conducted over many decades and the new theory of Basic Rhythm complicated the matter even further. Pfanne denies the need for the graphologist to investigate rhythm in order to do a good analysis. Pfanne acknowledges, however, the theories of Klages and admits that they merit further study. He feels that modern theories of movement and brain physiology replace the study of rhythm. According to Wirz, this is only partly true, and Mueller-Enskat have to be credited with the incorporation of Pophal's contraction and release into the theory of rhythm.

The first step Mueller-Enskat took was to distinguish between rhythm of movement, rhythm of form, and rhythm of space (or distribution). Mueller-Enskat see the connection between rhythm according to Klages and the contraction theory of Pophal in the substance of rhythm itself. The connection shows up, according to Klages, in the recurring similar pattern at similar intervals and by flowing transitions of polaric to and fro movements. The elastic to and fro movement serves

8 Grundlegung einer Kausalen Graphologie. Bouvier Verlag Herbert Grundmann. Bonn, 1985.

as the basis of the Klagesche Rhythm theory. Roda Wieser also acknowledges that the elastic to and fro movement is one criterion of the basic rhythm.

To describe script rhythm it is not sufficient to mention the grade of elasticity of the to and fro movement, because writing movement is not a simple occurrence like the waves of the sea, the heart beat, and breathing. Pophal pointed out that handwriting has to serve the form, for which a simple to and fro movement is not sufficient. To produce individual form the writer needs certain attitudes, certain contractions and singular movements. Form production requires a constant modification of the movement. The continuous modification of the movement alone does not guarantee rhythmic movement. Only when a periodic interchange of movement release and movement contraction occurs can we speak about rhythm. All graphological indicators that have opposites—for instance, large and small, wide and narrow, right trend and left trend, heavy pressure and light pressure, fast and slow, etc.—favor a rhythm which is dominated by the interchange between the opposing indicators.

Now we come to the rhythm of form. There is form rhythm present when we find similar repetitions of similar transformations which in turn are due to the rhythm of movement. If this is true, then the form rhythm is the molding of the movement rhythm. One has to look at it from the reverse side. It is not that the writing form is created by the movement rhythm but rather that the form forces the movement into its rules. Rhythm is the life force under the laws of nature. Movement rhythm is the drive which produces the stroke. Form rhythm is the creative power which produces the form. Space rhythm has as its objective to conform to the laws of structure. Space or distributional rhythm means the proportional distribution of the writing over the writing surface. Here also we find that the factor of similarity is the focal point of our observation, or in other words the similarity of the proportions between the empty spaces and the word bodies. Another way to express that would be to establish that the empty spaces produce an optical equilibrium.

The rhythm of a handwriting is strongest when the rhythm of movement, which means elasticity and periodically recurring movement patterns, is visible; when there is clear indication of good form rhythm; and finally, when the distribution of the writing over the writing surface produces a rhythmic picture. According to Mueller-Enskat, rhythm is a phenomenon of the movement, involving elasticity and periodic interchange of polaric expressions, which are also indicators of contractions. The interpretation of elasticity is adaptability in the widest sense. Elasticity also indicates that the writer possesses unconscious powers of assimilation, which in turn influence his ability to develop. Lack of elasticity would therefore allow an interpretation of lack of adaptability, resulting in disturbances in development, again in the widest sense. Script rhythm can not be the expression of vitality or fullness of life but rather relates to the relationship between vitality and spirit, the personal and the impersonal, the emotions and the intellect, the "self" and the "you." Form rhythm, according to Mueller-Enskat, indicates a fulfillment, a sense for convictions and imagination, joy in activity and achievement, the will to self expression, the will to work on oneself.

Good rhythm of space indicates that the writer had the ability to live successfully in his surroundings and that his attitudes and convictions were involved in shaping his outer world. Basic rhythm, a theory which was originated by Klages and Wieser, really is connected to the theory of the gestalt. Once this has been established it becomes obvious that everyone has an individual rhythm, which we call personal rhythm. In studying the basic rhythm of Roda Wieser, certain rules are manifested, whereby the basic rhythm is not an expression of tension itself but rather a measure of the change in the tension-release pattern. Wieser was guided to basic rhythm through her observation of criminal writings. The best explanation of basic rhythm according to Wieser would be that the more a handwriting leans towards rigidity and tension, or the more a writing leans towards slackness and looseness, the lower is the measure of the basic rhythm.

In order to teach students to see rhythm in the handwriting it was necessary to establish at least one aspect of rhythm in a visible pattern. As part of the similar recurrence of impulses in the handwriting, the manifestation of an impulse pattern became a valuable tool in order to start the understanding of rhythm in some form. An impulse occurs whenever the point of the pen touches the writing surface and is completed when the point of the pen leaves the paper. In other words an impulse can be as short as an i-dot or as long as a complete word. We can produce impulses in a rhythmic way or in an arrhythmic way. To see that in the handwriting is very difficult. However, when we produce an impulse pattern by connecting each beginning of an impulse with its end on a thin sheet of paper, we can establish one part of rhythm. It has been observed that one segment established in the rhythm may also show similar results in other parts of rhythm. As we divide the rhythm into three parts it becomes necessary to not only observe the impulses but also how proportionally the letters are formed and the space is disturbed. Finally, a very negative influence on rhythm would be any kind of extreme.

I can not emphasize enough that rhythm influences everything in the handwriting. If one were to point out rhythm's most important impact it would be on the individual's ability to develop. Development is the key to reaching one's potential, and rhythm is necessary for anyone to attain his or her potential. It is helpful to compare rhythm to the oil that lubricates a fine piece of machinery. As the machinery depends on the oil so does the maximum functioning of a writer depend on rhythm. Although extremes are detrimental to rhythm, the interchange between one end of the spectrum and the opposite end does not necessarily make a writing arrhythmic. However, that interchange must also come in a periodically similar fashion. There are so many ways in which rhythm can be described. One very important definition would be that rhythm is the interchange between the intake of energy and its output.

Werner Wolff, in "Diagrams of the Unconscious," has some very interesting points to make on the subject of rhythm. "One characteristic of rhythm," he notes, "is periodicity. The Russian scientist M. Bechterev, searching for fundamental laws which govern nature as well as man's psychological reactions, believed that rhythm is such a basic principle. Periodicity appears in the change of seasons, in the alternation of day and night, in phenomena of our body such as circulation of blood, heartbeat, respiration, the periodic processes of ovulation, of sleeping and waking.... In the sphere of feelings and moods, periodical alternations are known which, in the cyclothyme [person afflicted with abnormal mood swings] show an extreme state characterized by the constant alternation of elation and depression."

"Periodicity," Wolff goes on to say, "is not only characteristic of rhythm. Rhythm is not merely a regular repetition of stimuli or a regular succession of accents or tone-impulses, as in music, but also a phenomenon of grouping. Succeeding stimuli, such as the tones of music, can be perceived as a melody only if they are grouped. Different impressions of our visual perception can result in a perception of objects only if these single impressions are grouped and interrelated. Rhythm," he continues, "is a characteristic of our feelings and emotions ... (and) the feeling of rhythm generally increases with repetition."

There is a rhythm of the outer and of the inner world, according to Wolff and other researchers. Wolff says, "The immediate influence of outer rhythm upon organic changes is shown in ceremonial movements, marches and dances that lead to **ecstasy**. The two rhythms, that of the outer world and of the inner world, confront each other and are in continuous relationship. It may be observed that the most pleasurable rhythm is that in which the outer rhythm coincides with the inner one. In so-called rhythm-therapy, especially in cases of stammering caused by the fact that the subjective rhythm is not adapted to the objective one, cures have been effected by an environmental change and through treatment by adaptation. We may conclude," Wolff states, "that personal rhythm is determined by the rhythm of environment as well as by inner, organic processes; and that the degree of each of these rhythmical determinants is different, some persons being rhythmically more determined from without, others from within."

"The rhythmical manifestation of periodicity has the characteristic of a repetition of the same pattern, which we call consistency if it is repetition in time, and symmetry if it is repetition in spatial arrangement. But besides consistency and symmetry, rhythm has the characteristics of a definite movement pattern, just as a wave of sound or a bit of color has its definite frequency of oscillation. Every elastic body, be it a wooden beam, stretched string, glass jug, steel bridge, or a roomful of air, has its own natural period of vibration. A pendulum of a fixed length always makes the same number of swings in a second. If the rhythm in graphic movement were to show unvariable characteristics it might be compared to a natural period of vibration." In going on to discuss stability and change of rhythm, Wolff says, "The pattern of rhythm is not affected by transposition. When we have an acoustic rhythm, such as one long and two short beats, the pattern is not affected whether the sound be loud or soft, and whether the sound be performed by sticks, water drops or piano keys. However, the rhythm is affected by the change of intervals, that is, by a change of the relationship of beats. When we have visual rhythm such as a periodical alternation of a long and two short dashes, the pattern is not affected whether the relative size of the dashes be long or short or whether circles and dots (or other forms) be substituted. However, the rhythm is affected by a change of grouping, that is, by a change of the relationship of the elements … We made a similar observation in patterns of graphic movements: neither the change of the relative size nor a change in the use of form-elements necessarily affects the pattern of the proportions. The rhythmical pattern of movement is changed, however, if the relationship varies."

Wolff elaborates: "If graphic movement were an expression of personality we would expect both phenomena, stability and change of rhythmical patterns. The pattern of our personality remains stable for certain periods of time, longer for some people, shorter for others. It is through deep-reaching experiences that this pattern changes. For many years of his life a person may possess a fixed neurotic pattern of living, but through a penetrating experience or through the application of psychotherapy this pattern may suddenly change; for instance it may change from activity to passivity, from expression of movements to a withdrawal. Such changes appear also if a person becomes sick bodily or mentally. Changes of movement patterns produced by psychological changes have been observed experimentally."

"The extremes of psychic tension are elation and depression, exaggerations of feelings of happiness and unhappiness. The word 'tension' from the Latin 'tensio,' means 'the act of stretching or straining.' In elation this stretching of forces is a raising of level, and actually, the meaning of the word 'elation' is elevation of mind, while depression means 'the act of pressing down, a sinking of a surface;

a sinking of the spirits.' Experimental observations supported this insight of language. As G.V.N. Dearborn remarks 'in a pleasant emotional state there will be an extension rather than a contraction of muscles (to jump for joy); one will lean forward rather than recoil.'"

"H. H. Reamers and L. A. Thompson, Jr. asked students to draw lines on paper while thinking of pleasant events and unpleasant events. The lines drawn during pleasant thoughts were longer than those during unpleasant thoughts. The involuntary tendency toward extension or contraction of movement appears to be based upon emotional stimuli."

"J. E. Downey, who was the first in this country to experiment with handwriting, reports that she and another subject wrote their signatures every day for four months, at the same time indicating their mood. When, at the end of the period, Downey compared the different signatures in relation to the moods in which they were written, she found that the total graphic movement increased when made in an energetic mood. However, an extension of movement, combined with instability and irregularity, also appeared if the writer's control of movement diminished, as in states of exhaustion. Similar observations have been made in experiments on the estimate of length. According to H. Munsterberg, depressive states are related to underestimation, elated states to overestimation."

I will end this discussion of Wolff's chapter on rhythm in personality with his statement that, "all the findings on movement patterns under opposite moods demonstrate a positive relationship between emotional states and motor activity."

I want to live in Italy.
I remember hiding under a
Dining room table and I set
the chairs on fire.
I also recall seeing Castro
in the streets of Havana
and two men were spraying
the streets with guns.

[illegible]

September 17, 1955

ILL. 1

Dear Roger,
Wll, here's what
I ate for breakfast:
I had a little shakti
and a lot
of love and
some Coca-Cola
and fresh air.

ILL. 2

I want to go to Italy—

~~Sun~~—
water—
good food—

wonderful!

ILL 3

I want to go to Italy.
I remember when I was four
and being bounced on my father's
knee while he played piano.

Eric Ernst

ILL. 4

Dear Mr. Rubin:

Wish a very joyous Christmas season and
a peaceful New Year!

[illegible]

P.S. Please send my wish to Miss Sheppard.
And I hope she would be surprised by
the scarf.

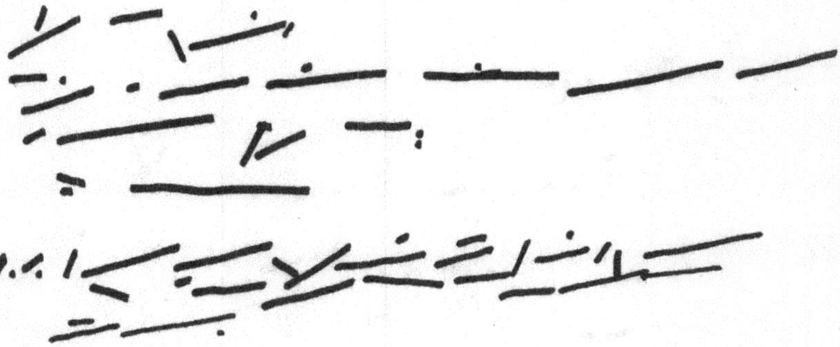

ILL.5

ILL. 6

May 30, 1986

Dear Roger,

I always look forward to our yearly visits - they seem to be touchstones for me. This year has been especially dramatic - a lot of work, my 2 months in the hospital, meeting JB and getting married. I'm pleased

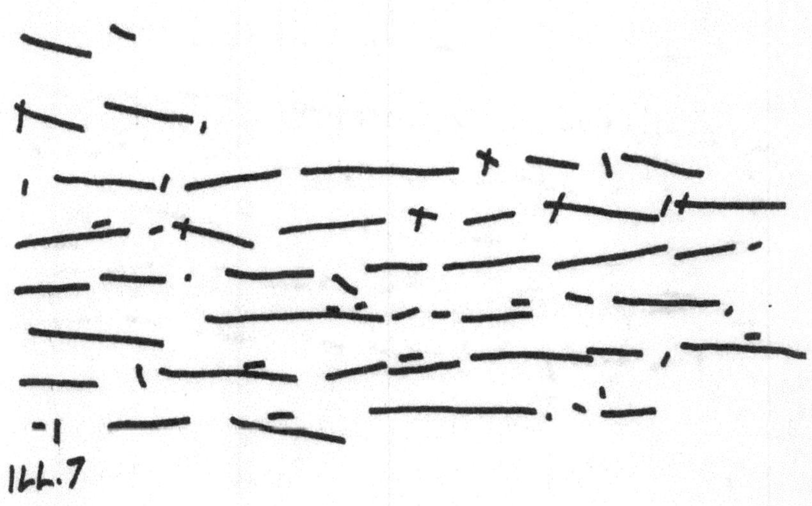

ILL. 7

I want to go to Italy.

When I was about four
years old I ran away
to the river where a bridge
building crew who were
eating at my great aunt's
boarding house were working.

ILL.8

My name is Kurt Melamed and
I've been writing for five
years although many people
dont know this. I believe
it though, as I've been
doing it all by myself.
So, I fell I do write
and perhaps this is
proof. Does this make
sense.

ILL.9

I want to go to Italy.

My earliest recollection is sitting out on the curb of our driveway. It was summer – we had just gotten icecream from the Good Humor man. What stands out in my mind is my brother Mike getting stung by a bee.

ILL.10

Don't go through the pain
and not learn the lesson
because each time you don't learn
the lesson, the pain is more severe

DESCRIPTION OF THE ILLUSTRATIONS

Illust. 1: FEMALE, 28, RIGHT HANDED.

It is very likely that the pattern of such an unusual writing will also be unusual. The extremes in the handwriting clearly show a difficulty in the rhythm. Looking at the writing will give you the impression of fluidity. It is also true that similar stroke formations occur in similar intervals. The pattern shows a clear difficulty, and from the writing it can be identified as a difficulty in the oral period. The writer is an airline hostess, very successful in her work.

Illust. 2: MALE, 22, RIGHT HANDED.

From the writing it could be expected that the pattern would be very poor. However, looking at the pattern it is almost surprising how well organized the arrangement of the lines is. According to the pattern, the person must be functioning. According to the writing there is a difficulty in emotional development which would not come across in the pattern. The young man is a musician, but because of the difficulty in his emotional release pattern he is an extensive user of Coca Cola and cocaine.

Illust. 3: MALE, LATE 50's, RIGHT HANDED.

As a first impression the writing is very fluid and surely is not arrhythmic. Looking at the impulse pattern it surely does not give the same impression. Trying to establish the profession of this person will most likely lead you in the wrong direction. He is a medical doctor, wanting to be different even in this field. He is a psychiatrist, a practitioner of rehabilitation medicine, who does "hands on" work with the body of the patient. His need for originality is clearly indicated in the pattern.

Illust. 4: MALE, 13, RIGHT HANDED.

Very little hope of seeing even a fair pattern can be expected from this handwriting. Extensions into the upper zone are so extreme that one surely would expect an extreme pattern. However, the pattern's rhythm is so well established that one wonders where this kind of rhythm can be seen in the handwriting. The answer is that at the age of 13 there is an extremely high intellect which would warrant the opinion that he should be in the sciences for his career. Both his grandfather and grandmother, as well as his father, are medical doctors.

Illust. 5: MALE, 30, RIGHT HANDED, JAPANESE.

The rigidity in this writing portrays a person who is used to working with details and is capable of extreme accuracy. It is a contradiction that he shows oral hooks in the writing, which is contrary to the compulsive regularity. This is the reason why the pattern is not regular. It clearly shows the difficulty in the emotional area.

Illust. 6: MALE, 33, LEFT HANDED.

This fragmented writing allows the prediction of a truly fragmented impulse pattern. The inability to relate to others caused him to become a drug addict. His profession was that of a professor of law.

Illust. 7: FEMALE, MID-30's.

Just looking at the writing will show the fine rhythm, which can be expected in the impulse pattern. Not only is this a certain indication of rhythm but also of the ability to use energy in a proper way. The big surprise comes when one looks at the capital I, which shows that her self image is poor indeed.

Illust. 8: FEMALE, 60, RIGHT HANDED.

The interruptions in this writing are not due to the copy but are in the original. Any undue interruption in the handwriting will not give a good impulse pattern. Whenever she interrupts, the impulse pattern will be very poor. When she does not interrupt and writes fluently, she will improve her pattern. This can be clearly seen by comparing the first two lines with the next four lines of the pattern. This woman is a retired nurse. She is quite unhappy because of her difficulties.

Illust. 9: MALE, 26, RIGHT HANDED.

It is almost superfluous to look at the pattern. There are so many inconsistencies in the writing that one would be surprised to find a good pattern. Lack of male identification is the original problem and because of it the writer became a homosexual.

Illust. 10: MALE, 28, RIGHT HANDED.

This is a handwriting which is also extremely fragmented. In addition to the fragmentation there is also threadiness, which on the one hand portrays a person with a high intellect and a high awareness level, but on the other with a very poor adjustment in the emotional area. The pattern is very poor and would indicate that there are serious problems.

Illust. 11: MALE, 29, RIGHT HANDED.

This writing is fluid, although it shows a poor middle zone legibility and a tendency towards thread. The left slant is contradictory to the rest of the writing. Poor adjustment in the emotional area would be the most important thing to mention here. Looking at the pattern, it is almost impossible to believe that such a pattern would come from this writing. The backward slant can not be seen in the pattern, so the contradictions are not detectable from it. It is not too difficult to determine from the script itself that the person has difficulty emotionally. He is a drug addict, using cocaine.

Bibliography

Klages, Ludwig — *Handschrift und Charakter*
(Johann Ambrosius Barth, Leipzig, 1929.)

Klein, Felix — *Elementary Graphology Course, Lesson VI*

Klein, Felix — *Rhythm, Groundrhythm, and Beyond*

Mueller, Wilhelm — *Mensch und Handschrift*
(Munz & Co., Verlag, Berlin, 1941.)

Wieser, Roda — *Personlichkeit und Handschrift*
(Ernst Reinhardt Verlag, Muenchen, Basel, 1956.)
Rhythmus und Politaritat in der Handschrift
(Ernst Reinhardt Verlag, Muenchen, 1973.)

Wirz, Ludwig — *Grundlegung einer kausalen Graphologie*
(Bouvier Verlag Herbert Grundmann, Bonn, 1985.)

Wolff, Werner — *Diagrams of the Unconscious*
(Grune & Stratton, New York, 1948.)

The Power of Form

Felix Klein

The Power of Form in Art, Art Therapy, and Handwriting

Form, from the graphological viewpoint, originates during the process of establishing one's individual handwriting style. When a child learns to write, he or she is concerned with how best to use energy in order to produce a rhythmic movement. Only when the child feels comfortable in producing the necessary energy without over-emphasizing its production, does it become aware of the possibility of individual letter formations. This, then, is the beginning of the foundation of a personal relationship to form, which will undergo developmental changes whenever development occurs in the writer's character. Here we have the basis of the concept of form for the graphologist.

In other areas, such as art, art therapy, and psychology, development of form takes on much greater importance. Form, or the understanding of form, is the basis of all the visual arts. In art therapy, the development of form not only allows for diagnostic conclusions but also can show difficulties in the unconscious mind. When drawings are produced by a subject in various stages of therapy, the subject's progress can be observed in the development of the drawings. Therapists often ask patients to do such drawings, and by interpreting them can discern the unconscious images translated from the patient's mind to the paper. Similarly, the Rorschach test, which uses ink blots in symmetrical designs, enables the therapist to diagnose problems according to the interpretation of the dots.

Form is not only an integral part of life, it is life. Good form is the basis of aesthetics. Aesthetics demands continuity and is strongly dependent on lifestyle and culture. John Dewey, in Art as Experience, wrote "Form is moving integration of an experience." Gilbert J. Rose, in The Power of Form, writes, "In clarifying the process of organizing space and time, in any developing life experience form elicits the quality of experience more energetically than does ordinary life itself." Aesthetics is an essential constituent of life, and is followed by the experience of growth. The need for form is intimately related to this experience. Form depends on:

(1) continuity
(2) conservation
(3) tension
(4) rhythm
(5) anticipation
(6) resistance

The same is true for all growth processes.

Growth is an organization of change in time, and form gives a dynamic nature to this organization. Form is needed in developing self image and imagination. In infancy, self image emerges from the child's efforts to distinguish its own body and internal processes from those of the external world. By achieving this separation and realizing that it is a separate entity from the mother, the infant gives form to its own perceptions. This early separation is the original meaning of primary narcissism, a terminology which is no longer used in this context. Since this is a normal process, and since the mother's constant care makes it possible for the child to overcome its feeling of "aloneness," the child comes to accept the separation without permanent ill effect. If, however, the child is physically separated from the mother because of illness or any other reason, the child feels abandoned and helpless, and the basis for what we in graphology and psychology call primary narcissism is established.

As we have noted, form is also needed in developing imagination. Creative imagination not only enlarges the dimensions of reality but also points toward universal truths. Imagination depends on the ability to create images, to re-create memories, and to combine them with new perceptions, thereby creating new forms. To make the meaning of the word form clear, we can say that it is synonymous with style.

In handwriting, form refers to an individuality. In other words, letter formations must differ from the school model. However, sense for form can be seen even in the accuracy of school model letters. In order to achieve a sense of beauty we must have organic unity. Organic unity contains within itself different elements, all of which contribute to an integrated whole. Every element must be purposeful; not even one can be unnecessary. Variety and unity must be in delicate balance.

"In dreams, jokes, and symptoms," writes Gilbert J. Rose, "Freud saw form as related to the id. In 'Creative Writers and Daydreaming', Freud reduced form and beauty to resistance and defense. According to him, form provides satisfactions external to itself. Thanks to form, dangerous drives may be neutralized, disguised, and thus gratified. Form sugarcoats an offensive content, bribing the critical powers with aesthetic pleasure (analogous to sexual forepleasure) and detouring the normal sexual aim into voyeurism or exhibitionism (as in a perversion).… Analytic sophistication will unmask the forbidden content concealed behind the form."

The truth of the matter, claims Rose, is just the opposite. For the viewer with a trained and appreciative eye, a work of art yields values that go far beyond the content. To equate aesthetics with "paying a bribe to the censor" is to degrade and trivialize all art. "Psychoanalytically speaking," Rose says, "aesthetics evolve within a theory of reality and of perception, rather than motivation."

Because form and growth are closely related, and because the mind works via both the primary and the secondary process, it is evident that we will be able to see these processes in handwriting as well as in works of art. The Freudian concept of the primary process is described in "A Comprehensive Dictionary of Psychological and Psychoanalytical Terms" as "the process, located in the id, by which there is immediate and direct satisfaction of an instinctual wish; or that aspect of conscious activity which represents it. It is supposed that the id does not discriminate between image and reality; hence, in the absence of an immediately satisfying object or situation, an imaginary satisfaction is produced. Not being oriented toward reality, the satisfaction is only temporary. The laws governing the primary process are different from those of consciousness. They are known chiefly from the study of dreams, which are wish-fulfilling primary processes—or, rather, they are the reflection of such processes in consciousness."

"The secondary process," the Dictionary explains, is "conscious activity; action guided by objective realities; activity in the preconscious or ego; or such activities taken collectively. Secondary the process may be, yet civilization is its product. The related term, reality principle, has more accurate implications."

Primary process is dominated by the id, secondary process is dominated by the preconscious and the ego, resulting in a manifestation of the superego. Theoretically there is no true primary process in art, because the moment the artist exercises the smallest control over the work it ceases to be primary. If we try to detect it in art, we would have to find it in areas where the id plays some part in forming the subject. For instance, when a person is deeply troubled in his unconscious mind he will sometimes release those unconscious images into his drawings, which then become part of his therapy. Another way of showing the primary process is through the previously mentioned Rorschach test and through the Wartegg Drawing Test, where eight separate panes of dots, curves and lines are presented to the subject for completion in any way his imagination chooses. These tests reveal the difficulties in the individual's primary process, which otherwise would not be detectable.

All art involves a certain amount of control, and hence is secondary process. Even prehistoric and primitive tribal art, which constitute a transition from the primary to the secondary process, contain elements of the secondary. But of course it is a matter of degree, and on a continuum we would see the most evidence of primary process in the prehistoric cave drawings in France and Spain, in the more recent tribal art of Africa, and—in our own day—the cubism of Pablo Picasso, the surrealistic dream worlds of Giorgio de Chirico and Salvador Dali, and the abstractions of Jackson Pollock. The product of the secondary process is said to be civilization, and with civilization comes the superego. Again, just as there is no purely primary process art, so there is no purely secondary, but on that same continuum we would see more of the secondary process in formal portraits, certain still lifes, and in strictly representational art such as that of Andy Warhol. In art of these types the reality principle is an obvious component.

Illustration I is a cave painting of a bull from Lascaux, France, c. 15,000–12,000 B.C. The prehistoric artist was expressing the pre-superego concepts of men and women who were so close to nature as to be a part of it. Animals are closely allied to the primary process, especially in the lives of early peoples.

Illustration II is a rock painting of a human hand with dots, with a later figure of a hunter superimposed. Rhodesia, date unknown.

Illustration III is a rock painting from Algeria, c. 5,000–1,200 B.C.

Illustration IV is part of a large rock painting from Rhodesia, date unknown. Succeeding generations painted over the work of their ancestors, so we have an interesting record of their development. The predominance of animals and hunters is a primary process characteristic.

Illustration V is the cover of volume I of the two volume work "'Primitivism' in Twentieth Century Art," published by the Museum of Modern Art. On the left is "Girl Before a Mirror," by Pablo Picasso, 1932. On the right is a tribal mask from British Columbia, date not known (but probably 19th century). The similarity is striking but not surprising, because Picasso was strongly influenced by primitive tribal art. Few modern artists so powerfully represent the primary process as did Picasso, but always in the service of the secondary process—a combination which was a part of his genius.

Illustration VI is the painting "Three Dancers" by Picasso. (In this, as in the following illustrations, the lack of color in the reproducing process detracts to a great degree from the impact of the works.) J. Cary, in "Art and Reality; Ways of the Creative Process," says of Picasso that "he passed from the age of true childish inspiration, through years of conceptual and technical training, back to the original vision which is not childish, but has all the originality of the child's eye combined with the far greater depth and richness of a man's experience."

Illustration VII is by Hieronymus Bosch (1450-1516), a section of a larger work entitled "The Temptation of St. Anthony." Few painters were as closely in touch with the primary process as was Bosch, whose fantastic canvases were crammed with nightmarish creatures and shocking images.

Illustration VIII consists of four paintings by Giorgio de Chirico (1888-1978). De Chirico saw himself as an oracle, and the eerie dream world of his paintings—which were his attempts at portraying the reality beyond reality—is in the realm of the primary process.

Illustration IX is "Hallucinogenic Toreador," by Salvador Dali (1904–). The name of Dali is synonymous with Surrealism and all that the term connotes. H. H. Arnason, in "History of Modern Art," says that most important for Dali's development was his discovery of Freud, "whose writings on dreams and the subconscious seemed to answer the torments and erotic fantasies he had suffered since childhood." The primary process is everywhere in his paintings, but his genius lies in its integration with the secondary.

Illustration X is "Portrait of a Lady," by Thomas Gainsborough (1727-1788). Gainsborough was the most sought after painter of pretty women in late 18th century England. The elegance and refinement of his portraits are characteristic of the secondary process.

Since the secondary process involves reality testing, and since reality testing begins in very early childhood, it is probably safe to say that there are none, except perhaps for the delusionally schizophrenic, who do not operate under the secondary process to some degree. We can also say that there are no handwritings, just as there is no art, that are not influenced by the secondary process. In the personality as revealed in handwriting, however, there must be an integration of the processes so that the secondary process is always in touch with the primary one. When we see a neglect of the lower zone, for example, with exaggerated emphasis on the upper, we know that the writer has cut off his instincts to the detriment of his development, and has handed control over to the restrictive superego. The writer who is closer to the primary process is motivated mainly by physical impulses and feelings, whereas the writer who emphasizes the secondary process is motivated mainly by logic and facts.

In considering the writing from a psychological viewpoint, we would identify primary process with the mother (the dual union and dependency), impulses, the past, the oral period, narcissistic tendencies, addictive tendencies, and sexual deviation. Secondary process is identified with the father (independence and individualization), control, release from the dual union, ego development, anal/phallic/genital periods, group relationships, and the future.

In graphology all indicators for character traits can also be divided into primary and secondary process.

Under primary process we would find:

- School type connections
- Left trend
- Excessive roundedness
- Wide spaces between words
- Separation of letters within words in low style evaluation writing
- Varying slants
- Misformations in the lower zone
- Lower loops not reaching the baseline
- Lack of margins
- Directional pressure from the past
- Emphasis on upper part of personal pronoun I and avoidance of lower part
- Poor rhythm
- Lack of fluidity
- Elaboration
- Irregularity

Secondary process is seen in:

- All connections except the school type
- Separation of letters within words in high style evaluation writing
- Right trend
- Lower loops reaching the baseline (except in strictly school type writing)
- Good margins

Simplification

Balance in upper and lower parts of personal pronoun I (or a simplified version of the PPI)

Over connectedness

Regularity

The original stage of development as far as handwriting is concerned is movement, and particularly the learning of movement control. Form is the subsequent stage of development for most people, although not all. Detecting sense for form in handwriting is much more difficult than seeing it in a work of art, since our eyes are constantly drawn to the meaning of the text, rather than to the individual letters in the writing.

Illustration XI is the handwriting of a 35 year old, right handed female. This handwriting is highly developed and therefore the primary process can only be seen in the difficulty in returning the lower loops to the baseline.

Illustration XII is an enlargement of a part of the writing which reveals the sense for form of this writer, a very versatile painter.

Illustration XIII shows that even a signature alone—as with this one of Elie Wiesel—can display the sense for form. The primary process can be seen in the unusual emphasis on the lower zone.

Illustration XIV demonstrates that a signature does not have to be legible. It often serves as a symbol, and the fact that one uses the signature as a symbol rather than as letters, makes it more of a primary process.

Illustration XV shows a rigid concept of form which has not been allowed to develop into an artistic expression. In the word "truly," for example, the letter y, which does not return to the baseline, shows indications of primary process. This is in spite of the over connectedness, which is an indicator of secondary process.

Illustration XVI is the handwriting (*67%* reduced) of a highly creative female painter, late 40's. The writing does not show a clear consciousness of form.

Illustration XVII only in the enlargement (of the above illustration), do the fine letter formations reveal her creative ability. The secondary process is seen in the simplifications, the balanced zones, the simplified personal pronoun I, and the good rhythm.

Illustration XVIII is the handwriting of De Es Schwertberger, prominent German artist, 46 years. The very pronounced tendency to make arcade formations, thereby allowing influences to come from the lower zone, is an indication of primary process. Otherwise, the handwriting is highly developed and therefore strongly secondary process.

Illustration XIX is the handwriting of a male painter in his mid 50's. The variations in the slant of this writing are indicative of primary process. The writing is highly simplified and highly developed, which shows that the artist has greatly developed his own style.

Illustration XX is the handwriting of Marcel Janco, Romanian painter and sculptor who was one of the founders of the Dada movement. He was in his late 60's when this was written. The form in this writing is interfered with by the disturbance in space, which is due to difficulty in emotional development.

Illustration XXI is the handwriting of a female, 22 years, right handed. She asked for vocational guidance and provided both samples, which were written at the same time. The upper sample is clearly more form conscious and more primary process than the lower. As a consequence, she was advised to go into more creative endeavors than she was engaged in at the time.

Illustration XXII is the handwriting of a 35 year old female. Although there is sense for form in this writing, the form has not been developed due to the fact that there were severe difficulties in the primary process, which were never overcome.

Illustration XXIII is the handwriting of a male in his late 60's, a painter and a designer of stained glass windows for churches and other buildings. This is an excellent example of where the secondary process has developed strongly out of the primary process, as seen in an emphasis on the lower zone without being unsightly or arrhythmic.

Illustration XXIV is the handwriting of Rembrandt (1606-1669). The fact that this writing is strongly influenced by the primary process is seen in the changing slants and the lower zone loops that do not return to the baseline. On the other hand, it is extremely rich in very original letter formations and very creative simplifications, signs of the secondary process.

In conclusion, it is necessary to establish that form is not only an indicator of creative ability but also an indicator of a developmental process. Although a child can possess a sense for form, a higher form consciousness is only possible after puberty.

ILLUS. I

ILLUS. II

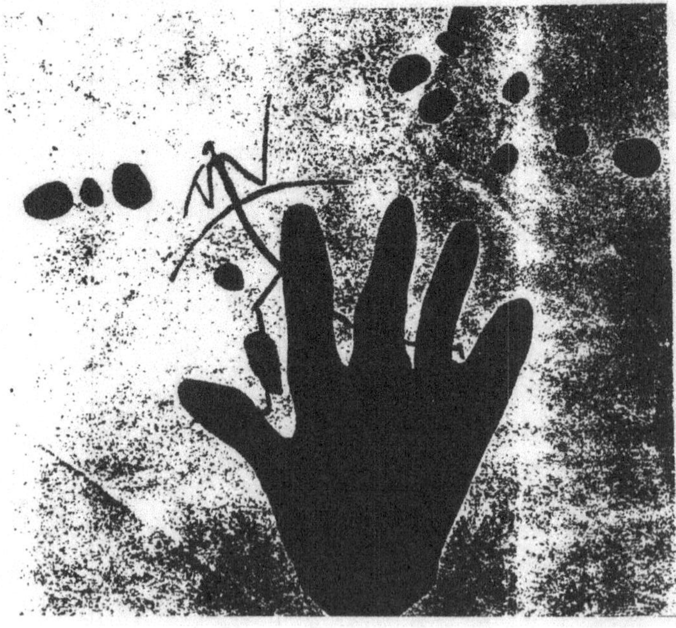

ILLUS. III

ILLUS. IV

ILLUS. V

"PRIMITIVISM"

IN 20TH CENTURY ART

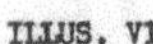

ILLUS. VI

ILLUS. VII

ILLUS. VIII

1

ILLUS. IX

Hallucinogenic Toreador, 1969–70

ILLUS. X

THOMAS GAINSBOROUGH - PORTRAIT OF A LADY

ILLUS. XI

Dear Felix & Janice,

Congragulations again —
It was wonderful to be
with you both again - my
course was really interesting
I can't thank you enough
for all I've learned & been
lucky enough to pass on
from you both. ——

Thanks for returning
my almost 2nd
lost

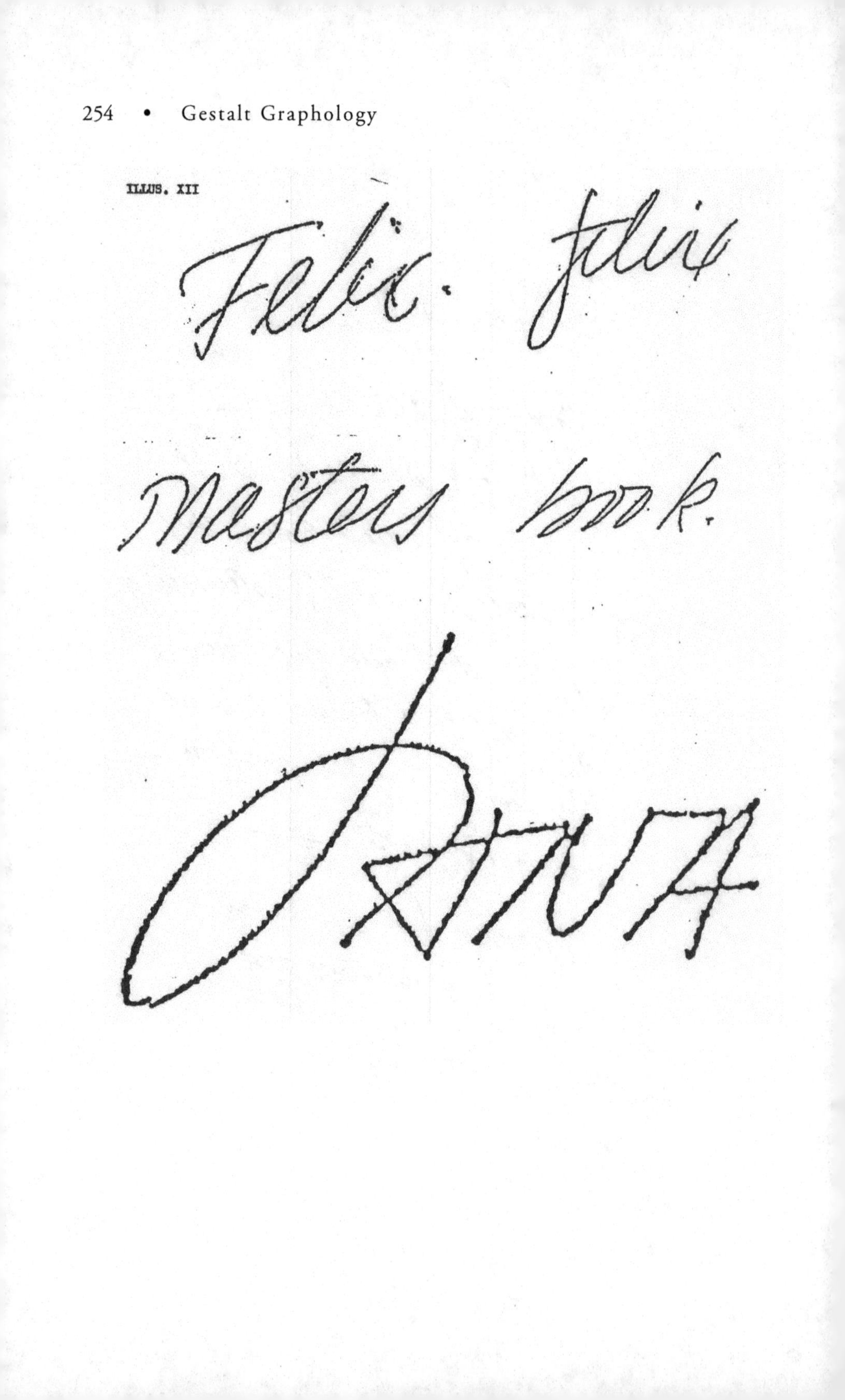

ILLUS. XII

ILLUS. XIII

sincerely yours,

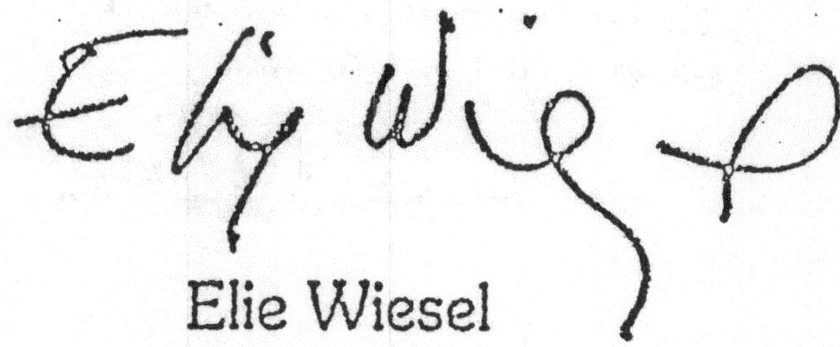

Elie Wiesel

Cordially,

ILLUS. XIV

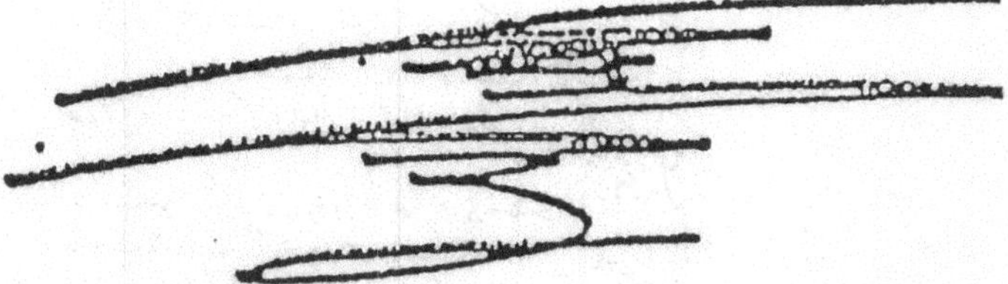

Alberto Andrade

ILLUS. XV

assumed respite's that one's retainer on outlayed "com
ive nature,, should address this matter business like.
operational ramifications; reciprocally... and thereby with
inform you, and/or counterparts its with Capitulary Co
to... assay of convessional: contrition wee just see it
sible inby contrivance to uphold continual gany c
mutually of ongoing inadvertencies.....

Very truly your's,
D.A. Ricketts; 296.40
DERMOT A. RICKETTS: PN

ILLUS. XVI

Aug 29th 86

Dear Felix,
You asked for my handwriting
before and after surgery.
The closest before - I could
find, are these notes, taken
at my last computer class.
Hope they are enough.
And, right here - is the
"after".
Of course, remember -
there was no malignancy.
Please, tell me if you
can see a difference.
I had to start this twice -
- because I was skipping letters

Love,
Sandra.

P.S. I need my notes back.
S.

ILLUS. XVII

Tell me if you
a difference.
I start this &
I was skipping
Love,
Sanda.

ILLUS. XVIII

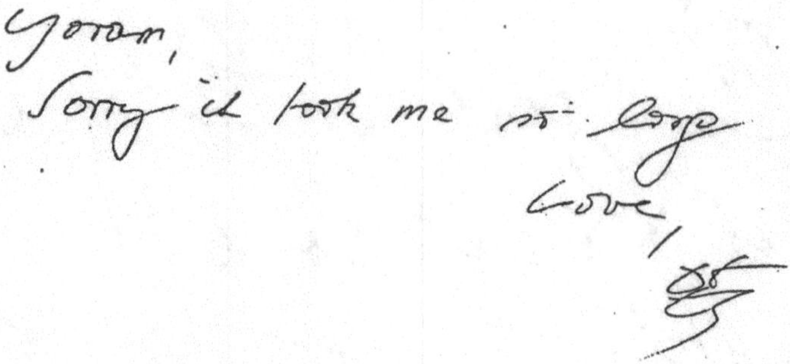

Yoram,
Sorry it took me so long
Love,
[illegible]

ILLUS. XIX

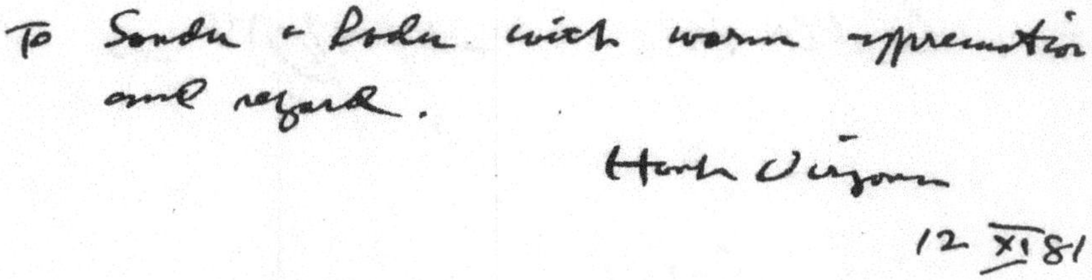

To Sonda & Rodu with warm appreciation
and regards.
[illegible]
12 XI 81

ILLUS. XX

27.9.68
Lui Sanda
urările mele bune de an
nou cu rugămintea de a transmite
acelaş lucru Dlui Fredkins. N'am aştept
at în zadar noi plecăm p. 1 luna
La revedere la finele octom
fie cu drag
Marcel Janco

Israel's army parade in United Jerusalem
Independence Day — 1968

מצעד צה"ל בירושלים המאוחדת
יום העצמאות תשכ"ח

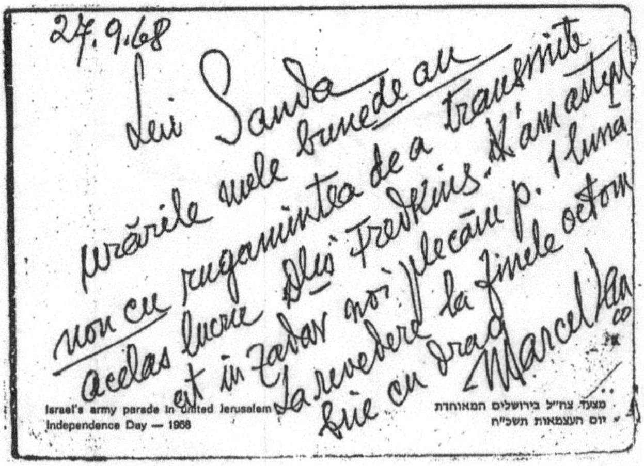

ILLUS. XXI

P.S. For some reason, I seem to
keep records i.e. checkbook, bills etc.
in this rounded script. Perhaps it's
because it's easier to read. I don't
know if its significant at all but
I thought I'd include it.

I want to go to Italy.

three years so I could join the work force,
but it's not what I thought it would be.
I haven't been feeling fulfilled at all
lately and I'm not sure if it's because
I'm still the "low man on the totem pole"
or if it's because I'm in the wrong business!
I still feel I have ambition but that
I seem to be lacking direction. I've been

ILLUS. XXII

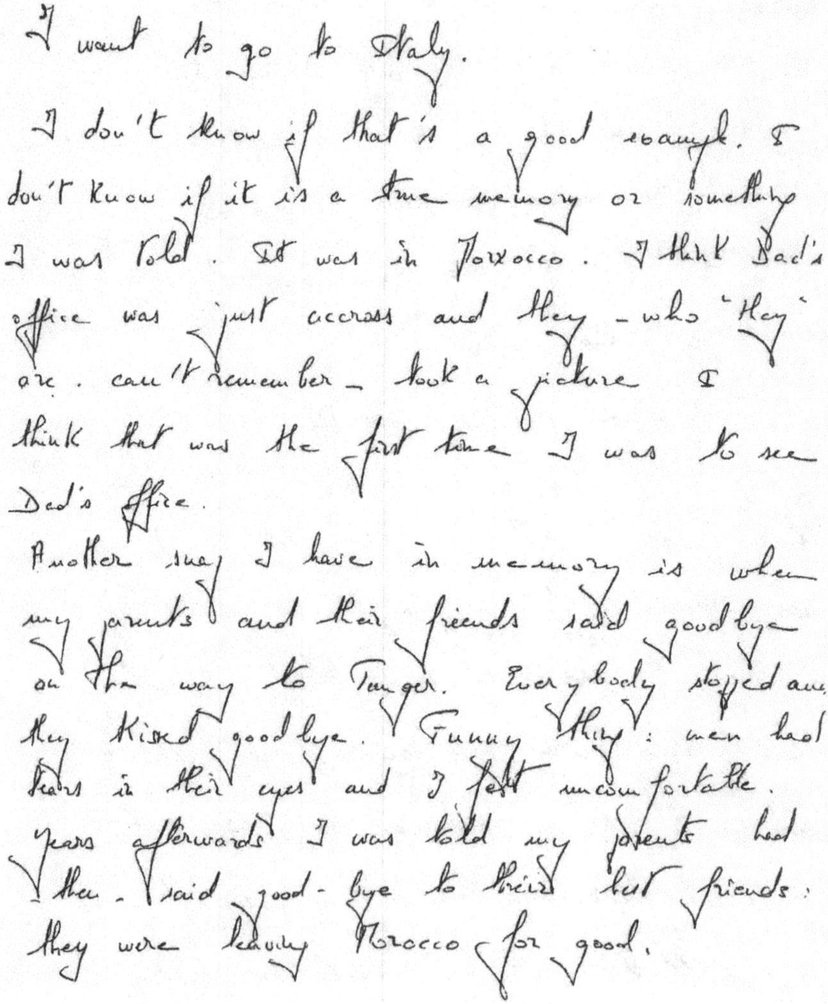

I want to go to Italy.

I don't know if that's a good example. I don't know if it is a true memory or something I was told. It was in Morocco. I think Dad's office was just accross and they - who "they" are. can't remember - took a picture I think that was the first time I was to see Dad's office.
Another one I have in memory is when my parents and their friends said goodbye on the way to Tanger. Everybody stopped and they kissed goodbye. Funny thing: men had tears in their eyes and I felt uncomfortable. Years afterwards I was told my parents had then said good-bye to their best friends: they were leaving Morocco for good.

ILLUS. XXIII

Es ist schlimm, dass ich Deinen lieben, guten Freundschaftsbrief noch nicht beantwortet habe. Beim Wiederlesen hatte ich die kurze Utopie nach Solingen zurückzukehren statt nach Köln, und Euch zu einem Abendessen einzuladen anschliessend bei Euch zu sitzen in der Kurfürstenstrasse und noch eine Flasche mit Euch zu trinken. – Was wäre und hätte sein können, wenn der Scheiss-Hitler Euch nicht vertrieben hätte. Nun gut, ich werde nach Köln zurückkehren, und überlegen ob ich eine Einladung nach Amerika annehme: im April-Mai 85. Ich lege Dir eine Fotocopie bei. Inzwischen habe ich nicht mehr recht Lust zu grossen Reisen.
Gerade waren wir 8.000. Kilometer in China im September. Es ist ein wunderbares Land, das mir sehr liegt. Es hat sich sehr verändert, Kolchosen und Kombinate sind abgeschafft und jeder kann Unternehmer sein. Allerdings sind die Industrielle im Zustand wie bei uns vor 80 Jahren. Kohlenabbau mit Handarbeit etc. Aber die Menschen wissen dass sie eine Zukunft haben Ökonomie geht über Ideologie und: wir wollen ja keine Weltrevolution wie die Russen, wir wollen dass unser Volk glücklich wird". Das ist die Tendenz, nach der auch praktisch sehr deutlich gehandelt wird.

ILLUS. XXIV

op dat ick mijn wel verdiende 1244 gulde
mocht een mael ontfangen sal ick sulx aen
met reverentij dienst ende blijckelijcke vrientschap altijt
soecken te verschuldigen hiermede ist dat ick mijn
Heer hartelijck groete ende wensche dat u.e.
God lanck in goede gesontheijt ende
gesontheijt ~~[illegible]~~

U.E. dienstwillige ende geaffectioneerde
Dienaer Rembrandt

ick woon op die binnen Amstel ende
suijcker backerij

1639

Bibliography

Arnason, H.H. *History of Modern Art*
(Harry N. Abrams, Inc., New York, 1986.)

English, Horace B. and English, Ava C. *A Comprehensive Dictionary of Psychological and Psychoanalytical Terms*
(David McKay Company, Inc., New York, 1958.)

Klein, Felix *Intelligence in Handwriting*

Klein, Felix *Pictures in Handwriting*

Klein, Felix *Psychology for Graphologists: A Study Guide*

Kuhns, Richard *Psychoanalytic Theory of Art*
(Columbia University Press, New York, 1983.)

Lommel, Andreas *Prehistoric and Primitive Man*
(The Hamlyn Publishing Group, Ltd. Middlesex, England, 1966.)

Rose, Gilbert J. *The Power of Form: A Psychoanalytic Approach to Aesthetic Form*
(International Universities Press, Inc., New York, 1980.)

Rubin, William (Editor) *Primitivism in 20th Century Art* (volumes I and II)
(The Museum of Modern Art, New York, 1984.)

The Unconscious in Handwriting

Felix Klein

The Unconscious and The Dynamics of Energy Distribution as Seen in Handwriting

In order to establish how much in our handwriting is due to unconscious material, we have to start by trying to establish what the unconscious is. In A Comprehensive Dictionary of Psychological and Psychoanalytical Terms, the unconscious is defined as "a part or region of the psyche (wherein) the activities are not open to direct conscious scrutiny but have dynamic effects on conscious process and behaviors."

Although the concept of hidden layers existing below the surface of consciousness had been explored by many European philosophers as well as ancient Greek and Oriental thinkers, it was Sigmund Freud who crystallized the general concept into a systematic and usable tool for the psychologist. As a neurologist by profession, Freud's original purpose was to use his research for medical ends. During his early years, particularly when he was a medical student, he was greatly influenced by the German physiologist Ernst Brücke, one of the leaders in the Helmholtz School of Medicine. It was from Brücke that Freud learned to regard man as a dynamic system subject to the laws of nature. He was also influenced and very stimulated by Jean Charcot's revolutionary views on the subject of hysteria. Among others who contributed strongly to the development of Freud's theories were Dr. Wilhelm Fliess and Dr. Joseph Breuer, with the latter of whom he did his first research on hysteria. Most important of all, however, was Freud's own self-analysis, a truly heroic undertaking that lasted from 1897, at the age of forty-one, until his death in 1939. "In my youth," Freud wrote, "I felt an overpowering need to understand something of the riddles of the world in which we live and perhaps even contribute something to their solution." Ernest Jones, Freud's official biographer, said of him, "He had a veritable passion to understand."

The term that Freud used for the unconscious part of the psyche was the "id," which was derived from the latin for "it."

"One might compare the relation of the ego to the id with that between a rider and his horse," Freud wrote. "The horse provides the locomotive energy, and the rider has the prerogative of determining the goal and of guiding the movements of his powerful mount towards it. But all too often in the relations between the ego and the id we find a picture of the less ideal situation in which the rider is obliged to guide his horse in the direction in which it itself wants to go."

In their book Theories of Personality, Gardner Lindzey and Calvin S. Hall give the following explanation of the id: "The id is the original system of the personality; it is the matrix within which the ego and the superego become differentiated. The id consists of everything psychological that is inherited and that is present at birth, including the instincts. It is the reservoir of psychic energy and furnishes all of the power for the operation of the other two systems. It is in close touch with the bodily processes from which it derives its energy. Freud called the id the 'true psychic reality' because it represents the inner world of subjective experience and has no knowledge of objective reality. The id cannot tolerate increases of energy which are experienced as uncomfortable states of tension. Consequently, when the tension level of the organism is raised, either as a result of external stimulation or of internally produced excitations, the id functions in such a manner as to discharge the tension immediately and return the organism to a comfortably constant and low energy level. This principle of tension reduction by which the id operates is called the pleasure principle."

For each one of us, the possibility of achieving the full value of our capacity depends on how efficiently we distribute the energy available to us in the id, or the unconscious. According to Freud's theory, this energy is distributed to the ego which may waste it, or hoard it, or—in the case of the mature personality—keep what it needs and distribute the remainder to the superego. Since the conscious effort necessary to produce handwriting reveals the unconscious mind of the writer, it is possible to trace the energy as it is released by the id and distributed to the ego and superego. The id, Freud explained, uses the energy for reflex actions and wish-fulfillment by producing images, and it is not capable of distinguishing between objects and images, which is the work of the ego. Because the only way instinctual gratification can be obtained is through the ego, more and more psychic energy is transferred to achieve gratification. However, as the ego has control over the spending of energy, it can use it for other purposes, such as perception, memory, judgment, discrimination, abstraction and reasoning to a higher level of development. The ego is also responsible for transferring energy to the superego, the guardian of traditional values and moralistic attitudes.

Drastic changes of energy distribution are both common and natural in the first twenty years of life, and the balancing of the available energy ideally with the maturing process. For many people, however, the balance is never established because of difficulties in the oral, anal, phallic, and genital periods, resulting in a lifetime of emotionally disruptive problems.

Since it is the ego which is the distributor of the energy from the id, and whose proper functioning is so vital to human development, let us explore the nature of the ego a little further. The first indication that a baby is developing an ego is when it smiles at the mother, expressing both its satisfaction and its dependency. The ego has two functions, the first of which is the reality principle, which serves to hold back tension until appropriate satisfaction of the need can be found. The reality principle is capable of temporarily foregoing the pleasure principle, which is designed to reduce tension. While the pleasure principle is only interested in determining whether an experience is painful or pleasurable, the reality principle distinguishes between true and false experiences. The other function of the ego is the secondary process, which produces a plan for the satisfaction of the need through realistic thinking. An example of this would be a hungry person experiencing the need for food initiated by the images produced by the id, and looking for the food in appropriate places. This is called reality testing. The ego controls the learning process and decides which of the stimuli from the outside world to respond to. The ego also decides which of the instincts will be satisfied and in what way. The ego is the organizer of the id and can not exist without it. The major function of the ego is the responsibility for maintaining life and for reproducing the species.

The superego is developed much later, and the first time a child becomes aware of the necessity for it is when the parent forbids it from doing something. Through the superego the child learns what is considered good according to the parents' standards and for which it will be rewarded if obeyed or punished if disregarded. The superego functions through two sub-systems. The conscience allows the child to distinguish between what is good or bad, and when he does something he was told not to do he feels guilty. The ego ideal, which represents not only what the child feels he ought to do but what he genuinely wants to do in his positive identification with loving parents, makes him feel proud of himself. Whereas the conscience will be identified with control of impulses, the ego ideal will be seen in the mature integration of the entire personality.

Summing up, the id represents the biological part of the personality, the ego represents the psychological part, and the superego represents the social aspect. We can see now that the distribution of energy depends entirely on the quality of the ego. Graphologically, the ego is usually recognized through a good middle zone, which is neither too large or too small, or better, which is in proportion to the other zones. The word balance may best describe it.

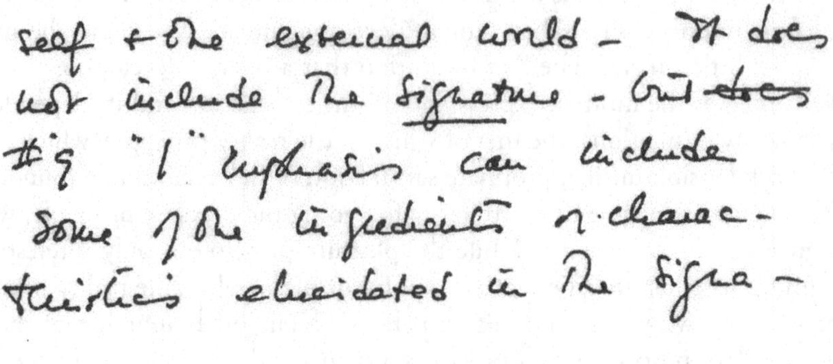

Illustration 1: Example of a good ego writing.

When a handwriting does not show a good ego, there are several possible consequences. The ego may not receive the energy from the id except for basic needs such as providing food, which will result in the energy remaining in the id and all actions becoming highly unrealistic. (This often occurs in adolescence.) The pleasure principle will govern all actions and destructive behavior will be the order of the day. A handwriting of this type would show a lack of control, very poor spacing and interlinear tangling, and a disproportionately large lower zone.

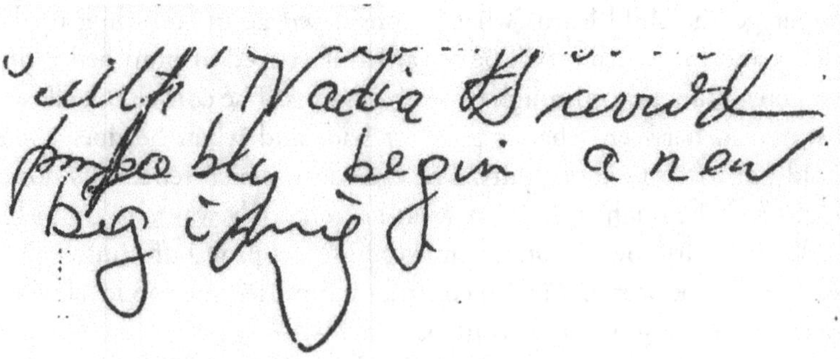

Illustration 2: Example of an id writing.

Another possible consequence of a poorly functioning ego would be the fact that the ego could hoard the energy, thereby allowing progress only in purely mental activities. The cerebral writing would show good simplifications, poor development of the lower zone, a better upper zone, and fluidity. This type of writing does <u>not</u> show rigidity.

framework to an interpretation of recent economic
and financial history. The main topics I deal
with are the transformation of banking from a
highly regulated to a less regulated industry

Illustration 3: Example of an ego that hoards the energy.

A poorly functioning ego can also result in the energy going into the superego, which will then produce varying degrees of compulsion. It must be borne in mind here that the superego acts to forbid and restrict, and causes one to do things over and over the same way without allowing for further development. There is no flexibility for making changes when the superego controls the energy from the id.

Graphological indicators for such writings would be a small middle zone, poorly developed lower zone, emphasis on the upper zone, and rigidity.

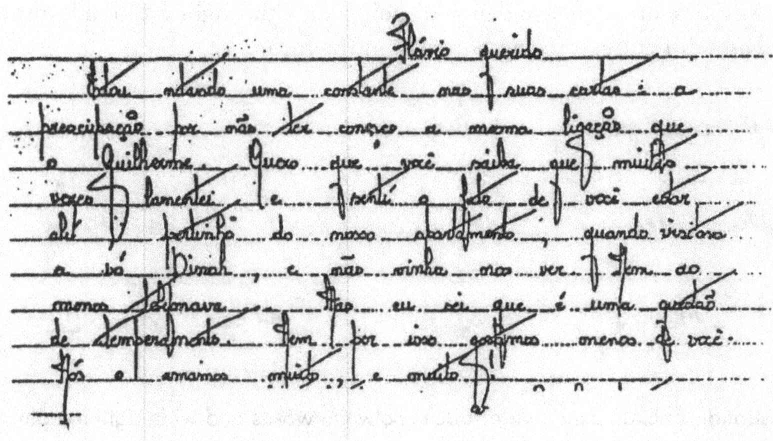

Illustration 4: Example of a superego writing.

To summarize, it is the first order of business for a graphologist who is interested in determining the distribution of energy in a writing to find the quality of the ego. Only then can we see if the writer is developing his or her own capacity or is being held back from it by the poor distribution of energy.

Now we must ask, how does other unconscious material manifest itself in the handwriting? The most obvious answer to this question is that anything that we do unconsciously, or in other words, without any intention or awareness of doing it, would be a reflection of the unconscious mind. However, this unconscious material has to be divided into two groups. The first group contains a summary of patterns that have been established over a long period of time in our brains. When we learn to make one letter in a certain way it becomes like a photographic image and we will reproduce this image without thinking about it. This is one way of showing unconscious material in the handwriting. The other way is a reflection of the unconscious without any previous image having been established. An example of this is the fact that the distance between two words remains an indicator of choice without any outside influence, and particularly not of the unconscious mind. Why is it that some people keep a very large distance between words even though they otherwise are extremely careful of how they use space? Every graphologist knows that the distance between two words is an indication of how close or how far we feel towards other people. So, the space left empty between two words is a clear manifestation of the unconscious.

Another indicator for the workings of the unconscious is the treatment of the right margin. We feel very strongly that the right side of the paper represents the future. Any hesitation or avoidance of going into the right hand side must be regarded as a difficulty in seeing ourselves in the future.

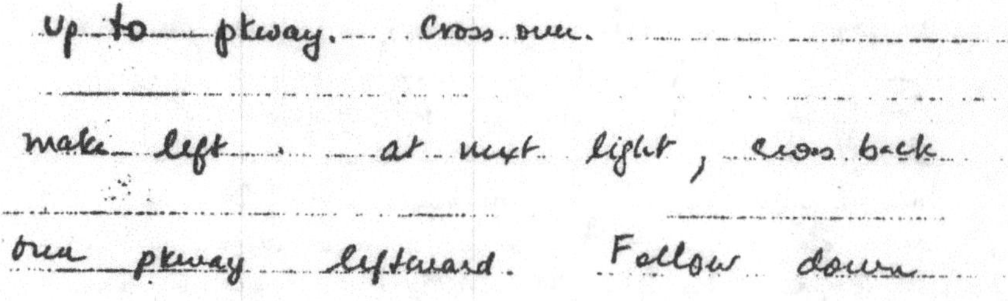

Illustration 5: Example of wide spaces between words and wide right margin.

Still another indicator of the unconscious in the handwriting is how we use the baseline. In our minds we identify the baseline with the ground that supports us. The baseline on a piece of unlined paper can he established by connecting the lowest points of the middle zone letters. When writers remain on the base line too long it is a sign that they feel insecure.

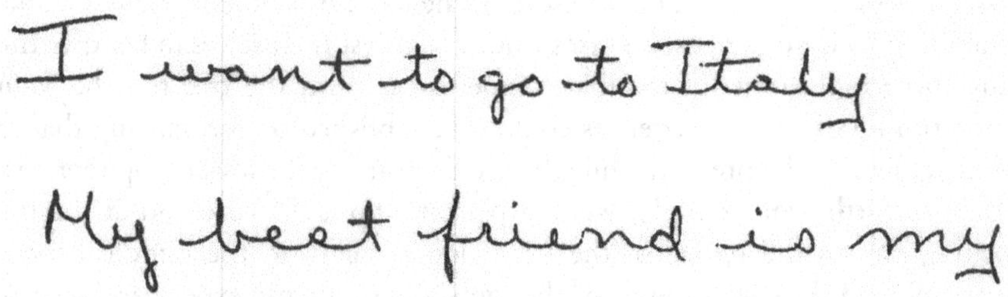

Illustration 6: Example of staying on the baseline.

Essentially, anything that will show unconscious material will show in the lower zone. It has been determined that the baseline is the line of reality, while unconscious material will often appear below the baseline. When we go from the baseline into the lower zone with the small letters "g" and "y," it is like asking a question in regard to the state of the unconscious mind. Upon returning we give the answer. When the material in our unconscious can be accepted into consciousness, the return of the lower loop will cross the downstroke exactly on the baseline as it goes into the middle zone. When the returning lower loop crosses the downstroke below the baseline it is a clear indication that the unconscious material can not be accepted into consciousness.

outrageous' and made the whole
night. I hope you continue your
singing and will remember us
when you become a big success.

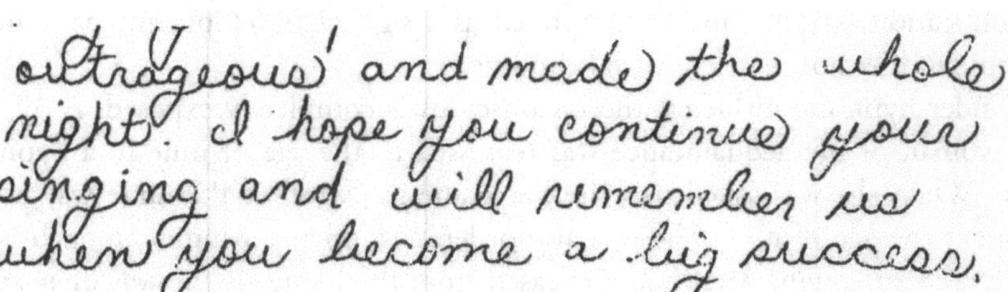

Illustration 7: Example of lower loops crossing below the baseline.

Some writers go as far as making a straight line below the baseline in the return of the loop, which can be interpreted as putting a lid on the unconscious.

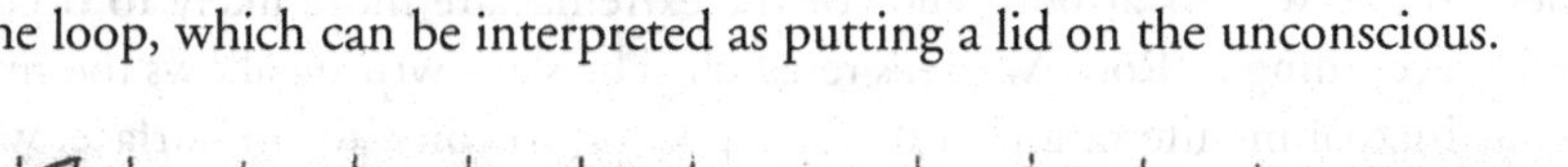

Illustration 8: Example of straight line on loop below baseline.

Over a period of many years of research, the late Dr. William Hallow worked to establish how traumatic experiences would manifest themselves in handwriting. Taking some indications of traumatic experiences from the tree test, he found that the timing of such experiences could be established by recognizing that the baseline represents the present, while the lowest point of the lower loop represents the time of birth. For example, when a person who is 30 years old at the time of writing crosses the return of the lower loop exactly in the middle between the baseline and the lowest point of the loop, the traumatic experience occurred during puberty, probably about the age of fifteen.

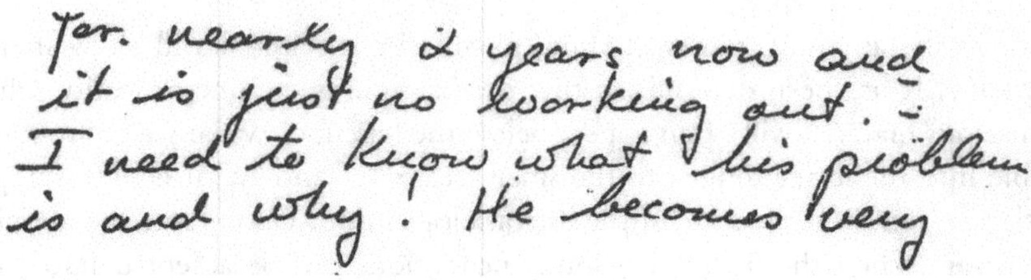

Illustration 9: Example of traumatic experience as seen in lower loop.

An exception to this observation is the avoidance of a lower loop at the end of a word when there is no return towards the baseline. This indicates a form of simplification, which can be interpreted as a sign of development, particularly because it does not interfere with legibility.

Under hypnotic influence the unconscious is completely exposed. A 32 year old woman of my acquaintance was regressed to the age of nine in a hypnotic state. When she was asked to write her name she wrote it the same way as she wrote at the age of nine. She was also ordered to open a window upon hearing the hypnotist cough. After being released from the hypnosis she was unaware of that instruction. As soon as the hypnotist coughed, however, she went over and opened the window, explaining, “It’s stuffy in here.”

The late Roda Wieser established a concept of basic rhythm (“grundrhythmus”) which is based on a continuum ranging from extreme rigidity (anal) to extreme slackness (oral). Writers at both ends of the extremes are more likely to become criminals, according to Roda Wieser’s research. The slack writing allows too much of the instinctual manifestation of the unconscious to come to the surface, without the censorship of the ego and superego. The very rigid writing, on the other hand, directs the energy into the superego, which can not have the benefit of the ego’s sense of realism. In simple terms, either of the two extremes has lost the concept of right and wrong.

Illustration 10: Example of rigidity.

Illustration 11: Example of slackness.

As we have seen, the ego is responsible for the distribution of energy, and consequently any person who has difficulty in that area must attempt to improve the ego before they can expect a proper distribution of energy. In order to improve the ego it is necessary to point towards achievement and to recognize that the achievement was due to the individual's own capacity. If the person can not accomplish this on their own it is necessary to go into professional therapeutic treatment. All therapy is designed to teach people to do things that are beneficial to themselves by using their energy productively.

Dear Mr. Jellinek =

Absolutely glorious program tonight on Strauss: sensitive, articulate, yet reverent to both your guest and your subject.

I have the highest respect for your vast store of knowledge, and your obvious love of your field. But to be able to combine all this in a beautifully produced radio program is also truly an art.

Many thanks from a small-league colleague, and big-league fan.

Very Sincerely,

Illustration 12: This writing portrays a difficulty in distribution of energy due to difficulties in early childhood, as seen in the large distance between words, the upright position, the narrowness between downstrokes in the middle zone, and the separation of letters within words.

The writing is an example of an ego that allows too much energy to go into the superego. It does, however, retain some for the ego.

Dear Mr. Sherman,

First, thank you for giving a repeat of your morning program with Evely Lear and Thomas Stewart. I wish you'd do it again – and how about repeati selected morning programs in the evening (so that non-artists who work regular hours can enjoy – and record)?

Lately I've been aware of some technical problems you've run into. This morning there seems to be an excessive flutter on your tape. It certainly sounded like a tape-quake. Yesterday at about 10^{20} a.m. there was a sudden reduction of hiss in the middle of a musical piece. The same, or much worse, happened last Thursday during the program "the vocal Sce. In the last piece hiss and noise came on and off, as though a dynamic filter of a noise reduction system was attacking and decaying every couple of seconds, or an auto-correlator was repeatedly falling out of lock. It sounded terrible!

There also seems to be some trouble with your microphones which sometim render a musical "bite" and, in particular with high amplitude and high pitched signals, give an annoying noise.

I hope you accept these notes as friendly remarks, not hostile criticism.

Sincerely Yours

Illustration 13: The ego is not properly distributing the energy in this writing. It is allowing the greater part of the energy to go into the superego.

He manages to stimulate interest and give a varied presentation of the material - whatever it is - even the commercials (which, by the way Mr. Edwards was sure to drive me away from). It's a pleasure to listen to the guy - and to be able to relax as one tries to gather oneself together in preparation for the day's tasks.

No question in my mind about WQXR being informative and being the best early morning shows for me. However, I used to listen out of necessity while now I listen by choice.

Viva Bob Lewis!

Illustration 14: This is an example of well distributed energy, with a sufficient amount of the energy being allowed to remain the ego.

Bibliography

English, Horace B. and English, Ava C. *A Comprehensive Dictionary of Psychological and Psychoanalytical Terms*
(David McKay Company, Inc., New York, 1958.)

Hall, Calvin S. and Lindzey, *Gardner* *Theories of Personality*
(John Wiley & Sons, Inc., New York, Second edition, 1970.)

Munroe, Ruth L. *Schools of Psychoanalytic Thought*
(Holt, Rinehart and Winston, New York, 1955.)

Pervin, Lawrence A. *Personality: Theory, Assessment, and Research*
(John Wiley & Sons, New York, Third edition, 1980.)

Progoff, Ira *The Death and Rebirth of Psychology*
(The Julian Press, Inc., New York, 1956.)

Bibliography

The Addictive Personality as Seen in Handwriting

Felix Klein

The Addictive Personality as Seen in Handwriting

I have been examining the handwriting of addictive personalities for many years, but when I came to prepare this paper I wanted to base my observations on the findings of someone whose career had been spent exclusively with such troubled people. By chance I came upon a small book entitled The Addictive Personality: Understanding Compulsion in Our Lives and I knew I had found the right source for my purpose. Craig Nakken, M.S.W., a certified chemical dependency practitioner and a lecturer at the Rutgers School of Alcohol Studies, has worked in the field of addictions for more than fifteen years. Everything that Mr. Nakken has discovered in his work with addicts bears out my own conclusions from a graphological standpoint.

The word addiction (which derives from the Latin word meaning "to favor") is familiar to everyone by now, although many of us tend to think of it as referring primarily to people who get hooked on drugs or alcohol. But, as Craig Nakken sees it, "an addiction is a pathological love and trust relationship with an object or event, and addicts are trying to get their needs for intimacy met through this relationship." Probably all of us have moments when we turn to objects for comfort, and we may jokingly refer to ourselves as being addicted, but we never reach the point where, like the practicing addict, we satisfy our intimacy needs through inanimate objects. "Addiction causes the addict to experience a predictable mood change," explains Nakken, which "gives the illusion that a need has been met." Instead of reaching out to others in a human relationship, the addict begins what is known as "acting out," engaging in addictive behaviors and obsessions that cause a kind of mental and emotional shift. The addict has come to feel that he or she has lost control of life, but that the control can be regained through the addictive acting out process. Of course this control is based on an illusion, but for a while it gives the addict the feeling that he has made some sense out of life. The acting out illusion helps him to escape, temporarily, from life's pressures and pains; he is seduced by the false notion that he can receive emotional nurturance from objects and events. Other people gradually take on the quality of one-dimensional objects to be manipulated, and an ever-widening gulf opens up between the addict and those who care for him.

What causes some people to fall into addictive patterns from which they may struggle a lifetime to escape? Science still is not sure if there is any biological cause that may make some more likely to do so, but we do know that everyone is born not only with a unique genetic makeup but also with a basic temperament that may incline one child from an early age to be more compulsive than another. Nevertheless, not every compulsive person becomes an addict, and what is more likely is that certain events may make certain people more susceptible to addictive influences. What is it in the addict's environment that triggers whatever natural inclinations may exist and produces a full scale assault of an addiction?

The word "loss" seems to be the key here—loss of a loved one, loss of status, loss of dreams and ideals, loss of familiar surroundings, loss of whatever it is in life that spells emotional security for that particular individual. In an effort to find relief from the pain caused by any of these losses, the addict falls for the false and empty promises of a mood change. As Craig Nakken notes, "Both washing dishes and gambling are events, but for most people washing dishes produces a much smaller pleasurable mood change. Milk and alcohol are substances but people don't become addicted to milk because it doesn't have the same mood changing quality as alcohol." What then is the difference? Gambling and alcohol, for the addict, produce a much greater intensity of mood change, and in their search for control over a difficult and painful situation, addicts mix up intensity with intimacy. Whereas intimacy produces a healthy and satisfying relationship with the world, but takes longer to develop, intensity works faster and seemingly more effectively for the moment. "Addicts," Nakken says, "feel very committed to the moment because of the intensity." If we think of a typical adolescent, struggling with a great number of difficult issues and aware of lacking control over them, we can get a clearer picture of the addict. Many addictions, of course, do start in adolescence, thereby compounding both the problems of adolescence and the problems that accompany addiction. The big difference between the problems of adolescence and the problems of addiction is that once the "normal" adolescent is through that particular stage, he or she is free to develop into a coping adult. But for the addict, there is no "outgrowing" the stage.

All of us, of course, experience mood changes that make us feel gloomy or out of control, but most of us handle these moods by talking to a friend, listening to music, painting a picture, or some similarly simple yet helpful activity. We don't expect to find total control, total perfection, total comfort in changing a mood, only satisfactory improvement. But the addict needs all of these totalities to produce a sufficient mood change to make life bearable again, A vicious circle develops as the addict, feeling out of control or helpless or in an imperfect situation, seeks out the object or substance that will give back the comforting illusion of control and perfection. It isn't enough for the addict to be human; he or she must be perfect. Of course perfection isn't available to any human being, and seeking it is a hopeless quest. On one level the addict realizes this and, in order to rationalize the pathological situation that is developing, creates what Nakken calls "addictive logic." Addictive logic develops as the individual attempts to justify and to cope with all the subtle and bewildering changes that are taking place. Through addictive logic the addict is able to deny everything; "there is no problem," he tells himself and others.

Inexorably addictive logic hardens into a delusional belief system, like a rigid cast that keeps the addict locked within himself. He can not get out and others can not get in. A behaviorally dependent lifestyle is now in place; everything must be done according to complex and unswerving rituals. "Healthy rituals," notes Nakken, "bind us to others, to family or friends, to helpful spiritual principles, or to a community based on helping each other. In this sense, addictive rituals are reverse rituals; their primary purpose is to isolate one from others." Rituals by their very nature are based on consistency and repetition, and a healthy ritual gives us a feeling of security and strength as it brings us closer to those we love. But the addictive ritual is practiced in terrible solitariness, hidden from the eyes of friends and family. Although the ritual is shameful to the addict, the shame is not enough to give the addict the courage to stop. As the addict retreats into his lonely world, those around him become increasingly confused and angry at his behavior. They find they can not "reach" the addict and his personality has changed so drastically that they scarcely recognize him. Derogatory labels are soon attached to the addict; he is "crazy" or "weird" or "out of it." Nakken explains that "family members are caught in a dilemma; they hate the Addict but love the Self within the person." The greatest sorrow, however, is that "no one hates the Addict more than a person suffering from the addiction." The greater the degree of the addiction, the deeper the addict's fear of being completely abandoned by those who love him. In a deep-seated addiction, the behavior is so extreme that it terrifies the addict himself. But, unable to make sense of his own behavior or to make changes in it, he lets himself be pulled into the devouring quicksand.

All segments of society must bear a portion of the blame that attaches to addictions because society is obsessed with the concept of perfection and super-achievement, especially in the realm of the body and the bank account. "You can never be too rich or too thin," is the often-quoted message that goes out to young women everywhere (and increasingly to young men). "Let me see bones," demands the ballet master. "Have a face lift and a tummy tuck and some liposuction" is the recommendation if we are less than young and slender and model-beautiful. You must be "perfect" to be accepted in many circles, and if not you must die in the attempt to become so. "The anorexic starves to death in search of perfection," says Nakken. "Bulimia can destroy the insides of its victims. Who knows how many people have killed themselves because they felt they weren't able to achieve perfection? Much pain is caused as people strive to be perfect. The stress of a life dedicated to perfection causes many people to seek the seductive relief found in the addictive process."

Another reason that so many people become addicted, adds Nakken, is that "relationships … in our society seem to have taken on a disposable quality. We live in a fast-paced, temporary society; as a result there is a lack of emphasis on relationships … and people tend to see others as objects." Just as our air and water is becoming so polluted as to be dangerous to our health, so the polluted attitudes of many people cause relationships to wither and die, and those who are victimized by these attitudes turn to alcohol or drugs or self-starvation in a vain attempt to escape the pain and to regain control of their lives.

While recovery from addiction is a long and difficult process, Craig Nakken believes that it can be found through what he calls Self-renewal. His encouraging message is that addicts are Addict-centered at a high cost to the Self, and that the road to recovery is through Self-care and a Self-relationship.

In graphology the addictive personality can be recognized by various indicators, but not without seeing the over-all picture, or gestalt, or described in psychological terms by Craig Nakken.

As with all addictions, the drug addict experiences a predictable mood change by taking drugs, either by mouth, by nose, or intravenously. Drugs alter both the physical and mental states of the addict. While in a drug-induced state the addict does not see his own problems but instead experiences a feeling of intense euphoria. In order to continuously experience the same effect the addict must increase the consumption of the drug. Because of this the addict is prone to reach a level of consumption that is fatal. It often happens that addicts who find that one drug fails to give them the original feeling of euphoria will turn to another drug in search of it. Psychologically speaking, it is the "hole" in the ego that the drug addict is attempting to fill.

It stands to reason that in graphology the first order of business in determining an addictive personality would be to look for difficulties in the ego, or let us say, to note that the ego is not developed. If a person shows difficulty in relating to others there is a greater likelihood of a potentiality for drug addiction, since the addiction not only requires no contact with others but indeed makes it impossible.

0n the one hand compulsive attitudes are a possible cause of addictive behavior. At the same time, however, the opposite of compulsion—which might be termed impulsiveness, lack of discipline, lack of control—can also be a basis for addiction. One is reminded of the theory of Roda Wieser, which considers the extremes of rigidity and slackness as parts of basic rhythm. We can conclude that the lack of basic rhythm not only allows for a greater possibility of criminality, as Roda Wieser believed, but also for a greater possibility of addiction.

The following handwriting sample is that of a 28 year old, left handed male, who is a cocaine addict. This handwriting shows a strong oral tendency, as seen in the emphasis on the upper (mother) part of the capital I. The poor male image is seen in the lack of sufficient horizontal movement to the right and the pronounced leaning of the lower loops toward the right (a looking for a father).

There is a noticeable slackness in the writing, observable in the neglect of form in the middle zone. The uneven and large margin on the right hand side indicates difficulty in the writer's own future orientation, This man had many problems, chief among them being a strong feeling of hatred for his father, and he turned to cocaine in his despair.

ILLUS. 1 COCAINE ADDICT

Male, 28, left handed

I would love to hear if there is
anything new in my handwriting sample

BUT YOU KNOW, USUALLY I PAINT SOMETHING LIKE THIS

What would you think about letting Anna
know if there any hope for me at all.

The handwriting of this artist, a 30 year old female who went from alcohol to cocaine addiction, shows a tendency to doing things on her own, as seen in the narrowness in the middle zone and the large spaces between words. Despite her creative tendencies (note the original letter formations) she has a poor self image, as evidenced in the neglect of form in the middle zone and her spoon "e," which not only shows difficulty in emotional release but also an ego problem. This writer turned to cocaine when alcohol no longer changed her mood sufficiently.

ILLUS. 2 CROSS ADDICTION (FROM ALCOHOL TO COCAINE)

Female, 30, right handed

> In now; I guess trying to be
> reasonable = work + forget me.
> That's what I am doing. An effort
> for nothing though + an [illegible]
> for not getting any worse,
> forgive me, let me try
> it the easy way or else you'll never
> get this letter,
> People here think I'm a great
> painter, a great expressionist

Alcohol is the most easily obtainable and socially acceptable substance that can lead to addiction. Since alcohol is found in many homes, even very young children have access to it and often become addicted. Alcoholism is probably the oldest form of addiction. Some societies have greater problems with it than others, while other societies have adopted strict religious taboos against the use of alcohol. This handwriting of a 43 year old right handed male shows greatest difficulty in the writer's lack of male identity, as seen in extreme roundedness, over-emphasis on the middle zone, and a strong horizontal movement to the left. These indicators give the impression of the writing of a young female, rather than that of a male.

The lack of sense for space indicates immaturity and poor self esteem. The writer worked as a stockbroker but lost his job because of his alcoholism. The loss of the job in turn caused him to develop a clinical depression.

ILLUS. 3 ALCOHOLIC

Male, 43, right handed

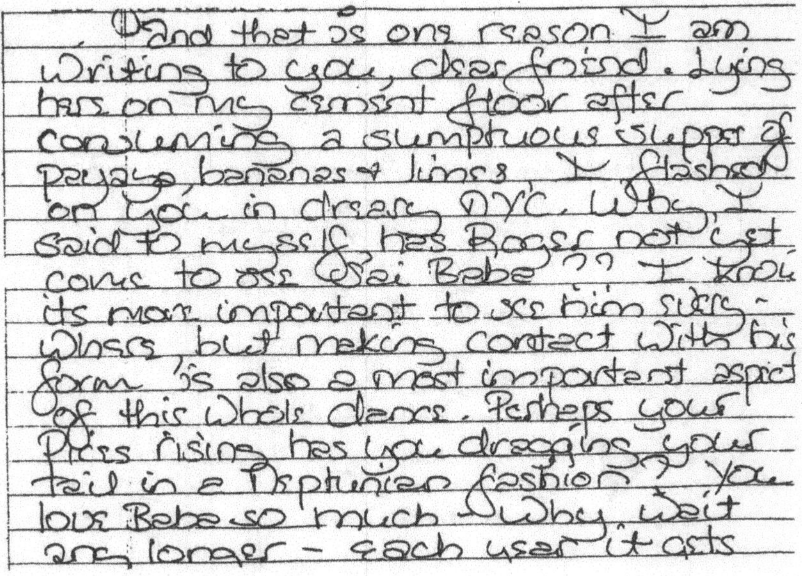

(1) And that is one reason I am
Writing to you, dear friend. Lying
here on my cement floor after
consuming a sumptuous supper of
papaya, bananas & limes, I flashed
on you in dreary NYC. Why, I
said to myself, has Roger not yet
come to see Sai Baba?? I know
its more important to see him somewhere, but making contact with his
form is also a most important aspect
of this whole dance. Perhaps your
Pisces rising has you dragging your
tail in a Neptunian fashion? You
love Baba so much - why wait
any longer - each year it gets

Also an alcoholic, the writer of this sample shows difficulty in his emotional development, as indicated by poor lower zone and emphasis on the upper zone. He shows a distinct neglect of form in the middle zone, evidence of a problem with self esteem and the ego. For him the alcohol is a substitute for the emotional release pattern. A stockbroker by profession, he is attending Alcoholics Anonymous meetings in an effort to overcome his addiction.

ILLUS. 4 ALCOHOLIC

Male, 40, right handed

the dog races
hockey game
whatever together.

Dear Lynn,

Knowing you enjoyed the card added gleam to the already brilliant day. How did you know which Lynn admiring Ted sent the card?

Daytime tele no. 774-
After 10 p.m 773-

Another one to Texas
Upon your return?
Ted

Another alcoholic, this writer is a lawyer and stockbroker. He shows strong persona qualities, indicated by rigid regularity and an avoidance of individualizing the letter formations. He was hired by a large brokerage house as a sales account executive but because of his alcoholism was unable to keep the job. A difficulty in emotional release is seen in the poor lower zone, malformations of the lower loops, and a leaning towards the left in the lower loops.

ILLUS. 5 ALCOHOLIC

Male, mid 30's, right handed

I believe that a career in the investment field can best utilize my academic training, and the skills I have developed through my work experience as well as personal qualities developed throughout my life.

Academically, my undergradute degree is in financial administration. As I'm sure you are aware, the program includes coursework in Financial Statement Analysis, Economics, Statistics and Computer Science as well as Management and Marketing. While in law school, I took advantage of the opportunity to expand on my undergraduate degree by enrolling in courses such as Business Planning Securities Regulation and all types of Taxation.

Prior to obtaining my law degree, I worked full time in the steel industry

This couple, both stockbrokers, are both alcoholics. The male is 51 and the female 30, and both are right handed. The male writing shows an extremely poor ego, as seen in the misformed capital I, neglect of the middle zone, and the backwards slant. The writer's avoidance of the right margin indicates difficulty in planning for the future and a problem in associating with others.

The female writing is slack, with a difficulty in the lower zone, neglect of form in the middle zone, an overdone right trend, and excessive speed beyond her personal rhythm.

ILLUS. 6 ALCOHOLICS (A COUPLE)

Male, 51, right handed

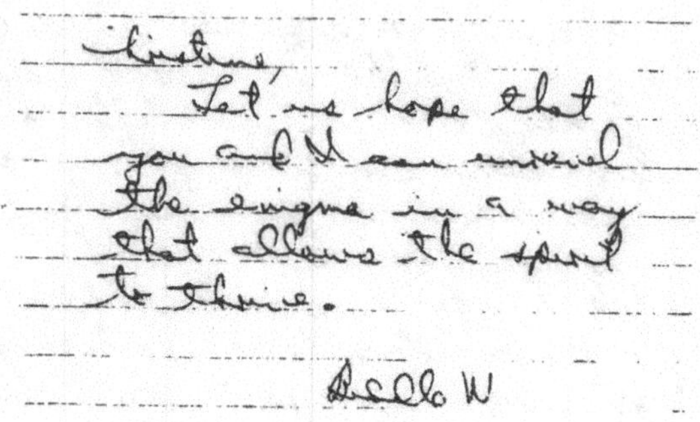

[illegible],
Let us hope that
you and I can unravel
the enigma in a way
that allows the spirit
to thrive.

[illegible]

Female, 30, right handed

For lunch I had
a dark chocolate candybar
to get over my hangover
Because I am driving myself
crazy.

Sex addiction is most commonly seen in people who are strongly oral. In females there usually is a difficulty with the father and with male relationships in general.

This handwriting of a 38 year old right handed female, a sex addict, shows an emphasis on the upper (mother) part of the capital I and the complete neglect of the lower (father) part. By avoiding a return to the baseline with the lower loops she indicates a reluctance to face urges coming from the unconscious. Her large right margin indicates her strong depressive tendency, which she can only overcome by engaging in promiscuous behavior.

ILLUS. 7 SEX ADDICT

Female, 38, right handed

I still feel close to Jim but realize, as an adult, at last, that this is not the right time for him or me. I find him one of the most interesting and fascinating people I have ever met. He's only 28 yrs old but has done so much that in many ways he is older than I am. He has had 3 major affairs. Since he was 18-19 he has lived with women. He needs this time to find out who he is, just as I do.

I am supposed to be working on my resume but felt I had to talk to you & tell you I feel good and am trying to learn to like myself. Went to one Bio-feedback session.

I wonder if this is the time to jump back into the business of N.Y.C. Cosmetics. Maybe I should look for a job I can do, taking it easy. I still feel I have a lot to learn about controlling my tension. It's distressing my teeth, (I grind them) my health (headaches, stomach aches)

Orality is the key to all food addictions. However, food addictions include not only overeating but also bulimia (eating, vomiting, purging) and anorexia nervosa (self starvation). Combinations of anorexia nervosa and bulimia are very common. In addition to an oral fixation, the handwriting of anorexics and bulimics will also show a strong sense for control, although to a lesser degree in the bulimic. The person who is exclusively an over-eater and overweight may show signs of slackness in the handwriting.

This writing of a 43 year old female, approximately one hundred pounds overweight, shows slackness, as seen in the difficulty in maintaining a regular base line and the carelessly formed letters with some threadiness. A difficulty in emotional release is seen in the incomplete lower loops and lower loops avoiding a return to the baseline. The writing clearly indicates that food is used as a substitute for emotional release.

ILLUS. 8 OVER-EATER

Female, 43, right handed

Dear Roger,
How delightful to be here listening
to music in you - Bach takes the spirit
into the beyond - pulling forth the greatness
of life together as the sun sparkles on the
water - in laughing manner - saying -
look - listen - smell - touch -
Tatiana A

This 46 year old female, a restricting anorexic (no vomiting, no purging) has been anorexic since college days. Briefly a nurse and a talented pianist, she is now unable to work and is on welfare. Despite a dangerously low weight for so many years and the absence of menstrual periods, she married and bore three children. Her weight is in the low 70's and her health is seriously deteriorating, yet she perceives herself as having no significant problems. The handwriting shows domination by the mother (emphasis on the upper part of the capital I), rigidity, malformation of the lower loops, a backward slant in a very rounded writing, extended initial strokes, looped garlands, and a generally low maturity level.

ILLUS. 9 ANOREXIC

Female, 46, right handed

Dear Mom & Dad -
Happy Anniversary to you both and
best wishes for a brighter, happier
year to come.
Last year was a trying one
for you, with the ups + downs of
health problems and family relationships.
I thought of calling you today,
but decided not to - didn't think
it was proper to charge you (collect
call) to receive your own anniversary
message. And, I figured you had
probably just received my long
letter so there wasn't much
of anything else to tell you.

The kids & Don are fine - and
school got under way this week. I was
able to talk to both school guidance

This handwriting of an 18 year old female bulimic shows avoidance of the baseline when coming up from the lower zone, extended initial strokes, school type formations, an i-dot on her signature, and a reversal of roles of mother and father as seen in the Capital I starting on the wrong side.

ILLUS. 10 BULIMIC

Female, 18, right handed

The Fear of Food

She felt so lonely and life was a cry,
Not even knowing that soon she would die,
She fell in a trap that wouldn't let loose,
Learning to late that there was no truce,
But still she persisted and made herself sick,
Finding the habit was to hard to kick,
It hurt her much worse then she thought it could
Most thinks it helps them so she thought it would,
Now that she's gone, just a lonely little tear,
We know she died in the trap of a fear,
If you knew what happened, you'd think it
was crude,
But that is what happens
when your fear is of food-
By Natalie K

Since addictions all have a common basis, it is difficult if not impossible to determine from the handwriting precisely what type of addiction a person will fall into. The borderline between an addictive personality and the potential for developing a full-blown addiction is very indistinct. We can only identify the potentiality. As graphologists we can never say that a writer is an addict, only that he or she has the personality basis to become one.

Bibliography

Diagnostic and Statistical Manual of Mental Disorders
Third Edition-Revised
(American Psychiatric Association, Washington, DC, 1987.)

Klein, Felix — *Psychology for Graphologists*
(Advanced Correspondence Course, lessons 5 through 10.)

Klein, Felix — *The Unconscious in Handwriting*
(Self-published, 1989.)

Nakken, Craig — *The Addictive Personality: Understanding Compulsion in Our Lives.*
(Harper/Hazelden, San Francisco, 1988.)

Rubin, Roger — *Character Structures and Defense Mechanisms*
(Self-published, 1985.)

The Psychology of the Handwriting of the Child

Felix Klein

The Psychology of The Handwriting of The Child

Periods of Childhood

In the development of the child we will divide the time into different periods, according to his possible achievements and developments. These are:

The First Year

Two to Four Years

Five to Eight Years

Nine to Thirteen Years

Fourteen to Nineteen Years

What do we know about a newborn baby? Many books have been written and many people have spent a lifetime trying to understand a newborn child. Many a mother looks at her crying child and listens, to be able to interpret the sounds the child is making. A famous Broadway actress of the fifties, Honey McKenzie, became well known for her study of baby cries and the way she was able to imitate them. I was fortunate to hear her do them and from her imitations it was quickly possible to understand the particular need of the child. A mother learns this also. The crying is the child's language. The crying for food is different from the crying of fear. It may not be so different from the crying of general discomfort. The crying is a form of expression. These expressions are completely basic, particularly designed to let the person that is responsible for his well being know what he wants. The first positive reaction to the outside world is the smile. This happens as soon as the child is able to focus his eyes sufficiently to recognize the face that takes care of him. The first two months of the baby's life are completely passive from the point of the psyche. A momentary reaction can only be achieved by the strongest stimulus.

In the third month we see the first psychic activity in the observation and recognition of objects. Things and people are now being actively acknowledged and disturbances are being actively rejected. The world around him takes on shape and his own function is being formed through his own activities. The second half of the first year finds the baby with activities through new impulses and aims by touching objects. He establishes contact with the people around him by his smile and his stammering. So he learns how to manipulate objects and how to get people to react to him. At the age of nine months the child may be able to crawl and his ability to grasp and manipulate objects improves. He has become increasingly aware of the social world by learning to say "no."

The First Year.

At one there is a distinct slowing down of the development. At this age there is more of the social development which adds to his self-confidence. He enjoys an audience. Now comes the time where he learns to walk. His motoric abilities improve.

Two to Four Years.

Age of Two.—The age of two finds him understanding most everything and able to express himself particularly when he wants to express his wishes although his demands are not quite as strong as they were.

Age of Two and a Half.—The age of two and a half finds the child already making attempts to scribble, particularly if so directed. It is good for a parent to know that this is a time when the child does things, contrary to what the parents expect. The child is inflexible. He wants what he wants when he wants it. It is the age of extremes, it is the age of learning willpower, it is the age where conflicts become the daily routine. It is also the age of perseverance. The child wants to go on doing things even from one day to the next. Patience is needed for this time.

Age of Three.—Only when he turns three, things quiet down. He becomes more flexible, he learns the word we, not only "I." Not everything has to be done his way. He becomes more social minded, likes to make friends. The increase of his ability to use the language helps.

Age of Three and a Half.—And then three and a half again brings a difficult period where the child becomes unsure of himself, where tension sets in and may cause all kinds of reactions, like stuttering, blinking of the eyes, biting his nails or picking his nose etc. And his relationship to others gets affected also.

Age of Four.—And then the four year old, all you can say: "out of bounds." He hits, he kicks, he throws stones, he breaks things and he runs away. And the language. He uses words that you would not know where he got them from. He seems to enjoy them, even if they are inappropriate. There is a need to restrict the four year old, the question is: how much. Not too much, he has to be given a chance to test himself.

Age of Four and a Half.—By four and a half they show a further improvement of their controls. This is often expressed in their drawings.

Five to Eight Years.

Age of Five.—The age of five is a blessing. The child is not unpredictable. The mother becomes the center of the world. He now knows his limits and he only tries to do what he knows he can accomplish.

Age of Six.—The age of six is tumultuous. The parents find that the child is difficult to deal with. One minute he loves you and the next he hates you. The mother is not the center of the world anymore. Much goes wrong because he is too demanding. His responses to others become extremely negative. He needs to be praised. He is having a difficult time within himself and a lot is being done for him by realizing just that.

Age of Seven.—At seven there is a tendency to withdraw. He has calmed down and he is easier to live with. He now likes to be alone and he wants a room of his own. He is exploring with his mind and with his hands. The tendency is to feel that people are against him.

Age of Eight.—At eight the time of withdrawal is over. The eight year old goes out to meet the world. Now he overestimates his abilities. He is constantly busy and active, trying new things and making new friends. He is not only interested in how others treat him but also in the relationship with others. At the age of eight we are getting the first real glimpse of what he will be like later.

Nine to Thirteen Years.

Age of Nine.—At nine he will be more quiet, more within himself. Often the friends seem to be more important than the family, and their opinions too. Nine is a year of complaining, also of rebellion and some do it by withdrawal.

Age of Ten.—Ten is the year of "yes." He has a good relationship to his parents and he tends to be satisfied with the world.

Age of Eleven, Twelve and Thirteen.—Eleven, twelve and thirteen mark the preparation and the start of puberty. The changes in the body cause changes in the emotional behavior. It is not true that a boy becomes a man at the age of thirteen and a girl becomes a woman. The maturing process is a long one.

Fourteen to Nineteen Years.

The age of puberty is a critical age indeed. The age of finding a place in the world, the age of finding himself. No attempt will be made to go into the problems of the adolescent. This subject must be treated separately. Even for this period of the growing process the deep knowledge of the child is essential. Without it, the teenager and his problems cannot be understood.

Why Children Scribble

In her book "What Children Scribble and Why," Rhoda Kellogg, a supervisor at the Golden Gate Nursery School in San Francisco, has made a study based on thousands of samples of children's scribbles. She says: "children's scribbles have become meaningful or meaningless, depending upon the adult who is considering them." As a means of communication between the child and adult, scribbling is not yet too satisfactory.

Just as art is preverbal, a child can "draw" and look at art before he can speak. We are all consciously and unconsciously affected by lines, marks, symbols, smears, smudges, shapes, light and shadows and all concrete forms in the arts. According to Herbert Read, art is "mankind's effort to achieve integration with the forms of the physical universe and the organic rhythm of life." In art we use terms like impressionistic, non-objective, surrealistic, cubist, and many more. For the art of the pre-school child we do not have a general vocabulary.

The adult's mind so controls the eye's interpretation of marks on the paper, that the observer can record what he sees only in words that make sense to himself and his followers.

We classify, analyze and interpret children's drawings too heavily in the observer's imagination. The adult is unaware of his lack of capacity to observe objectively. The eye is controlled by the brain and records what it sees, only according to mental systems recorded in brain cells, as learned memories. The child's eye and brain are in the process of being trained; that is, of interpreting back and forth from eye to brain, that such and such a mark is square or a "house" and another is a circle or a "ball." We cannot know what the child sees.

The concept is advanced that the child draws what he knows, not what he sees. Read says that the child has "no bases in immediate visual experience." The chances are that the preschool child draws what his eyes have seen many times before on his own scribbled paper. If this is true, then the child's visual experience in relation to his own drawing does influence his further work. The child draws what he sees in his own work, but the structural aspect of scribbling is "lost" to the adult. It is during the work of the two and three year old child that he acquires most of the basic structural images with which he works from then on, as a child and as an adult. The very young child does not draw reality objects and this is disturbing to adults.

If the great significance of preschool art is the potential value as a means of better communication between children and adults, then, to understand what these scribblings mean, to read "their works objectively, there must be a method or system for analyzing pre-school scribblings and drawings, and these must be applicable to any and all groups of children."

Studies have shown, says Hilde Eng, that children's drawings have taken the same course in their main outline in all countries. To come up with common denominators, some 100,000 pieces of work were studied. These include markings with fingers, crayons or brush as creative expressions. The adult should never treat these as junk. The effect is belittling to the child as well as to his work.

How do we apply this to graphology? We say that our writing is brain writing. If so, when did this learning process first start? We must go back further than when the child first went to school and start to interpret his first scrawls.

Rhoda Kellogg had first sorted out the various scribbles into 20 basic scribbles.

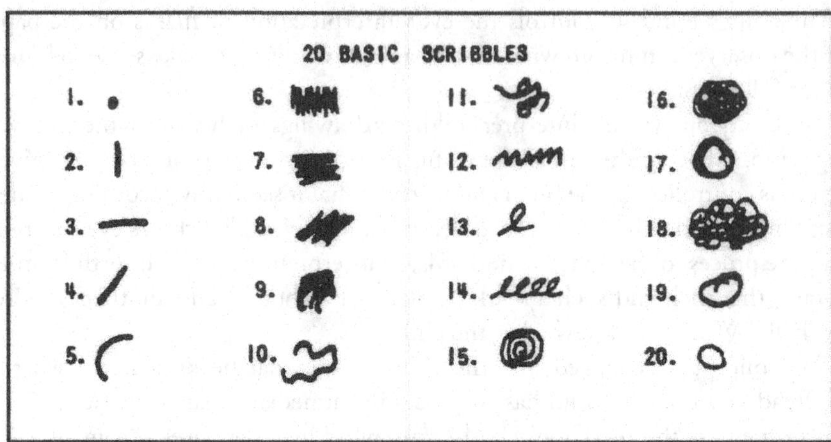

Looking at these 20 basics graphologically we can see at a glance all the elements found in our handwriting. These are the scribblings from two to four and a half years. As the powers of coordination improve, the child builds on these 20 basics to form 6 basic diagrams. This is usually achieved by the age of three.

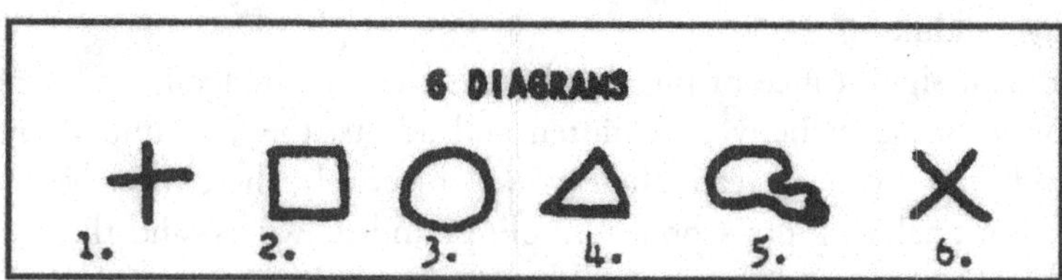

The six diagrams include:

1. The Greek cross (from scribbles 2 and 3)
2. The square and rectangle (from scribbles 2 and 3)
3. The circle and oval (from scribble 5)
4. The triangle (from scribbles 2, 3 and 4)
5. The odd shape (from scribbles 10 and 11)
6. The diagonal cross (from scribble 4)

The child goes from the diagrams that include scribbles to combines:

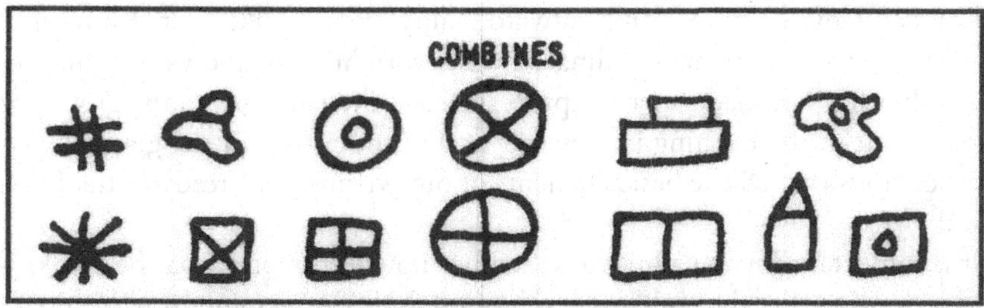

Then the child advances to aggregates, simple and mixed.

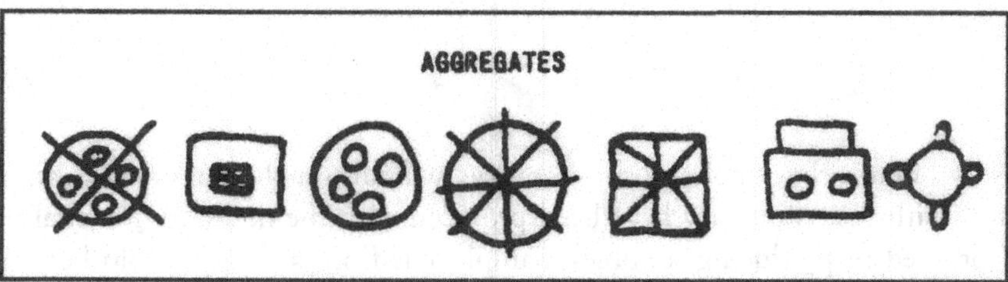

The mentally retarded child at a much older age has never advanced beyond the simple aggregates. As the child's kinetic ability improves along with various muscle groups and with the increased extent of his attention span, he normally advances to achieve from the basics (20), to diagrams, to combines and aggregates, from which a multitude of shapes can evolve, using the various basics, diagrams and mixed aggregates. This level should be achieved between one and four years.

"Mandala," means magic circle, which has been divided into either four or eight parts by lines radiating from the center. From this evolves the sun, then the face figure.

From an abstract circle a human face is developed to which legs, feet and arms are added and later the torso is incorporated, also definite details, as hair, teeth and others. Flowers, houses and outward reality seem to take on meaning in the form of boats, cars, airplanes, animals, houses with humans and various mixtures. The author has not made an attempt to associate these designs to the growth and development of the learning process per se. From the view of the graphologist it seems obvious that all the basic elements of our writing are already in the first 20 basics.

It is important for the adult to remember not to interpret what he thinks the child is drawing. Let the child express himself as the images appear to him.

There is a close relationship between scribbles of children from all lands. For the graphologist it might be worthy of consideration to follow these early efforts and see how personality develops and what brings about harmony or disharmony.

* * *

Very often a child, not yet of school age, will answer the question: "Can you write?" with yes. After they have been provided with the necessary material they will proceed in producing scribbles. Sample 1 is from a 4 ½ year old boy, and sample 2 is from his 5 ½ year old sister.

Sample 1. (half original size)—The boy first framed it with a line which is not too straight due to his lack of writing skill. He then continued by putting in the middle of the writing space a maze of criss-cross lines with great speed. The writing instrument was handled with such pressure that the paper was torn in places. The criss-cross lines are connected by sharp angles. Other writing tests with this child produced similar results.

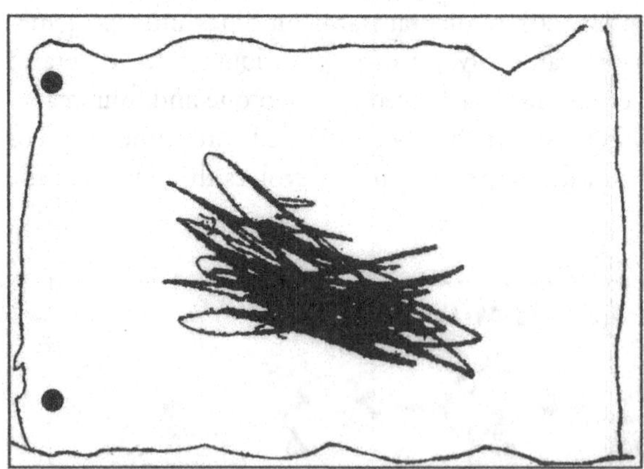

The graphological interpretation is: His thoughts are concentrated on what he wants to do. He divides the space according to a plan. His motion impulse is intensive. The movement in itself is forceful, rather jerky than gliding. According to the arrangement he is capable of deliberation, he has a sense for the distribution of space and he has a desire for expression. According to the pressure and the speed of movement, there is emphasis and liveliness. The jerky strokes always portray an urgency in moving ahead and the criss-cross lines reveal passionate impulses that seem to have a disturbing effect on his quiet and smooth activities and in finding his proper place.

Even with such a primitive writing product we have been able to define the developing character sufficiently, so that the pedagogue and the psychologist should have it easy to find the proper guiding principles for the upbringing of the boy.

Sample 2. (half original size)—The girl used the pencil with a light, almost floating and slow movement producing soft lines all over the paper. This writing image seems to express delicacy and unclearness. Through the aimlessly moving strokes we see a lack of planned concentration. The delicacy of the strokes indicates psychic delicacy, sensitiveness and little energy. The slowness and softness of the writing movement indicates indecision and impressionability. The wildly extending strokes indicate imagination.

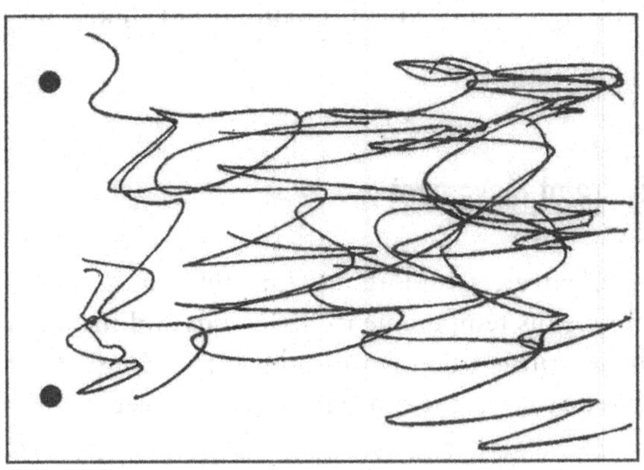

The graphological interpretation is: The above indicators create a picture of a delicate child with a lively imagination, a child which is impressionable and open to influences, poorly equipped for the struggle of existence. Only an appropriate training of her willpower would help in this respect.

The boy, however, has a sufficient amount of self assertion, almost too much of it, possibly constituting a danger to the harmony of living with other people. As far as he is concerned his upbringing must concern itself with the channeling of his willpower into a productive work pattern.

The above mentioned analyses of the two scribbling samples were found extremely accurate by the parents of the children.

Tables for Children's Graphology

Zones.

Upper Zone.—The zone of the spirit, the intellect and the mind.

Middle Zone.—Should be seen as the zone between the upper and lower zone, between the mind and the instinct. It is the "personal" zone, the zone of the soul and the zone that shows how the writer feels about himself.

Lower Zones.—With the child also the erotic, materialistic and sexual zone.

In the analysis of children's handwritings the division of all the indicators into three picture groups is essential: picture of movement, picture of form, and picture of space.

Picture of Movement

The picture of the movement is of greatest importance for children's graphology. Unknowingly the child expresses his temperament, his moods and his inner controls. In comparison to the handwriting of grown-ups the handwriting of the child is more dynamic, less inhibited as far as the movement is concerned.

Large—Small.

The absolute height for children's writings is the same as for grown-ups, 3mm for the height of the middle zone letters. The tendency of the child is to write larger in earlier stages of development in line with the fact that control is needed to reduce the size of the writing. We have to distinguish between genuine and artificial height. A proportionate ratio between middle zone height (3mm) and overall length of long letters (12mm) would indicate a genuine height. Any disproportion either way would have to be regarded as an artificial height and such a writing of a child would not fall into the category of a small or large writing.

Large Writing.—(More than 12mm long letters, more than 3mm middle zone letters.) Indicates: clumsiness, seeking of contact, optimism, extroversion, childish carelessness.

Large artificial (disproportionate) writing in adolescent age group often indicates a search for their own "thing."

It is important to remember that extreme differences in size can be an indication of difficulties with vision.

Small Writing.—(Long letters 6mm or below.) Indicates: reflective type, analytical, commencing self-critique, tendency to keep distance, introversions, pettiness, sense for criticism, inferiority complex.

Speed—Slowness.

It is well to remember that the handwriting of even a very lively child will show signs of slowness as long as the process of achieving a high degree of writing agility is not completed. Signs of speed: right slant, wideness, curvy writing, slim forms, extended final strokes, i-dots comma-like, i-dots to the right, increased width of left margin.

Speed.—Indicates: liveliness, eagerness, alertness.

Too Speedy.—Indicates: superficiality, haste, impatience, flightiness. Combined but indistinct forms, neglect of forms and letters, omission of important parts of letters.

Slowness.—Indicates: lack of drive, slow mentality. It is often caused by inefficient writing skill and lack of knowledge of the forms. Slowness can also be the result of gripping the writing instrument too tightly.

Extreme Slowness.—Indicates: mental heaviness to mental retardation. Extreme slowness combined with distinct faulty writing results in numerous mistakes, corrections, uncleanliness and double starting impulses.

Wide—Narrow.

The width (wideness) is the relation of the height to the distance between downstrokes of the middle zone letters.

Wide Writing.—Wide writing is mostly a spontaneous expression of the conduct of the child. Often pert children, who want to talk and answer without knowing the answer, write wide. It seems to be established that children with pre-school activities (kindergarten) have a tendency to write wider than those without such experiences.

Widened Writing.—Lack of self-consciousness (at easeness), readiness for experiences, openness, receptiveness, cheerfulness, sociability, brightness, also: spirit of enterprise, uninhibitedness, imagination. Emphasized widening can be an indication for pretentious self-reliance.

Narrowness.—(Can often be seen in scribbles.) Indicates: often upbringing too strict, inhibitions, self-consciousness, self-control, reflectiveness, "inside child," often shy to contact and touch, oversensitivity.

Heavy Pressure—Light Pressure.

Heavy Pressure.—Heavy pressure in a child's writing often is the result of a tense gripping of the writing instrument. It usually produces an uneven pressure. When it is possible to see the writing efforts of the child the observation can be made if the child holds the pen very far down which also produces uneven pressure and usually is an indication of an attempt to stay with the copy book form which also should be evident in the writing. Only if the pressure is combined with a rhythmic movement can we deduct vitality and willpower.

Displaced Pressure.—Displaced pressure, particularly along the base line, is an indication of vanity, distrust, early developed sensuousness (particularly in the age of puberty).

Distinct Spotty Pressure (or swellstrokes).—Distinct spotty pressure in puberty indicates inner disturbances due to secretional changes.

Light Pressure.—Indicates: agility, delicacy of feeling, high sensitivity, indecision, unsteadiness.

No Pressure.—Indicates: general weak vitality, lack of energy, oversensitivity. In combination with falling word endings or descending lines or both, could be a warning signal for an inability to cope with reality.

Connectedness—Disconnectedness.

Connectedness.—The degree of connectedness indicates the train of thoughts. To the normal child the connection of a few letters is no problem. Even in the handwriting of a child it can be observed that the capital letter stands separated from the rest of the word. This should not be regarded as a form of disconnection, only if the disconnections also occur frequently in the middle of the words. Just as with the grown-ups the good connectedness means an ability of flowing oral expression. With the increase of the writing agility the child finds original letter combinations.

Disconnectedness.—Complete disconnectedness does not occur in the handwriting of a normal child. However, large spaces between words are indicative of an unwillingness for contact with others. Inability to connect or constant separate connective strokes must be regarded as a sign for low intelligence and poor memory. Strong disconnectedness in the writing of teenagers often indicates an unwillingness for logical thinking, a lack of understanding of mathematical principles—but often artistic tendencies.

Pastosity—Sharpness.

Pastosity.—Pastosity is something to be expected in the writing of a child. It indicates a natural way of talking to others and readiness for perception. Heavy pastosity bordering on smeariness is an indicator for body malfunctions. Constantly increasing pastosity can be an indicator for the beginning of a sickness.

Sharpness.—Sharpness is rare in children's writings. In the writings of youth it indicates a preference for reasoning, self-discipline and ability for abstract thinking but also sense for cleanliness and order. If combined with lack of pressure: delicacy of feeling.

The Stroke in itself must be examined very carefully. The type of stroke does not undergo changes. It remains the same from the pre-school scribble to old age.

Picture of Form

The picture of form can only manifest itself after the mechanical difficulties have been overcome and the writing act has become more or less automatic. Only then can we expect to find what a child is suited for or where his talents are. It is quite natural for one child to establish his original form earlier than another. The writing agility is not the only criteria. The progress of emotional development is another.

The Connections.

Garland.—A true garland will not appear in a child's writing before the child acquires an individual style of his own. The type of movement the writing of a garland requires is very basic to the child. Tests have shown that 85% of the children prefer the garland movement over the arcade movement.

Arcade.—The basic movement of the arcade is more or less away from the "you" particularly when you look at the end of it. This kind of attitude in a child is contrary to the basic goals in the upbringing of a child. If an arcade appears in an early age it can be assumed that the child feels a pressure from his immediate surroundings. Many of these cases will show other signs of "closed up" tendencies or even signs of lying.

Angles.—Angles in the writing of children usually indicate a refusal or inability to adapt themselves. A child of such a description usually needs a "stronger hand." Softness will be "used" and most likely laughed at. Emphasized angles where curves are expected are an indication of stubbornness.

Thread.—Thread is not rare in children's writings. Generally, it is the acceptance of the wishes of the grown-ups that will be the indication there. A very distinct thread connection over a number of years should be regarded as a warning signal for things to come. In the handwriting of teenagers the thread often indicates increased activities and a strong desire for things to happen. Also the willingness "to take things in" without proper consideration of the possible consequences.

Fullness—Meagerness.

Fullness.—Fullness can often be observed in bulgy loops. These indicate a need for communication and expression. Combined with slowness it should be regarded as a sign of playful procrastination. A sample showing fullness in the middle zone indicates a child with reserve of strength, and usually the efforts do not have to be great to achieve results. The overemphasis of the ego will be seen in the fullness of the middle zone. Upper zone fullness should indicate a capacity for illusions and fantasies. Fullness in the lower loops would show the strong connection the child has to the past, also fantasy about it.

Meagerness.—Meagerness as seen in the loops and narrowness of the curves would be an indication for emotional inhibitions, fear, shyness, self-consciousness, and a child that is difficult to reach. Meagerness in the writings of teenagers can indicate clear, abstract and critical thinking.

Embellishments—Simplifications.

Embellishments.—Embellishments will often show up in the initial or endstroke. Completely embellished letters are often due to efforts of a group of youngsters in one class wanting to attract attention. This seems to be the case more often with girls than with boys. In such a case it can be deducted that a need to be admired is already present. Vanity plays a part here also. The scrutiny of such forms is highly necessary to determine the degree of originality and genuineness of form. The higher the degree of originality the higher will be the ability to express in some form of the arts. If you should find a sample where the capitals are playfully embellished while the middle zone letters are neglected, this should be an indication for you that the child has difficulty in concentrating.

Simplifications.—Simplifications as we see in the writings of grown-ups are not expected to appear in a child's writing until the child has reached an agility so that the writing becomes "automatic." Such simplifications indicate sense for the essential, sense for efficiency, intellectualism, also good taste and sense for style. The neglect of form exists in children's writing also and can mostly be found in the writing of teenagers. The indications then are: carelessness, superficiality, love for comfort, impatience and unreliability. There are such cases where depressive tendencies and fatigue can be deducted.

The Picture of Space

Regularity—Irregularity.

Regularity.—Regularity is an achievement which also depends largely on the writing skill. Once that writing skill is established the child's character and attitude will determine the degree of regularity. You should not interpret regularity at all if it was achieved through extreme care and slowness. A child with good writing agility and regularity in his writing has learned to fulfill his obligations. It does not occur too often that children get to rigid regularity. If they do, it usually is an indication that they do not want to reveal themselves or that they even want to disguise their feelings.

Irregularity.—It is again necessary to determine the degree of writing agility before judging the irregularity as a character trait. Generally irregularity is an indication that the child is easily distracted and easily influenced. There are extreme cases where the child disregards every rule of regularity and so shows that there are emotional difficulties often due to outside changes or due to a resistance to the values of the educator.

Slant.

Upright and Left Slant.—It has been observed that the tendency toward a more upright writing exists even without the consideration that many of the school systems are advocates of a more upright slant. The change of slant results from the development and the relationship of the child to the outside world. A natural upright position allows the judgment of an even tempered child, in combination with slow speed even phlegmatic and with lack of initiative. A sudden change to upright or even left slant often is a sign of insecurity or inhibition. The child is not able to act naturally but rather out of compulsion. Upright and left slant often appears in the writings of teenagers, more in girls than in boys, indicating often a desire for being "different," more sophisticated or stylish.

Right Slant.—Right slant should be regarded as the "normal" slant for a child. This is the child that is open and often says things that are even embarrassing to the grown-ups. With the oncoming of feelings the child is unaccustomed to, the slant can undergo changes. And an increase of the slant toward the end of the words would be an indication of a temperamental child that wants to have self-control but needs to "let go" once in a while.

Right Trend—Left Trend.

Right trend and left trend are not as strong indicators here as in the writings of grownups. It is also to be considered that left-handedness has a definite tendency to produce left trend. Generally the indications are the same for children as for grown-ups.

Emphasis on Upper—Lower Length.

Upper Length Emphasis.—Indicates: agility, receptiveness, sensitivity, active mind.

Lower Length Emphasis.—Indicates: sense for practical things, ability to adjust to the demands of every day school life.

Spaces Between Words.

It is also part of the picture of space to look at the distance between words.

Large Spaces Between Words.—Large spaces between words can indicate a sense for clarity, sense for reality in a very positive writing. In a more negative writing it would be an indication of laborious thinking and inhibition of expressions.

Small Spaces Between Words.—Small spaces between words would indicate in a positive writing quick comprehension, ability to concentrate on his work, in negative handwritings strong dependency.

Bibliography

Becker, Minna — *Graphologie der Kinderschrift*
(Niels Kempmann Verlag, Heidelberg, 1926.)

Buehler, Charlotte — *Kindheit und Jugend*
(S. Hirzel Verlag, Leibzig, 1930.)

Ilg, Frances L., M.D. and Bates, Louise, Ph.D. — *Child Behavior*
(Harper & Row, New York, 1955.)

Kellogg, Rhoda — *What Children Scribble and Why*
(N.P. Publications, Palo Alto, Cal. 1955.)

Klein, Felix — *The Analysis of the Stroke,* a lecture.

Koch, Paul — *Kinderschrift und Charakter*
(Brause & Co., Iserlohn, 1932.)

Schelenz, Erich and Lotte — *Padagogische Graphologie*
(Ehrenwirth Verlag, Muenchen, 1958.)